Marlborough's Sieges

MARLBOROUGH'S SIEGES

To   Rod

with Best Wishes.

by

James Falkner

James Falkner
16 April 2007.

Foreword by His Grace the Duke of
Marlborough

SPELLMOUNT

British Library Cataloguing in Publication Data:
A catalogue record for this book is available
from the British Library

Copyright © James Falkner 2007
Maps copyright © Spellmount Ltd 2007
Editor: Thomas Chidlaw

10 ISBN 1-86227-340-5
13 ISBN 978-1-86227-340-5

First published in the UK in 2007 by
Spellmount Limited
The Mill, Brimscombe Port
Stroud, Gloucestershire GL5 2QG

Tel: 01453 883300
Fax: 01453 883233
Website: www.spellmount.com

1 3 5 7 9 8 6 4 2

The right of James Falkner to be identified
as the author of this work has been asserted by him
in accordance with the Copyright, Designs
and Patents Act 1988

Printed in Great Britain by
Oaklands Book Services
Stonehouse, Gloucestershire GL10 3RQ

Front jacket image by kind permission of His Grace the Duke of Marlborough

Contents

Foreword

Blenheim Palace.

Much as he strove to achieve decisive military action, far more of Marlborough's time was actually spent in siege than in battle. At Blenheim Palace we are aware of one siege in particular – his last, at Bouchain, in 1711. As the author points out, here once again Marlborough displayed his military genius. He completely hoodwinked Marshal Villars in a brilliant crossing of the lines of 'Non Plus Ultra' and then, totally against the odds, completely dominated him in the siege which followed. Marlborough's awareness of his success is illustrated at Blenheim. Of the ten huge tapestries here that he commissioned to show his major achievements no fewer than three are of Bouchain.

We are aware of a sad irony here too. Far from enhancing his reputation this success gained him nothing. It was conveniently ignored. His political enemies brought to a head a sustained, government-inspired, public campaign of criticism and vilification – and brought him down. In a matter of weeks he was dismissed from all his posts.

The book appeals because it puts Marlborough's sieges in perspective. It has been suggested that Marlborough engaged in costly sieges for purposes of prestige and financial gain. The author makes it very clear that Marlborough had no choice. Vauban, the military engineering genius, had put in place an entangling belt of highly sophisticated fortresses to defend the French frontier. This meant that Marlborough was not able simply to march into the heartland of France to force final victory. He first had to reduce the garrisons supporting arms in his rear; he was too vulnerable otherwise. This book, detailed but always of interest, is a compelling account of these campaigns. Marlborough laid twenty-six sieges and was successful in every one.

Marlborough

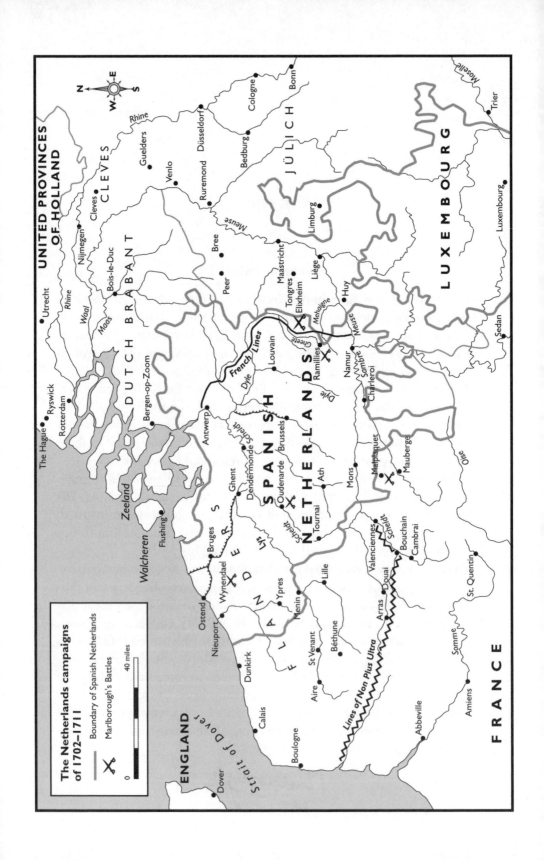

The Netherlands campaigns of 1702–1711

Boundary of Spanish Netherlands
Marlborough's Battles

0   40 miles

UNITED PROVINCES OF HOLLAND

The Hague
Ryswick
Rotterdam
Utrecht
Nijmegen
Cleves
Guelders
Venlo
Ruremond
Düsseldorf
Bedburg
Cologne
Bonn
Trier
Moselle

CLEVES
Rhine
Waal
Maas
Rhine
Meuse

DUTCH BRABANT
Bois-le-Duc
Bergen-op-Zoom
Bree
Peer
Limburg
Maastricht
Tongres
Liège
Huy
Namur

JÜLICH

LUXEMBOURG
Luxembourg
Sedan

Antwerp
Scheldt
Ghent
Dendermonde
Brussels
Louvain
Dyle
French Lines
Elixheim
Gheete
Ramillies
Mehaigne
Meuse
Sambre
Charleroi

SPANISH NETHERLANDS

FLANDERS
Zeeland
Walcheren
Flushing
Bruges
Wynendael
Ostend
Nieuport
Dunkirk
Calais
Boulogne
Ypres
Menin
Lys
Oudenarde
Scheldt
Tournai
Ath
Mons
Malplaquet
Maubeuge
Lille
St Venant
Béthune
Aire
Valenciennes
Douai
Arras
Bouchain
Cambrai
Scheldt
Lines of Non Plus Ultra
St. Quentin
Somme
Amiens
Abbeville
Oise

ENGLAND
Dover
Strait of Dover

FRANCE

Introduction

The Sieges and Marlborough's Reputation

John Churchill, 1st Duke of Marlborough, while he was in command
of the Anglo-Dutch armies between 1702 and 1711, fought six major
battles against the renowned Marshals of France.[1] These were the
critical years of the War of the Spanish Succession, when the Grand
Alliance formed by England, Holland and Austria sought to limit
the overbearing power of France and achieve a division of the vast
empire of Spain. Marlborough, Queen Anne's Captain-General, was
successful in each clash of arms in open field, and he was able to
send his troops delving into northern France in the later years of
the war. Louis XIV was forced to offer his opponents almost all that
was demanded of him, and a triumph for the Alliance was only
missed due to some careless miscalculation of the character of the
old French King. This was an astonishing military achievement by
Marlborough, for France had established a well-merited tradition
of victory during the previous fifty years. The French troops were
the best trained and most magnificently equipped and mounted; the
Marshals of France the most accomplished of commanders – victory
in all its stately magnificence was what was expected of them; they
had become accustomed to delivering those victories to their King
in his wonderful palace in Versailles. Instead, with his successes
over them, Marlborough was acknowledged as the undisputed and
foremost Captain of the age, and French commanders, made wary
by defeat, were eventually ordered not to challenge him in battle, no
matter how good the odds in their favour might be.

In addition to his famous victories in open battle, the Duke of
Marlborough also conducted or supervised no less than twenty-six
formal sieges during this same period of long years of the war (see
Appendix 1). Many of these sieges were major operations, some of
them were on a vast and bewilderingly complex scale comparable

to his major battles, and arguably greater military achievements; once again the Duke was successful on each and every occasion. In addition, he seized a number of important cities and towns (Brussels, Louvain, Bruges, Courtrai, Oudenarde) by skilful campaigning but without really having to fight for them. By this simple arithmetic it may be felt that Marlborough's reputation should rest just as much, if not actually more, on his sieges as on his battles. On the one hand, there was the deathly chance in a single day of battle to ruin a French army; on the other hand, the capture of a valuable fortress, prominent symbol of sovereignty and authority, might lay bare the very heart of France to invasion – this danger, in itself, should bring on the need for the increasingly cautious French armies to fight an all-or-nothing battle in the open, in defence of their borders.

Marlborough once wrote to Hiensius, the Grand Pensionary of Holland, 'There is no comparison between the advantages of a battle and what we can reap by a siege.'[2] He was not necessarily implying that the one kind of operation was more advantageous than the other. Despite his natural preference for the chance to overwhelm an opponent in open battle, the Duke realised that he had to engage the French, not when and where he wished, but when and where he could get them to stand and fight. On rare occasions, this might be facing him in the field, with regimental colours bravely flying and drums tapping, in a hailstorm of musketry and canister. More frequently, however, the soldiers on both sides fought their battles in siege operations, crouching in wet trenches and behind stone and earthen walls, as the mortars rained death from above and miners dug the deadly, unseen tunnels in murk and mud beneath their feet. The dynamics of the war required the Captain-General to bring Louis XIV to the negotiating table, humbled and ready to submit to whatever demands the Grand Alliance chose to put before him. As the war progressed, it became evident that in no other theatre of war but that where the Duke commanded would this happen. Only Marlborough and his army could do this; and his were the campaigns that came to matter most. Victory was required, and whether it was to be brought about by battle or by siege, it made no difference.

Beyond question, Marlborough never laid siege to a French-held town he did not then take. These were formidable places, and this simple record ranks as a major military achievement. However, the Duke's undoubted success against the daunting fortress belt in the Spanish Netherlands and northern France can be seen with the valuable advantage of hindsight to be something of an illusion. That illusion of success was dangerous, both for the Grand Alliance and for the Duke, for when linked to his victories in open field it led to an easy expectation of outright and inevitable victory that was not in fact there to be had. Apart from river lines, the border with the Spanish Netherlands was devoid of major natural obstacles of the kind that protected France elsewhere. After extending by conquest France's borders into Artois, Picardy and Flanders, Louis XIV had in the 1670's given the master French engineer Sebastien le Prestre Vauban the task of preparing a new defence for the region. Vauban constructed, with scientific skill and at enormous labour and expense, a thick fortress belt, what might be regarded as a complex stone entanglement. A snare was laid to catch any attacker rash enough to try and take advantage of that lack of obstacles which, by their very absence, laid the northern borders of France invitingly open to attack.

Marlborough's victories in open battle created an understandable euphoria amongst the otherwise level-headed victors, men who had until recently been very doubtful of obtaining success at all. This was particularly so in the aftermath of the astonishing triumph at Ramillies, in May 1706. The French and Bavarian army in the Spanish Netherlands collapsed and fled, and the Duke went surging forward in pursuit of his broken opponents. The troops of the Grand Alliance soon stood on the very borders of France with almost no-one to oppose them. It was an extraordinary situation, unimaginable only a few months earlier. The Duke had lunged forward to take full advantage of his victory – he could not really have done otherwise. He wrote to his good friend, the Lord Treasurer, Sidney Godolphin, during that exhilarating summer 'God has blessed the beginning of this campaign beyond what the thoughts of man could reasonably suppose, so it must be our duty to improve it as far as occasion shall offer.'[3] To improve in this case meant to thrust onward, and this thrusting took him into the French fortress belt designed and constructed by Vauban. In time, the apparent helplessness of the French generals when faced with his daring strokes proved to be a tantalising mirage, drawing the Allied armies ever onwards but not to final victory. Marlborough, once committed, never extricated his army from Vauban's entanglement during long years of bloody, expensive, and increasingly exhausting siege warfare.

By 1708, Marlborough was at the pinnacle of his powers and influence. Undoubtedly he was the military marvel of the generation, and was simultaneously conducting Britain's foreign affairs almost single-handed. However, his position at Court in London was being slowly undermined by a fading friendship and failing influence with Queen Anne. His success also bred jealousy amongst those who had at one time been supporters. This would not matter, for victory in the war – outright victory that is, with the French submissive to the demands of the Grand Alliance – would set all to rights for the Duke. If this victory was not to be had, people asked to what effect then was the escalating cost and labour of the war. Caught in Vauban's entanglement, unable to quite shake himself and his army free despite his numerous tactical successes, Marlborough drew heavily – too heavily – on his capital balances of trust, confidence and goodwill while pursuing these heartbreaking operations. There was no bright campaign for the Duke beyond the fortresses. Out on the wide open fields of Artois and Picardy that beckoned but remained tantalisingly out of reach, there was no repeat at the gates of Paris of the glorious triumph at Blenheim – the elusive knock-out blow that would bring Louis XIV to his knees and the war for Spain to a triumphant end. This failure, so unexpected in the warm afterglow of Ramillies when everything seemed possible, was loudly recognised at the time by his opponents at home and critics abroad. As much as anything, it brought Marlborough down in the end.

Marlborough, with his successes at Blenheim (1704) and Ramillies, procured an astonishing and, as it happened, wholly unexpected success over France for the Grand Alliance. The Allies, it was soon found, had no plan in place for such a welcome situation. They did, however, quickly add demand on demand to what was required of Louis XIV, and became absurdly greedy with the victory handed to them by the Duke. Having achieved this success, which no-one was on hand to take and convert by judicious negotiation into a proper peace, Marlborough then proved unable to force a submission from the King and his resilient armies – one that was sufficient for the Allies to dictate the terms to their heart's content. In the bitterness of the uncalled-for disappointment that ensued, the Duke was never forgiven.

It has been easy and very tempting for Marlborough's many admirers to see the waspish comments of his detractors as being politically motivated, or the result of suspicion, prejudice and mean envy of a great and gifted man. However, although their motives may often have been less than noble, the Duke's opponents put their fingers neatly on what was perhaps the key factor in his eventual fall from favour and his abrupt dismissal at the end of 1711 by a tired, ailing, and disappointed monarch. That Marlborough's reputation was allowed to fade, his achievements partly forgotten and neglected by some historians, and his career eclipsed by later commanders (most notably the Duke of Wellington who did achieve, at Waterloo in 1815, courtesy of Napoleon's fumbling, that valuable knock-out blow) is perhaps explained by this failure to bring about a neat and convenient conclusion to the war for Spain. Just as Louis XIV looked to his Marshals for victory, so the Grand Alliance looked to Marlborough. Nothing short of a complete victory was demanded of the Duke: nothing less would do. Marlborough found it difficult to lay to rest the charges levelled against him that, for his own narrow, selfish reasons, and at the expense of both Queen Anne's Treasury and the lives of his soldiers squandered, he wished to perpetuate the war. It was maliciously claimed, and not sufficiently refuted, that the Duke engaged in costly and unnecessary sieges to prolong the war, in order that he could retain his position at the head of the Allied armies with all the prestige, advantages and financial remuneration that came with the post.

At the level of grand strategy, however, it can be seen that Marlborough's efforts actually met with success, little though it was acknowledged at the time. The main aim of the Grand Alliance, as envisaged by King William III and negotiated, at least in part, by the Duke when he was Earl of Marlborough, was not the installation of an Austrian prince on the throne in Madrid. What was sought was a partition of the moribund Spanish empire so that neither France nor Austria should gain too great an accretion of power from the death of the King of Spain in 1700. This had at one point also been an aspiration of Louis XIV, as envisaged under two Partition Treaties agreed between England, France and Holland in the last years of the previous century. When his grandson was offered the throne and empire undivided the French King found himself unable to resist that offer. As the resulting war for Spain came to an end twelve years later, the partition of the empire was achieved and the feared growth in French military power in the process had been checked for a generation or more. Austria meanwhile happily took its gains in northern Italy and the Southern (Spanish) Netherlands, and through necessity turned to the east to face the Ottoman threat, losing interest in the old Habsburg empire of Charles V in the west. Therefore the outcome of the war, largely as a result of the Duke of Marlborough's efforts, was a real success in the strict sense that neither France nor Austria gained unduly from the will of the late Carlos II of Spain.

However, the young French prince (Philip V) remained in Madrid, and that ran counter to the new war aim for the Grand Alliance – one that had been carelessly developed as the conflict progressed – that an acceptable peace could only come with the installation of the Austrian claimant (Carlos III) on that throne. 'No peace without

Spain' had become the dangerous war-cry in the capitals of the Alliance, and once let out it could not be put away again. So, the ground had shifted significantly under Marlborough's feet – a shift that he found, in fact, he could work with. The Duke saw no difficulty in the Alliance espousing the Habsburg claim to the throne, particularly as it wedded the Imperial armies and the valuable services of his comrade, Prince Eugene of Savoy, to the common cause against France. Also, if the French armies could be defeated often enough, it was surely not an unrealistic aim to have.

In the realm of day-to-day tactics, Marlborough's campaigns of siege warfare succeeded also, as fortified town after town fell to his ruthlessly efficient operations, and the best efforts of Louis XIV's commanders failed to prevent the Duke's armies from thrusting into northern France. Even the great city of Lille, cherished conquest of the King when a young man, fell to Marlborough's army. It was at the wider level that the Duke fell short. He was unable in the time available to him to break through the belt of French fortresses and get out into the open. Only there could he hope to repeat the thrilling successes of Blenheim and Ramillies and thus impose the will of the Grand Alliance on that of the French King. For all his brilliance, Marlborough was held to have failed in the task he was given and had readily accepted. Nothing else counted and he was angrily pulled down by others who, with their own character and abilities, could not dream of attempting such a task. Even the Duke's loyal soldiers, whose faith in his abilities never dimmed, eventually came to pray 'God to put an end to these troubles and to grant us a happy, long and lasting peace, that every man may once enjoy the fruit of his own vine.'[4]

It can be said that an army commander should not undertake tasks that with reason he cannot expect to achieve; otherwise the labours of that commander are put to waste, as are the lives of his men. Marlborough was not blind to the enormous task in which he was engaged, and may have understood that the ultimate chances for success were slim. Nor was he blind to the attractions of alternative strategies. Rather than battering his way through a fortress belt, he several times drew up plans to invade France through the Moselle valley, and in 1705 actually made the attempt to do so, only to be foiled elsewhere. He also put forward plans to use the flexible power of the Royal Navy to undertake a 'descent' on the Pas de Calais and Normandy coastline, in combination with a deep thrust by land across northern France to the gates of Paris itself. This would side-step and leave behind, massive but irrelevant, the fortresses constructed by Vauban. The Duke's colleagues, even the intrepid Prince Eugene, would have none of it; such a project was felt to be laden with too much risk. They were probably right – a French army in the field is not to be trifled with, especially when the supply and communications of their opponents are dependent upon either ships lying off-shore, on the one hand, or on miserable roads threading their precarious way across territory sprinkled with unconquered enemy fortresses on the other. The risk attendant on such a joint land and sea operation was huge. Marlborough's close colleagues were against the notion and, almost inevitably, he was persuaded to turn away from it.

When considering Marlborough's record during the long years of the War of the Spanish Succession, it is plainly necessary to look closely at his many siege operations alongside his major victories in open battle. The Duke is understandably best known for these astounding triumphs, most popularly those at Blenheim and Ramillies, although arguably his most daring achievement was at Oudenarde in 1708. However, the technical, tactical demands of a protracted siege operation were considerably greater and hardly less hazardous than in the cut and thrust of a hectic day of battle. If an opponent will not or cannot be made to stand and fight, then a determined army commander, when pressing a campaign forward, must take his opportunities as they come. If that opportunity was a siege then so be it, and very often, the pursuit of one kind of operation, whether battle or siege, would lead to the other. Speaking in a parliamentary debate in 1712 over whether his successor as army commander in Flanders, the Duke of Ormonde, could rightly engage in a siege but not fight a battle, Marlborough said 'I do not know how to reconcile the orders, not to hazard a battle and [yet] to join in a siege, to the rules of war, since it is impossible to make a siege without hazarding a battle.[5]

The repeated loss of valuable fortresses would be bound to induce an opponent, however deficient in manpower and resources, to take the risk of a battle to stop the rot. So, the siege of Lille in 1708 led to the brief but fierce battle at Wynendael that September, while the murderous battle at Malplaquet in 1709 was intended by the French to prevent the siege of Mons. 'The cost is not to be considered,' Louis XIV wrote to Marshal Villars, demanding that he save the place.[6] Despite the increasingly threadbare state of French armies in the later years of the war, there were few occasions when Marshal Villars did not at least try to deflect Marlborough from his siege operations, although he failed most obviously at Bouchain in 1711. On the other hand, much as the loss of these places would be hard to accept, if the fortress belt was deep and strong enough the time for war might pass by without a decisive military result for either side. The more successful commander, for all his tactical virtues and successes, might still be foiled and unable to break through into open country and victory.

The inconvenient lack of a neat final conclusion to his campaigns should not obscure Marlborough's actual achievements while making war in this way, for his record was certainly impressive. The fortresses that Marlborough and his armies attacked were perhaps the most sophisticated and cunningly constructed ever seen before or since: massively built, often using extensive water obstacles, and well garrisoned with veteran soldiers led by aggressive commanders. That every place the Duke set his troops to take fell into his hands must speak volumes – not only for his energy, enterprise and skill, but for the bravery and fortitude of his soldiers, fighting in what were very often appalling conditions. These successes in siege warfare demonstrated generalship of a very high order. Like any commander, the Duke had to push forward the actual siege operations himself, with all the laborious squalor of fighting in trenches, and command the covering army, which simultaneously foiled the attempts of the enemy – often superior in numbers – to relieve the garrison. A formal siege was a huge operation. The successful result was never to be regarded as a complete certainty and the submission of any garrison was recognised as a major achievement. What makes Marlborough's achievement in this kind of warfare stand out is the massive scale and complexity of the defences he overcame. Given the extent of the task and the numbers and abilities of those ranged against him, Marlborough should not have got so far by any considered measure. Accordingly the abilities – and also the genuine limitations – of Marlborough when operating as a great commander are rarely seen to better advantage than when studying his siege operations during these long, deadening, years of war.

It is easy to assume that the triumphant battles which Marlborough fought in open field were of greater importance to his reputation than his sieges operations, and it occasionally seems that only one really counts anyway: the victory at Blenheim in August 1704. This is quite understandable, as successes on the field of battle certainly seem to be more clean-cut than protracted sieges with all their measured complexity, baffling technical phrases, and jargon. The battles have also the convenient neatness of occupying only one day on each occasion, and (in all but that of Malplaquet in 1709), the Duke's victories were very evident and to a great extent glorious. His inability to fight more battles in the open is often put down to the reluctance and hesitation of his cautious Dutch allies to go out and fight.[7] It is to be concluded that with greater freedom to act on his own initiative, the Duke would have fought more of these battles. In so doing he would surely have brought the war to a successful conclusion, although it is not certain that victory would be had on all occasions, good though his known record undoubtedly was. The whole question of the Dutch and their cautious attitude can certainly be over-stated. They were energetic men and brave enough, but had most to lose. Also, the question does not really address the true basis on which the Duke's reputation should properly depend.

Blaming the Dutch, and their views on how the war should be fought, overlooks the degree to which the French anticipated the very sort of campaign on which Marlborough embarked. Marshal Vauban had laid the most careful plans to foil any hostile army approaching the northern borders of France. It is usually acknowledged that it was imperative that Marlborough should neutralize or destroy the French fortress belt Vauban created before he could get on with any march to Paris and Versailles – the longed for, but ever elusive, war-winning stroke. The Duke could not afford to have French garrisons – and French field armies drawing support from those same garrisons – active behind the rear areas of his own army, and sat across his lines of communication and supply. Well, if that that was so, and it is hard to argue against the military logic, Marlborough unavoidably was 'fixed' in military parlance, obliged to besiege the fortresses and engage in a campaign dictated to him by the (now deceased) Vauban. With Marlborough's quickness of mind and mental flexibility under pressure – seen to such astonishing effect for example at Ramillies – these measured, intensely laborious, campaigns deep in the French fortress belt must have presented more of a challenge to his skill, and placed great demands on his patience. This was a challenge which the Duke repeatedly met and came through with honours on each occasion, leaving an ever growing number of captured fortresses in his wake.

Marlborough's victories in open battle must be seen alongside his successes in siege warfare. They are two sides to the same coin, and when considering the basis on which the Duke's reputation should justly lie, the litany of sieges in which he engaged between 1702 and 1711 are, at the very least, no less important than his victories in open battle. Given the scale of the challenge the Duke faced, the sieges may even be thought to be more significant. It is, of course, very tempting to view Marlborough's achievements in the glittering light of his astonishing victories in open battle. His successes in siege warfare, the result of sustained calculation, skill and fortitude, are less obvious and more complex; they tend to be overlooked, and that is a pity.

However, the story is not straightforward, for there is another consideration to take into account when studying the Duke's command of the Anglo-Dutch armies. The time available to Marlborough to win the war for Spain was strictly limited, and he was aware of this. It can be seen that the man who thwarted him and helped, perhaps more than any other, to bring about his downfall, was the designer and builder of the fortress belt that held him ensnared for so long – Louis XIV's engineer genius, Marshal Vauban.[7]

NOTES

1. The Schellenberg and Blenheim (July and August 1704), Elixheim (July 1705), Ramillies (May 1706), Oudenarde (July 1708), and Malplaquet (September 1709). Wynendael, fought in September 1708, saved Marlborough's huge siege operations against Lille, but John Webb commanded on the field that day, with the assistance of William Cadogan. The French commanders who faced Marlborough were tough and talented men, and although they were invariably beaten, they learned lessons quickly and studied his methods, so that the Duke's successes became more qualified and expensive as time went on.

2. C.T. Atkinson, *Marlborough and the Rise of the British Army*, 1921, p. 449.

3. W. Coxe, *Life of Marlborough*, Vol I, 1848, p. 431. Given the stunning success at Ramillies, Marlborough could not and would not let slip the opportunity to thrust forward deep into the Spanish Netherlands. The speed of that campaign was the military wonder of the age, but it unavoidably drew the Duke into the French fortress belt. He had foreseen this eventuality and hoped to avoid it when pressing for a major campaign in the Moselle valley, which would conveniently avoid Vauban's entanglements. For a variety of reasons, this was never to be.

4. W.S. Churchill, *Marlborough, His Life and Times*, Vol II, 1947, p. 455.

5. D.G. Chandler, *Marlborough as Military Commander*, 1976, p. 251.

6. D.G. Chandler, *Blenheim Preparation*, 2004, p. 189.

7. Marshal Vauban, Sebastien le Prestre, (1633–1707) Louis XIV's chief engineer and designer of thirty-three new fortresses and fortified towns. He also improved over 150 other places and conducted fifty-three separate siege operations, at twenty of which Louis XIV was present in person. As Governor of Lille between 1667 and 1670, Vauban massively augmented the defences of the city and constructed the vast new citadel. A dashing, even reckless, commander in his youth, Vauban also possessed cool and calculating skill; like other great military engineers, he came to wage war at one remove, his fortifications being his weapons. 'Engineers, unlike other warriors, do not have the satisfaction of exchanging blow for blow … they have to remain calm in the midst of the most alarming dangers.' See C. Duffy, *Fire & Stone*, 1975, p. 147. Not that the engineers lacked energy or courage, far from it, and Vauban would often be found in the most forward and exposed positions 'The engineer must be outstandingly bold and outstandingly prudent.' Vauban was made a Marshal of France in 1703, but fell from favour with the King soon afterwards.

I

The Stone Entanglement

*The enemy lay within a series of fortresses, of
all types, that controlled the battlefield.*[1]

It may help to tell the fascinating story of the Duke of Marlborough's
lengthy campaigns of siege warfare, and to allow what his achievements were in that onerous, heartbreaking task to be more clearly
understood, if the scene in which he and his soldiers conducted
those operations is set. It is not intended however to give a detailed
description of the complex art of siege warfare in the early years of
the eighteenth century – others have already provided this valuable
service, and their enjoyable works on the whole vast subject are
listed in the bibliography. It is worth remembering what were the
purposes of any fortress: in the main, they provided a visible element
of defence for a border region or an area otherwise of particular
importance. For much of history, monarchs and rulers had sought
to define their dominions and protect their 'natural' frontiers with
imposing man-made physical defences. Fortresses also provided
depots for stores, munitions and equipment from which a field army
might conveniently draw sustenance without having to reach back
too far into the rear areas to do so. Lastly, fortresses were often the
administrative and civic centre of a region – important not only as a
symbol of enduring authority (authority which was weakened when
a place was lost to an opponent) but useful for the gathering of taxes
and other state revenue.

   To capture a town or fortress was a significant military achievement, with wide implications, extending the control and influence
of the successful army over stretches of an opponent's territory. This
impinged on the sovereignty of that opponent, and hampered the
ability to campaign to good effect in the region or to raise taxes. Any
movement into an opponent's territory would usually require the
clearing out of any fortresses that might otherwise lie dangerously
close to the lines of supply and communication of the advancing

army. The fortresses therefore provided a very real symbol of forward defence, a marker across which an opponent must not be allowed to march lightly. When peace came, as inevitably it does, any captured place would serve as a useful bargaining counter in the negotiations. Siege operations also offered the prospect of military success at supposedly lesser cost than fighting battles in the open and importantly for many commanders, at less risk to professional reputations. Cautious generals, ever mindful of their carefully crafted reputations, had a tendency to prefer the steady procedures of the formal siege to the rigours of outright battle. There was no telling what might happen in the smoke and dust of a hazardous and difficult to control day-long clash of arms in open field, but there were measured and, on the whole, commonly-understood rules for siege warfare. Sieges apparently held less risk.

The significant development of artillery, and its increasingly effective use in military operations over the period from the fifteenth to the seventeenth centuries, had brought about a revolution in fortress design. This was intended to bolster the resilience of defence against the burgeoning power of the artillery attack. The besieger, courtesy of this technological advance, was in a position of superiority over the now vulnerable defender. Upright, exposed stone-walls, impressive enough at first glance but of themselves not sturdy or proof against artillery, no longer offered protection. Castles in the classic mould became obsolete embarrassments in military terms, appearing to offer security and protection when in practice they offered none. As a result, the necessary choice of military engineers became the development of low and wide defensive embankments of either stone or earth, better able to avoid, withstand and absorb the fire of cannon. Massive sloped defences became the norm in Europe, not only in the north and west, but in the Ottoman empire to the east also.

The second half of the seventeenth century had seen a tremendous development of scientific fortification, and it became an age of great military engineering. The two outstanding engineers of the period – the Frenchman, Sebastian le Prestre Vauban, and the Dutchman, Meinheer van Coehorn – thoroughly developed the existing theories for extending the power and influence of the static defence. This led to increasingly complex geometric designs for fortifications. While offering as meagre a target to enemy gunners as possible, the defenders were enabled to sweep all approaches to their works with interlocking and overlapping arcs of artillery and musket fire. There was to be no dead ground, no inch of grass that the attackers must cross that was not exposed to fire. By extending outwards the layers of defence, the battering guns of an attacking army were progressively distanced from the heart of the fortress: the citadel. Inevitably, any successful outcome of a siege was delayed as a result, and in a period when the campaign season depended upon the use of dry roads, such delay could kill a campaign off just as surely, but rather less spectacularly, as inflicting a defeat in open battle.

This terrific development of imaginative fortress design, and the expense and care lavished on new construction, was such that it became apparent by 1700 that the artillery arm had not kept pace with these new techniques and tactics. Until the gunners caught up in this contest for supremacy – establishing once again the penetrating power of the gun over the endurance of stone – then a modern Vauban or Coehorn-designed fortress would be a bafflingly complex and difficult objective for any military commander. Success was by no means impossible to achieve, for in theory no fortress would stand a well conducted and sustained siege for ever (if all else failed the garrison might be starved out), but that success would demand in return a very high price in effort and in the lives of men. Most significant from a military point of view would be the loss of time:

> The sieges of the wars of Marlborough and Eugene in the early part of the 18th century, may be taken as giving a fair index of the resisting power of fortresses at a period following lavish expenditure on permanent fortifications, and when Vauban's method of formal attack and defence met on more equal terms, and these sieges may almost be regarded as crucial tests of the defensive efficacy of the fortifications of the time.[2]

So the actual power of a fortress – in itself an amalgam of physical defensive works, the bravery and skill of the garrison troops who manned the walls, and the mental robustness of their commander – lay in its ability to endure. By enduring, this shackled the freedom of choice of their opponent, who was forced to stand and attack them on ground that had been chosen and prepared long in advance. In any battle in open field this choice of ground is taken to be an important factor; it is no less so with a fortress.

It might seem obvious that the driving force in siege operations was provided by the attacking army; by their very nature the defending garrison appear to have the lesser, more passive, role. This is something of an illusion. All commanders seek to 'fix' their opponents, not in the sense of pinning them against some physical object but by taking away their freedom of choice. By doing so, the more accomplished commander will impose his will upon the other, even if only for a limited time, while a certain object is obtained. The general who is fixed in this way is obliged to react to the moves, however mundane, of his opponent and must wait in hope for his own opportunity to come. In the classic mould, a commander became victorious by defeating an opponent in open battle. To have to devote resources, effort and time to reducing fortresses instead was a major distraction from the principal aim, but to draw off, and leave those places alone, might be to compromise an otherwise promising campaign.

To embark on a formal siege might well be an unavoidable choice. By threatening valuable fortresses, the defenders' main army may be drawn out into the open to fight a battle – Louis XIV wrote to one of his generals in the post-Ramillies summer of 1706 'The Duke of Marlborough attacks places in the hope of enticing you thither.' Just so, the Captain-General was indeed hoping to fix the Duke of Vendôme by forcing him to come forward with his weakened army and fight to save French-held fortresses in the Spanish Netherlands. In those particular circumstances, the French might suffer a second catastrophe, one that could not be made good: the entire loss of their field army. Hence the King's caution; he would give up fortresses at a price, but had to save the army. However, Marlborough too was fixed, in a wider sense, as his victory at Ramillies impelled him forward into Vauban's fortress belt, where his particular skills at both strategic and tactical level would be blunted with time. The French engineer had planned for this thirty years earlier, knowing that one day an attacker would have to take this route. Although it was not immediately apparent at the time, such was French disarray and despair, Marlborough's freedom of choice at a strategic level was taken away, and that was to be fixed militarily.

Fortresses had become a device, massive, expensive and complex, with which to delay an opponent so that the chill weather of winter would overtake the unfinished campaign and force a withdrawal of the attacking army into warm quarters. This being so, it followed that a garrison should not be expected to fight it out to the death; submission on honourable terms, after a decent period of resistance, became an acceptable course of action. This was possible as the common practice of hanging the garrison from the walls of a captured fortress was no longer thought to be right, at least in western Europe. Men who fear for their neck will fight harder and longer. For the garrison commander, the knowledge that any defence, however devoted, would eventually fail without some external factor coming into play (such as a lack of supplies for the besiegers, or sign that a relieving army was coming to lift the siege), had to be set against the certainty that no fortress should be lost prematurely through default or neglect. There were certainly widely understood, and apparently rather convenient, conventions for this kind of warfare, but these included the strict requirement for both opposing commanders to do their utmost at the risk of their professional reputation, and this often entailed bitter fighting and heavy casualties.

Although it was understood that a defended place could not be expected to hold out for ever, Louis XIV felt obliged to write to the town governors of his frontier fortresses, reminding them that he expected them to resist more firmly than was becoming the tendency. Certainly they should not just give up as soon as honour had been seen to be satisfied. On 5 April 1705, the King sent a message to his governors, that 'They are strictly forbidden to yield their places until there is a large breach on the main parapet and they have withstood at least one assault.'[3] On one particular occasion, Comte de la Motte, a very competent commander charged with the defence of Ghent in the aftermath of the fall of Lille late in 1708, was urged by the French Minister of War to stand firm or risk his professional reputation, but he still gave the place up after a rather perfunctory defence. The Comte could claim in justification that his commanding general was intent on going into winter quarters, and making no effort at all with the field army to relieve the town. All the same, on the other side of the hill, Marlborough was anxious at the onset of cold weather and agreeably surprised when the place was given up so soon. A more enterprising commander might well have made the Duke's troops freeze in their trenches for a while longer, but these decisions can be finely balanced, and in this particular case the morale of the garrison was very fragile and the citizenry had turned hostile.

Marshal Vauban did more than design and build first-rate fortresses. In addition to his engineering talent, he was in many ways a very aggressive commander with a keen interest in the potential superiority of attack over defence. He developed, and set out in a logical way, the previously rather impromptu methods of conducting the siege operations of the day. These had been characterised by insufficient preparation, inadequate provisioning and dispersal of effort, together with a tendency to launch rash massed infantry assaults as soon as possible on inadequately degraded defences. As a result, siege operations were often ill-prepared, protracted, costly and unsuccessful. Vauban set out in simple form a model timetable as a form of practical guide for besieging commanders to follow in operations against a specimen six-bastion modern fortress, well-appointed and firmly held. The proper time to be expended if matters were properly conducted, was calculated to be:

To invest the fortress, collect stores and construct the lines of circumvallation and contravallation	9 days
To open the trenches and to reach the covered way	9 days
To capture the covered way	4 days
To cross the ditch to reach the demi-lune	3 days
To create a breach by battery or mining	4 days
To capture the demi-lune	3 days
To cross the main ditch	4 days
To site forward batteries and breach the main defences	4 days
To capture the breach and flanking positions	2 days
To accept the capitulation of the garrison	2 days
To allow for unexpected delays	4 days
Total time to be allowed	48 days[4]

There was an obvious risk, one that became reality on several occasions, that these overall guidelines (for they were meant to be no more than that) would be taken as a literal programme dictating what a garrison commander was expected to do. The implication was that, having reached the required point in the timetable, it would be acceptable just to submit without further effort. Louis XIV's comment of April 1705 reflects his growing concern at this tendency amongst his garrison commanders, although some in the past could not claim to have held out this long. However, those officers had to balance this instruction and the suspicion that not enough might have been done to save a place against that of leaving things too late. This would put the besieging army to the cost and trouble of a storm, with the consequent horrific risk of a sack of the town and massacre of the garrison.

Given the short time available each year for active campaigning, the loss of fortresses was certainly not a foregone conclusion, no matter how meticulous the arrangements of the besieging army might be. If no relief was in sight, however, and a storm of what was known as a 'practicable breach' in the defences was in the offing, a garrison commander was able, expected even, to ask for honourable terms to yield. The garrison that had acquitted itself well in defence was entitled to expect good terms and the soldiers to be permitted to return to their own lines without molestation or giving their parole not to serve further. That the modern first-class fortresses to which Marlborough turned his attention should have been overcome (in most cases, but not all) well within the 48-day guidelines suggested by Vauban, says much for the Duke's skills at this methodical and positional kind of warfare. Still, the prolonged, difficult, and expensive operations against Lille (1708), Tournai (1709), and perhaps most starkly at the dreadful siege of Aire (1710), show us the other side of the story. These were, in effect, very protracted pitched battles, fought over a period of weeks in which neither side flinched, and often hideously more expensive in casualties than a single day of combat out in the open. That to engage in sieges was not to wage war cheaply by timetable is plain from these operations.

Although in a strategic sense fortresses provided security, and were an important physical symbol of sovereignty and power, tactically the purpose of a fortress had become to gain time – that most valuable and irreplaceable military commodity. The fortress would impose delay while the enemy's campaign tired throughout the long summer and eventually withered away with the approach of autumn and winter. Fortresses would be stoutly defended, to be yielded at the appropriate moment. Ground would have been traded in exchange for time, and military goals would have been achieved in measure depending upon how successful the opposing commanders had proved to be. Given the practical limitations on those generals when maintaining an army in the field at this period (not least in supplying their horses with forage), and with the virtual impossibility of campaigning throughout the winter, a steady series of defensive operations anchored on a fortress belt would eat up the good campaign months of summer, and could be a very effective strategy indeed. Without necessarily having to fight a major battle, a commander on the defensive could frustrate his opponent until the fine weather was over and the dusty roads turned to bottomless mud. For the commander on the offensive on the other hand, the prize of taking a number of fortresses before calling a halt in the autumn, apart from demonstrating military expertise in the art of siege warfare, could be more than enough to sustain a professional reputation. After all, the capture of a fortress was no meagre thing, and these places were certainly useful bargaining counters. Many generals, as a result, became particularly impressed with the merits of siege warfare, both from the point of view of the offence and the defence. Relatively few commanders in the early eighteenth century sought to fight both ways, however.

The outer part of a fortress was the glacis, an area of sloping ground about 300 yards in width, kept entirely clear of anything that could shelter an attacker. This glacis was bounded on its inner side by a parapet and firing step known as the covered way, the first formal part of the defence, and this was crowned with a fence of sharpened stakes known as palisades or palisadoes. From there, infantry and dismounted dragoons would be stationed to sweep the open area of the glacis with musketry fire. The security of the covered way was of particular importance for the defence. Once this was lost or compromised to any real extent, the besiegers could bring forward their heavy artillery to batter at close range a breach in the main defences, preparatory to making an assault on the fortress. Once that breach was open, the game was all but up for the garrison commander, who was left with the choice between managing a negotiated submission or facing a storm.

Behind the covered way was the ditch, often filled with water and, at about twenty feet deep and one hundred feet wide, a major obstacle in itself. Occasionally there would be forward secondary ditches to take the force of a besieger's operations. The outermost inward-facing wall of the ditch was the counterscarp, sometimes pierced with galleries and loopholes from where defenders could fire into the backs of any attackers who had managed to clamber down into the ditch. Once the counterscarp was taken, however, the besiegers had a good 'jumping-off' point for the next phase of their attack on the main defences. The innermost outward-facing wall of the ditch was usually lined with stone or brickwork and was known as the scarp. The ditch area would often contain secondary defensive works, such as demi-lunes and ravelins (see Appendix 2, glossary of terms), which were in place to protect potentially vulnerable parts of the fortress and to keep the besieging artillery at as great a distance as possible. The main defences – the curtain wall and the major bastions – were wide, low, structures with multiple-angled faces, intended both to deflect artillery fire and to enable defenders to fire into the flanks of attacking troops. Although these works were low, the depth of the adjacent ditch added to the actual height, making them both difficult to scale and less vulnerable to battering fire than a tall structure would have been. The simple concept of layered defence meant that a series of obstacles of this kind, particularly with a major city, would confront an attacker. At the heart of the fortress was the citadel, a stronghold on its own merits, which could often hold out long after the defences of the town had submitted – as was the case with Liège in 1703 (and 1705), Lille in 1708, and Tournai in 1709.

The first task for any besieging army after investing the garrison, as far as could be managed cutting them off from contact with the surrounding countryside and their friends outside the walls, was to sweep clear the immediate neighbourhood of forage and crops, to prevent the defenders getting their hands on these supplies. The besiegers then had to prepare their own camp against any attack, either by the troops inside a fortress or from a relieving army that might approach from a distance. The army undertaking a formal siege would therefore construct for itself, after a fashion, its own fortified camp. Defensive lines built around the town and facing outwards against any approaching enemy army were known as lines of circumvallation. These would soon be matched by lines of defence facing inwards to the town, which were known as lines of contravallation. The area between these two sets of lines became the camp for the besieging army. Vauban was however rather scornful of the real value of these lines, considering them to be too passive. Rather, he preferred that active covering forces should manoeuvre freely to shield the siege operations, and prevent interference by relieving armies. By so doing of course, there was always the chance that the enemy could be made to stand and fight it out in the open, although this was not what all generals hoped for by any means. During the siege of Mons in 1709, Prince Eugene was so scornful of the ability of the French army after the battle of Malplaquet to interfere in the operations that he did not bother to construct these lines. He relied instead upon Marlborough's covering army to provide the security necessary.

The beleaguered garrison commander would be on the watch, and the knowledge that a relieving force had approached but been unsuccessful and drawn off for whatever reason, would often be the sign that terms for a capitulation had to be sought before long. For the besieging commander meanwhile, as his men constructed the lines of circumvallation and contravallation, the immediate task was to select the most promising point in the defences against which to direct his efforts. In practice, there would usually be two 'attacks', a left and a right, so that the defenders' fire would be split between them, and the besieging general would be able to keep his options open as events unfolded. On occasions, for the same reasons, there would be more than two attacks; but this risked diffusing the besiegers' efforts, breaking the siege up into penny packets. As the operations progressed, it would gradually become apparent which attack had the most prospect of success, and most resources would accordingly be devoted to that effort. Professional rivalry might however mean that an unpromising attack had to be kept open, otherwise the officer commanding that part of the operation might take offence at the implied slur on his reputation and efforts. This happened at Béthune in 1710.

Once the heavy guns of the siege train had arrived, the ground would then be 'broken' – in effect trench digging would begin – usually at night so that the darkness would help to shield the soldiers and pioneers from the unwelcome attentions of the garrison. Occasionally – although strictly speaking against the conventional wisdom – the digging would commence before the artillery arrived. A communication trench would be dug between the starting points for the attacks, to facilitate easy passage from one to the other as the besieging general shifted the weight of his effort day by day. This trench had no tactical significance other than that of convenience. Forward of this, the first 'parallel' trench, wide and deep, would be constructed so as to encircle the besieged fortress at a uniform distance along its whole course. This would vary with the demands of topography, but would be sufficiently out of range for the defenders' fire not to seriously impede the work or harass the occupants of the trench. The first parallel would be connected to the lines of contravallation by another communication trench, and provide the starting point for subsequent operations. Here the siege guns would first of all be placed and begin their counter-battery work – wearing down the defenders' artillery in particular – and where stores and ammunition could also be gathered in relative safety but conveniently ready for use. Reserves of troops, ready to repel any sortie by the garrison, would also be held back in this area, ready to move forward into action as required.

The next move would be to advance the entrenchments from the first parallel trench towards the defences of the fortress, by means of a 'sap' or secondary communication trench. The direction this took would again depend on the terrain and the water table, as workings would flood in low-lying ground remarkably quickly. Because of the high water table in much of the Southern Netherlands, the normal practice, of necessity, was the placing of gabions (large wicker-baskets filled with earth or stones) to make a barricade and sheltering parapet. Although the placing of these devices was a hazardous business if the enemy were on the alert, it was certainly quicker and less tiring than digging a deep trench, even when this was practical.[5] Care would be have to be taken that the defenders could not shoot very far down the length of a sap, so that a zig-zag course would usually be taken, and the 'sappers' could labour in relative safety. When enough progress had been made towards the fortress a second parallel trench would be dug, again at a uniform distance from the defences, and the zig-zag sap then continued forwards to a third parallel. At various intervals rudimentary fortified posts would be constructed, and secondary, short, parallels dug off at right angles to the sap, which could be manned quickly at times of emergency, such as when the garrison attempted sorties. Soldiers in these posts could also to a fair degree provide covering fire for the sappers as they made their way forward. This was especially so if these posts were built up into what were known as 'cavaliers', with soldiers standing on bundles of fascines, able to fire over the palisades into the ranks of defenders lining the covered way. To avoid being caught in a cross-fire, able to be shot down the length of the sap as the labourers got closer, the 'attack' would often be aimed towards the projecting salient angle – the most prominent and exposed part of the defences. To ignore these angles and go instead for the main curtain wall would, under Vauban's system, inevitably expose the sappers to fire from one flank or the other or even from both flanks simultaneously. It is plain that sapping was an art fraught with risk and the men engaged in the work were no mere labourers.

Sapping was obviously a time-consuming and laborious business, and the technique that was developed was for the sappers, the pioneers or workmen, to crouch behind a stout, mobile, timber screen on wheels known as a mantlet. Sometimes, a gabion laid on its side (being roughly cylindrical, the cumbersome device could be pushed along with some effort) would be used, but this was rather less effective than a proper mantlet. Pushing this rudimentary protection in front of him, the leading man, on his knees, would scoop out a shallow trench with his shovel as he went, his comrades immediately behind him improving the trench both by deepening the excavation and by building a makeshift parapet on the side most exposed to the enemy with gabions and the spoil from the digging. The normal practice was to dig down about three feet, the men coming along gradually being able to stand rather than kneel or stoop as the work of building the parapet progressed. The gabions, once in place on top of the spoil, would provide another three feet or so of cover. All but the tallest man would in this way be provided with shelter from observation and fire, and often a firing step would have to be constructed to allow the soldiers in the trenches to use their own muskets against the garrison.

In this way, slowly and carefully but with some reasonable element of shelter, the saps could be pushed forward, almost literally inch by inch. The danger from the garrison's gunners being able to shoot down the length of a trench was such that the course of the saps was calculated with utmost care. The officers would do well to keep a close eye on the men engaged in this task. 'Sappers often intoxicate themselves at the sap-head' Vauban wrote 'and are then slaughtered like beasts as they take no care what they do.'[6] As much work as possible was done with the cover of darkness, but inevitably a lot had also to take place in daylight, exposed to observation and fire from the garrison. The leading men sometimes wore protective armour on the head and upper body, indicating the hazardous nature of the work they undertook, and for which they often received bounty money.

The creeping progress of the sap would quite naturally attract the close attention of the besieged garrison, who could be counted on to keep the pioneers under a heavy fire with musketry from the soldiers lining the covered way, the first real line of defence. Artillery and mortars could also be used; but powder was precious, the saps were meagre targets, and the gunners in the fortress were better employed trying to demolish the partly constructed besiegers' batteries. Any sign of slackness amongst the sappers however (clumsy handling of the gabions perhaps, an imperfect alignment of the zig-zag course taken, or a failure to build the usual protective redoubts at intervals along the saps) would encourage the garrison to make sorties to interrupt the work. Night-time was the obvious first choice for such vicious operations, with the darkness giving protective cover against the artillery of the besieging army. However, mid-day was also favoured as the sappers would be tired after their morning exertions, perhaps snatching a bite to eat and not really on the alert. Alternatively, a new shift of sappers might be taking over from their tired comrades, with all the disruption and lack of attention that such a brief period of change holds.

The natural inclination of an aggressive garrison commander to mount sorties of this kind, and so try and delay the sapping work, had to be weighed against the inevitable cost in killed and wounded that was entailed. Vauban warned against rash or pointless attacks that might achieve little other than the inflicting and receiving of a few casualties, and have little real impact on the rate of progress of the siege. Unlike the besieging army which could, to a degree, replenish its depleted units with fresh troops, the invested garrison was a finite resource, gradually wasting away as the siege went on and without much hope of replenishment. On occasions this did take place, however, as when Marshal Villars managed to slip fresh troops into Bouchain in 1711. This was only possible because the Allied lines were incapable of being completed due to the close proximity of the French main army and the marshes of two major rivers. Despite this evident concern at the relative lack of numbers in any garrison, sorties were a regular feature of siege operations. Close-quarter fighting in the saps and parallels often took place, slowing the besiegers' work and putting off the critical moment at which either the garrison had to yield or face the horrors of a storm.

As the third parallel, that closest to the defenders' covered way, was completed, the besiegers would look for signs of submission. Time would be getting short for the garrison commander, who in turn would be scanning the horizon anxiously for signs of relief. The siege artillery would be prepared to be dragged much closer to the main defences, so that the battering work of the big guns and mortars could begin in real earnest. In the absence of any indication from the garrison that they wished to ask for terms, a final double-sap might be pushed towards what would have been identified as the most vulnerable point on the edge of the covered way. This sap would then branch out at that point to right and left, just outside the grenade-throwing range of the defenders, and this would provide a convenient jumping-off point for an assault on the palisades of the covered way, the counterscarp and ditch. The storming party for such an effort was commonly reckoned to have to be eight or ten companies of infantry to be effective (600–800 men, usually grenadiers), with a similar number of reserves ready at hand in the second parallel, able to move forward once the stormers had stepped off in their attack. Once enough of the covered way had been secured, the big guns would be dragged forward and the breach opened out ready for the greater, general storm when the artillerymen had done their work.

If necessary, the final double-sap might be pushed further forward again, encroaching further into the covered way itself. If the defensive ditch was dry, this sap could be dug sloping down through the earth of the covered way, with timber brought forward to shore up the sides and roof, so that the attackers could get at the counterscarp and into the ditch in relative cover. If the ditch was flooded this was plainly not possible and the attackers would have to go 'over the top', once again led by sappers pushing forward a mantlet, just as in the digging of the approach trenches, until the point was reached when the defenders could be rushed. This was of course a highly dangerous operation as the range between the sappers and their infantry supports on the one hand, and the defenders on the other, progressively lessened. Lengthy battles between grenadiers at this point were common; one advantage though, was that the closer the saps came to the defences, the less likely it was that the garrison would blow their deadly counter-mines against the encroaching entrenchments, as these would damage their own defensive works in the process.

Simultaneously with the digging of the saps, the besieging troops would construct the batteries with which to fire at and breach the main defences. The big guns would usually require a stout wooden platform to be constructed so as not to sink unto the soft earth. The materiel necessary for these platforms had to be manhandled forward, with all the associated risk, before the siege artillery could even come on the scene. The amount of timber and other base material was carefully calculated, and a single 24-pounder siege piece was typically placed on six or seven 18-foot long logs laid side by side. An eight gun battery of the big 24-pounder guns required a frontage of sixty yards (occasionally, larger guns were used but they had no more breaching power and were more expensive in powder use). Once again, to protect the pioneers from counter-battery fire, the preparatory work was done at night and had therefore to be completed in less than twelve hours. Magazines for explosive shells and gunpowder would be constructed close at hand with protective coverings, although round-shot (not being susceptible to the elements) was often stacked in the open. Mortars, those highly effective engines of siege warfare, were emplaced in a similar fashion, although their high-angle trajectory, so useful and deadly in operation, meant that the timber platforms had to be particularly strong, using deeply dug foundations made up of massive timber beams.

Once all this was in place and the ammunition, shot and powder necessary for sustained battery firing was stored nearby for ready use, the siege guns, firing from their allotted places in the parallels, would begin their work. Firing from positions at the first parallel initially, the gunners would soften up the defences and suppress the defenders firing against the sappers. As the saps got closer to the covered way, the breaching batteries would be progressively brought forward to intermediate ricochet battery positions and then to the third parallel, as close to the defences as possible. Massively protected positions would need to be constructed to shield the gunners from the fire of the garrison at such close range. The principal aim now was to achieve a 'practicable breach', incapable of being defended, and it was calculated, with scientific nicety, that a twelve gun battery of 24-pounder guns would produce a breach in twelve to fifteen days when firing at the rate of 100 rounds each day. Others, however, calculated that twenty-two guns, firing at the same daily rate at the closest range, should produce that same breach in 48 hours.

There were two principal techniques employed by the gunners: direct fire by siege guns using round-shot, and high-angle mortar fire with explosive shell. The use of mortars, both large siege pieces and the small variety known as coehorns, was widespread, with the ability of these simple but cruelly effective weapons to search into dead ground otherwise hidden from direct-fire artillery.[7] Effective in throwing explosive projectiles deep into a fortress, well-directed mortar fire could turn a place into chaos in a very short time – as at Liège in 1702, Huy in 1703, and Ostend in 1706 where Royal Navy bomb vessels off-shore soon set the town alight, to the dismay of garrison and population. Although the smaller coehorns were also often used by defenders, their effectiveness was not the same as in the attack, as the target area against trenches was less than that presented by a fortress or town. Much of Vauban's system for complex fortification design was intended to lay out the defence so that an attacker could not easily push his saps and parallels forward, safe from the garrison's artillery firing down the length of a trench with appalling and deadly effect. Of course, the besieged garrison would also employ artillery pieces in the defence, but these were commonly of a smaller calibre than the breaching artillery of the attacking force. Guns firing 12- and 16-pounder shot were often used, equal in range to the big guns of the besiegers, but of course less expensive in powder consumption.

As the breaching work progressed and the hard face of the defences – whether made of hard-packed grass covered earth, stone or brickwork – was broken open, the gunners would switch from solid round-shot to explosive shell, and the mortars would begin to play a larger part in the bombardment. To continue using round-shot from the 24-pounders (although they too could use explosive shell when required) would just compact the earth core in the developing breach. Mortar bombs or shells fired with reduced charges on the other hand were more likely to settle, explode and then collapse the earth into the ditch, producing the gentle slope up which attacking soldiers could scramble – the much sought after 'practicable breach'. In the normal course of events, unless repairs could be made this development would be the signal for the garrison commander to think very carefully about asking for terms to be granted for an orderly capitulation. He would watch with care the creeping progress of the saps and for signs that preparations for a storm, perhaps the ostentatious assembling of scaling ladders in the parallels, were being made.

Direct fire (the simple battering of the defences with round-shot) is fairly easy to understand, but a variation often employed was ricochet fire. In this particular way, the projectiles were fired at a low trajectory across the ground to bound over the defensive works and career on into the fortress. If sited in enfilade (firing from a flank) this could be devastatingly effective against defending troops, whether infantry or gunners, who were manning a parapet. Accordingly, ricochet batteries detailed for this purpose would be sited very carefully. These gunners would try, as far as was possible, to shoot down the length of the defences, clearing out the defenders in the process, rather than those who were firing at close range at the face of the defences to produce a breach. The intention was just the same as defenders trying to shoot down the length of a sap or parallel, and the ricochet technique had the added advantage that the powder charge required for such fire was, as with explosive shells, rather less than for straightforward battering work with round-shot. The guns could therefore be worked for longer with the powder supplies to hand, and the wear on the artillery pieces was correspondingly lessened. The brass guns in use at the time would, after periods of sustained firing, also begin to droop and warp with the heat. However, the ricochet technique had its obvious limitation, as Vauban-style defence relied on having no very long straight lines.

Breaching by means of artillery was the favoured method in sieges, but mining was often also used where the geological sub-strata and the height of the water-table permitted. Mining was an ancient technique, and defensive walls would occasionally still be collapsed by tunnelling underneath and then burning out the timber supports – as in medieval times. This particular method was less effective once low earthen and stone-faced ramparts, intended to counter the increasingly powerful artillery, replaced high castle walls and towers. More common in the eighteenth century was the use of explosive charges to demolish an earthwork or section of defensive wall, and with good luck the defenders would simultaneously be blown sky high in the process.[8] As with breaching by artillery, the spoil thrown down into the ditch by the explosion of a mine would help the attackers to mount the breach. The response of the garrison to such a threat would often be to counter-mine, or dig outwards towards the attackers, and disrupt their tunnelling, either by blowing them up with counter-charges (*camouflets* as they were known) or by breaking into the enemy galleries.[9] Although mining was often the technique favoured when attacking a fortress, it was also particularly valuable as a defensive measure against sapping work. While expensive in powder and labour, it was relatively inexpensive in men, and invested garrisons were by their very nature composed of a limited number of soldiers. Such counter-mining was quite cost-efficient in the numbers of men at risk. In addition, the besiegers were often working in very poor conditions, labouring to construct the parallels and battery positions in bad weather, and to attack these activities with mines could seriously disrupt the timetable of a besieging general, in what was always a limited campaigning season.

There in the mud and the darkness things would be fought out hand to hand, and the favoured weapon of choice was often a sharpened spade, useful both for digging or hacking as required and more handy than a sword or pistol. The siege operations that Marlborough undertook between 1708 and 1711 saw extensive mining and counter-mining, and the casualties on both sides were very heavy. These operations were regarded with particular horror, and the Allied troops were plainly less adept at them than the French; the progress of the sieges were prolonged, and the tally of casualties lengthened, as a result. Any tunnelling was a time-consuming business, and mining teams would normally comprise eighteen miners, each man an expensive asset, together with thirty-six labouring assistants. Whether besieged or besieger, to kill any number of these expert workers by means of a counter-mine or by breaking into their tunnels to fight in the darkness would often be well worth the effort.

Enormous care was required by the besieging armies to overcome the extensive and ingenious use of water obstacles used in formal defensive works. These were often added to by the extemporary flooding of meadows and fields adjoining a threatened fortress. The water used as an obstacle in this way was, quite naturally, drawn from local rivers and canals, and these could be diverted by the besieger with careful cutting through the banks to run the water off and away from the defences. Sometimes the sluice gates in a region, used routinely in time of peace to vary the water levels as required, would be seized or broken down. Frequent battles, some of great ferocity, were fought by opposing forces for control of these small but important devices. When the defensive ditches could not be drained off or the connecting watercourses dammed up enough, the attackers would have to prepare and lay huge quantities of fascines to create temporary paths and bridges over the flooded obstacles. Such exhausting work imposed serious delay on the progress of a siege, and crossing them under fire entailed great risk.

As a siege went on, the defenders would seek in quiet periods and often at night to repair the damage caused by artillery fire and mining, but the rate of repair would not usually keep pace with that of the damage inflicted. Once the 'practicable' breach was made, the garrison commander was expected to yield. This was a perfectly honourable thing to do, as long as the siege had been dragged out long enough. Although there was a general expectation that an active garrison commander would stand at least one attempted storm of a breach before giving way, as Louis XIV had ordered his town governors to do, in practice many did not do so. The existence of a breach and clear signs that a storm was being prepared often proved to be the point of capitulation if no relief was in sight. Sometimes of course, tactical considerations drove events on faster than the accepted convention of the age, as when Colonel Haxhusien stormed St Ghislain, 'sword in hand' the night before the battle of Malplaquet in September 1709, so that Henry Withers could march straight onto the battlefield the following day without hindrance.[10] It was found that attacks mounted at night taking advantage of the cover of darkness were worthwhile. However, the lack of visibility also imposed a real handicap on command and control, and night attacks were prone to breaking down in confusion. This was certainly seen at Lille in 1708 where several well-prepared night attacks failed, but a subsequent attack, sent in broad daylight, was a surprising success.

The two main parties engaged in any formal siege were, quite obviously, the garrison holding the fortress and the besieging army trying to take the place. The latter's covering army, free to manoeuvre, protected the troops engaged in the siege, and ensured that regular supplies got through. They in turn would be matched against whatever relieving army might be sent to help the garrison. There were two main options open to the commander of such a relieving army: either to close with the besiegers' covering army and force a confrontation in open field – a course of action that was fairly uncommon – or alternatively, the relieving commander could threaten the besieging army's ability to feed itself. Although ultimately unsuccessful, this was the course pursued with such vigour by the Duke of Vendôme in 1708, during operations along the Scheldt river in an attempt to save Lille. Otherwise, a relieving army could move to threaten some sensitive point elsewhere, intending to draw off the besiegers from their target. This was attempted by the Elector of Bavaria, again in the autumn of 1708, when he attacked Brussels, hoping to draw the Allies away from Lille. In that particular case, Marlborough, entirely at the height of his tactical powers at the time, moved swiftly to drive off the Elector. He did so, while at the same time managing to maintain the siege operations without the least interruption, even though the number of troops left in the trenches had been drastically reduced.

The provisioning of their armies was an understandable, constant concern for commanders on either side, each of which laboured under the same difficulties, more or less. However, a besieging force, unlike a garrison, was relatively free to forage for supplies.[11] When the region around a fortress was exhausted, their supplies had to be dragged from depots and magazines deep in the rear areas along the miserably poor roads of the day. If available, the waterways could be used, but these assets were recognised for the value they had and were stoutly held, becoming the scene of prolonged and expensive fighting as one side sought to keep the waterways open and the other sought to close them down. The beleaguered garrison of course could not resupply itself but had to subsist on the stores held in the fortress itself, and to a very limited degree on what it could gather by foraging raids into the immediate area. As the days of siege lengthened, the daily rations for the soldiers would be progressively reduced to eke out the stores, and occasionally the besieging troops would have the same privation. Finally, as a desperate expedient when all else had failed, supplies could be forced through the besiegers' lines to replenish the garrison and enable them to endure a little longer. Resupply operations by relieving armies were certainly attempted, as with the infamous and reckless 'affaires de poudre' at Turin in 1706 and again at Lille two years later. Dragoons draped bags of powder over their saddle bows and tried to force and bluff their way through the lines of besieging armies to resupply the garrisons. Despite the apparently desperate nature of these operations, and against all the odds, they were quite surprisingly successful, although only serving as a temporary measure.

The capture of a fortress of Vauban's design required enormous preparation, effort and the most careful tactical arrangements. It was calculated that a besieging army 40,000 strong, assisted by 10,000 conscripted peasant labourers, when engaged for forty days in a formal siege of a modern fortress (with set scales for rations of meat, bread and beer or wine) would require a total of 3,300,000 individual rations just to feed itself. The gunners would need 40,000 round-shot for the 24-pounder breaching guns and 800,000 pounds of gunpowder, with an immediate reserve of another 150,000 pounds of powder, just in case of need. Amongst other miscellaneous stores was 550,000 feet of assorted timber for revetting the entrenchments and building the gun batteries, and 18,000 tools for the labourers.[11] The sheer number of wagons and draught animals, required to bring all this gear and munitions up along bad roads to the vicinity of the fortress before operations could start, can well be imagined. Those very supplies, essential in every respect for the progress of the siege, were continually vulnerable to raids and interruption by opposing forces, and had to be protected on the road and in camp.

As the supplies in a fortress ran low, so the thoughts of the garrison commander would inevitably turn to a negotiated submission, even if the breaching operations had yet to reach an advanced stage. To starve out the garrison however would usually take far too long, unless an inexplicable mistake had been made and the provisioning of the fortress was seriously lacking in some respect. The scale of stores necessary for a defended place was therefore carefully calculated, the general rule being that one man required two pounds of bread, one pound of meat, eight pints of water (for washing as well as drinking) each day.[12] With less than this, the ability of the soldiers in defence was recognised as being at risk. Also important was the supply of such luxury items as tobacco, as it assisted in keeping up morale.[13] On occasions when a siege was not expected, as with Douai in 1710, the garrison commander was left with an inadequate number of troops for the task, and magazines and store-houses poorly stocked. His ability to resist would be limited as a result.

Fortresses in their classic, timeless role provided security and demonstrated sovereignty. As siege methodology and refined artillery and mining techniques in particular advanced, the ability of any defence to withstand a resolute attacker began to fail. In time, to cater for this development, fortress design improved immeasurably and the power of the defence came into its own again. Still, that same resolute attacker, if he were persistent enough and had sufficient resources and time, would eventually always succeed. So, the garrison commander discharged his duty by imposing on his opponent the penalty of delay, and this ability to impose delay became of major importance given the short campaigning season in each year. Vauban laid his plans to defend France in an otherwise indefensible region and built his complex fortresses with the utmost care. Marlborough ventured into the stone entanglement that had been laid in readiness and took those fine fortresses one after the other, but the time available to him was perilously short.

NOTES

1. G.H. Bidermann, *In Deadly Combat*, 2000, p. 68.

2. G. Clarke, *Fortification*, 1907, p. 9.

3. C. Duffy, *Fire and Stone*, 1975, p. 153. See also D.G. Chandler, *Art of War in the Age of Marlborough*, 1974, pp. 245–246. A hundred years

or so later Napoleon would codify this practice, and his garrison commanders would imperil themselves if they did not stand at least one attempt on a breach.

4. S. Vauban, *Traites de la Defence des Places*, *(1706)*, 1779, pp. 51–54.

5. Meinheer van Coehorn, the Dutch 'fighting engineer', simplified Vauban's formal and overly complex (as he saw it) geometric defensive designs to incorporate to a rather greater degree substantial water obstacles. This made a virtue out of necessity when having to build fortresses in the water-logged terrain of the Netherlands. Unless the water could be drained off, the obstacles had to be bridged under the fire of the garrison. Coehorn also favoured the extensive planting of detached bastions to keep an attacker at a distance from the main defences.

6. D. Chandler, *The Art of Warfare in the Age of Marlborough*, 1976, p. 255.

7. As an alternative to firing explosive shell, the mortars were often loaded with fist-sized stones, which acted as a kind of crude grapeshot, and were dreadfully effective. The stones fired in this way were sometimes found to have penetrated the ground in the target area to a depth of six or more inches, even when the earth was hard packed. Mortars specifically designed to use stone projectiles in this deadly way were known as 'perriers'. See C. Duffy, *Fire and Stone*, pp. 83–84.

8. The first recorded use of gunpowder in a mine was by Florentine troops in 1403 at the siege of Pisa, but as powder was scarce and expensive, under-mining and burning out remained the technique for many years. Vauban laid out the size of the charge and optimum depth at which mines should be set in his treatises on attacking and defending fortresses. For example, a *fougasse* – a defensive anti-personnel mine packed with stones – was to be laid at three metres depth, any deeper and it would be classed as a *mine* proper. A *camouflet* was specifically designed to be blown against enemy mine workings, by attackers or defenders.

9. The French garrison commander of Béthune in 1710 wrote: 'Flames came out of the Allied parallels for several yards, after he blew one such device against their miners.' See J. Reeve, *Siege of Béthune, 1710*, 1985, p. 204.

10. The storm by a German brigade under Colonel Haxhusien of the relatively minor, but well-garrisoned, fortress of St Ghislain on the night before the battle of Malplaquet in September 1709 shows that, when circumstances required it, a formal siege was not undertaken and all-out assault took its place, regardless of loss. In this particular case, however, casualties were quite light, St Ghislain being quite a modest place to defend.

11. D. Chandler, *Blenheim Preparation*, 2004, p. 148.

12. All armies, up until quite modern times, have, to a greater or lesser degree, had to subsist off the country in which they operate. Cattle, horse, draught animals, crops, fodder, firewood and supplies of every kind were systematically sought out and seized by the quartermaster's foraging parties. Often, but by no means always, the goods were paid for, but even when this was the case, it was likely that there was nothing left for the unfortunate citizenry to buy – starvation and destitution resulted. Given the nature of soldiery, the womenfolk of the region would also be at some risk. Understandably then, campaigning armies were feared and resented by the local people unfortunate enough to be caught up in these huge events, the success or failure of which would often mean little to them. 'A corporal in the Hanovers' John Deane remembered, 'was caught by the Boors [peasants] and hanged up dead in a tree.' It did not do for a soldier to stray too far from the camp, especially when alone. There was also the deliberate pre-emptive strategy in some cases of having commanders literally 'eat up a country', and so devastate and pick it clean of supplies and shelter that no other army could operate there for some time. Louis XIV, in his campaigning heyday, had used this to terrible effect on a number of occasions. See R. Hatton, *Louis XIV and His World*, 1973, p. 113. One of Marlborough's veterans wrote home in 1703 'Tis hardly possible to keep an Army from plundering when they are near an Enemy. My Lord Duke has given the strictest orders against it that can be, and yet some little places that are nearest to us have been most barborously ruined.' S. Johnston, *Letters of Samuel Noyes 1703–1704*, 1959, p. 68. There was until quite recently a tradition, in parts of Limburg and Brabant, to burn the Duke of Marlborough in effigy, as symbolic punishment for the looting and foraging of his armies, 300 years or more ago.

13. Vauban calculated that one pound of tobacco would allow 28 soldiers to smoke four pipes each day. 'Tobacco' he wrote, 'is essential for keeping the soldiers content. Indeed, they have become totally dependant on it.' See S. Vauban, *Trait de la Defense*, *(1706)*, p. 92. General John Pershing, commander in chief of the American army in Europe in 1917 and 1918, shared Vauban's high opinion of the value of tobacco in keeping up the morale of the troops. He rated the regular supply of tobacco as only slightly less important than that of ammunition.

II

This is the King of Spain: The War of the Spanish Succession, 1702

The throne of Spain became vacant on 1 November 1700 when the childless King Carlos II died. That sickly man and his advisers had been increasingly susceptible in his last years to French influence, particularly as Louis XIV's unrivalled military power seemed the most certain guarantee that the Spanish empire would not be dismembered when the King was dead.[1] Spain was militarily almost impotent, and a strong ally would be essential in the inevitable period of uncertainty to come. Shortly before his death therefore, Carlos dictated a new will which offered the throne in Madrid when he left it and the whole undivided Spanish empire to Philippe, Duke of Anjou, the youngest grandson of the French King. In this way, it was hoped that the empire, which Spain was incapable of defending with its own resources, would remain intact under French protection.

The problem of who should eventually succeed Carlos II had been recognised throughout western Europe for some years. The First Partition Treaty, drawn up between France, England and Holland, had with the Treaty of Ryswick brought to an end the seemingly interminable French-Dutch wars of the 1690s. Amongst its provisions was that a young German prince, Joseph-Ferdinand Wittelsbach (son of the Elector of Bavaria), should succeed to the Spanish throne. Both Spain and Austria, neither of whom were consulted over the treaty terms or the plain intention to partition the wide Spanish empire once Carlos II died, were offended at the apparently high-handed manner in which these things were so coolly settled. However, while the treaties might be imperfect, they would probably avoid dangerous friction between France and Austria over the whole difficult matter. Everyone wished to avert a resumption of a ruinously expensive war. Yet the whole carefully crafted arrangement over the succession to

25

the throne came to grief when Joseph-Ferdinand suddenly died of smallpox.

So, in late 1700 there was not one claimant for the Spanish throne but two, the other contender being Archduke Charles, younger son of the Austrian Emperor Leopold I. The Second Partition Treaty, negotiated after the death of Joseph-Ferdinand, set down that the Archduke should have the throne in return for valuable concessions being made to France in northern Italy. In this complex dynastic matter, each young man, whether Bourbon or Habsburg, arguably had as good a claim as the other and the whole affair plainly had to be handled with the utmost care. Unless there was some neat diplomacy on all fronts and a degree of co-operation between the nations concerned, there was bound to be renewed trouble. Unwanted war might come over whether Philip V or Carlos (Charles) III, the Frenchman or the Austrian, should sit on the throne in Madrid. That was the danger; everyone knew it, and it quickly proved to be just what would happen.

The Spanish empire was no longer of major significance as a military power and the finances of Spain were so poor as to resemble national bankruptcy. Nonetheless, the empire included extensive important regions, not only in the Iberian peninsula and the islands of the western Mediterranean but also in strategically desirable areas such as Naples and Sicily, the Milanese in northern Italy, lands all across the Americas, and the rich and populous Southern (Spanish) Netherlands. Louis XIV was well aware of the potential danger in allowing his grandson to accept the offered throne, throwing over the Second Partition Treaty and offending Austria in particular. Concern was bound to be felt across Europe at such an extension of French influence. The King was at first reluctant to give his consent, but the Grand Dauphin – the King's only surviving son – was particularly insistent that the glittering offer to his own youngest son should not be turned away. Louis XIV was persuaded to permit Anjou to accept, and the Duc de St Simon wrote in his memoirs of how the fateful announcement was made to the assembled courtiers at Versailles:

On Tuesday, 16th November, the King publicly declared himself. The Spanish ambassador [Castel del Rey] had received intelligence, which proved the eagerness of Spain to welcome the Duc d'Anjou as its King. There seemed to be no doubt about the matter. The King immediately after getting up, called the ambassador into his cabinet [private chambers] where M. le Duc d'Anjou had already arrived. Then, pointing to the Duc, he told the ambassador he might salute him as King of Spain. The ambassador threw himself upon his knees after the fashion of his country and addressed to the Duc a tolerably long compliment in the Spanish language [which Anjou did not understand]. Immediately afterwards, the King, contrary to all custom, opened the two folding doors of his cabinet, and commanded everyone to enter. It was a very full Court that day. Then, glancing majestically over the numerous company, he indicated the Duc d'Anjou, 'Gentlemen' said he 'This is the King of Spain.'[2]

The dilemma that the French King had faced was plain to see. Under the terms of the will, if the offer to his grandson was rejected, the throne of Spain, and the Spanish empire, would go undivided to Archduke Charles. An old heartfelt fear of Habsburg encirclement of France to the north, east and south would reemerge. The division of Charles V's empire in the mid-sixteenth century had relieved France of the immediate danger of encirclement, but an Austrian prince on the throne in Madrid might bring that threat right back again.[3] Louis XIV's near neighbours, having suffered at his hands in the past, were nervous of French intentions and on the alert, but the King was equally and quite genuinely concerned at what he regarded to be an unjustified and aggressive attitude over the succession on their part.

The Marquis de Torcy, the French foreign minister, set out rather well Louis XIV's dilemma over whether or not to permit his grandson to accept the offer of the throne:

If the King refused to accept the will, this same deed transferred the entire succession to the Archduke Charles. The same courier that had been despatched into France would proceed to Vienna; and the Spanish nation would, without any hesitation, acknowledge the Emperor's second son for King. The House of Austria would re-unite, betwixt the father [Leopold] and the son [Archduke Charles] the ancient power of Charles V, a power formerly so fatal to France.[4]

The eventual French acceptance of the offer may be seen almost as inevitable – what else was he expected to do? Louis XIV wrote to Madrid: 'We accept in favour of our grandson the Duke of Anjou, the Will of the deceased Catholic King ... we will cause the Duke of Anjou immediately to depart, that he may the sooner give his subjects the satisfaction of receiving a King.'[5]

Despite such heartening sentiments, this decision broke the most significant provision in the Partition Treaties: quite apart from the question of which of the two young men should be king, this treaty provision laid down that the thrones of France and Spain would always be kept separate. This was now in considerable doubt, with a French prince, susceptible to the bidding of his grandfather in Versailles, about to be installed in Madrid. A formal union between France and Spain was not a realistic prospect of course – the Spanish people had no desire or intention of being dictated to by the French, and the Duke of Anjou would, on accepting the offer from Spain, irrevocably renounce any claim to the throne of France if his elder brother, the Duke of Burgundy, died without an heir. However, there was suspicion that this irrevocable renunciation might in fact be capable of being revoked if it suited the French. The increase in Louis XIV's influence – if not actual domination – in Spain and her empire in these circumstances was obvious. Real concern at the impending extension to the reach of Versailles was felt throughout western Europe. Many of France's neighbours began to look about them to form new alliances to guard against what was seen as a renewed, unavoidable, and rapidly growing danger.

At the other side of the political, dynastic and military divide, Louis XIV was anxious to avoid renewed war; the recent lengthy war with the Dutch had not been worth the enormous effort, and the French Treasury was in a sorry state. With some astute diplomacy a new conflict could in all probability have been avoided. However, Vauban, the brilliant creator of France's formidable fortress belt along the northern border, stepped forward and argued, no doubt with great sincerity, that these defences still had insufficient depth to provide security in a region devoid (apart from river lines) of natural defences. While the southern Netherlands were a Spanish possession there was little to be done. Certainly no-one had wanted more trouble with the Dutch (for whom the region provided their Barrier against French aggression), but now that Anjou was on his way to Madrid to claim his inheritance, things seemed to be rather different. In February 1701, cloaking the move with the declared intention – which was at least partly true – that he simply wished to protect his grandson's new possessions, Louis XIV sent French troops northwards to occupy a string of important towns: Charleroi, Oudenarde, Maastricht, Ath, Namur, Nieuport, Mons and Luxembourg. This operation provided a comforting forward strategic posture for France deep in the Spanish Netherlands, but the dangerous reality was that those very same towns had been held by the Dutch as a vital part of their own highly cherished Barrier. The French threat had come again very quickly.

Great offence was given to the States-General of Holland – already on the alert over the question of the Spanish succession – by this abrupt and unwise campaign of seizure. The Dutch garrisons, some 15,000 troops in all, had rather meekly submitted and withdrew, unharmed but under French escort, to Holland. Maastricht alone of the Barrier Towns held out, and the governor refused the summons to yield the place. Foiled, but in no position to storm the citadel, the French promptly pulled back from the town. William III, King of England and Dutch Stadtholder, had been told of the intended French moves in advance, but for his own reasons kept the information to himself and did not divulge it to the States-General. It is at least possible that he was not averse to creating trouble between the wary Dutch and his old adversary, the King of France. England and Holland, under the terms of the 1668 Treaty of Triple Alliance (Sweden was also a signatory), were each required to come to the aid of each other if attacked, so William was subtly binding the two states more closely together, ready for another effort against the French when the moment was right. If Louis XIV was given enough leeway, he might stumble into a renewed conflict that he did not want.

As the threat from France seemed to grow ever more oppressive, Holland, England and Imperial Austria agreed in September 1701 the terms of a Grand Alliance to meet the challenge.[6] Diplomatic efforts continued though, and Louis XIV was at pains to reassure both the English and the Dutch that their own national interests were not put at risk by his grandson's accession to the throne in Madrid. In fact, both Holland and England had now recognised as a *fait accompli* Philip V as the King of Spain. William III certainly seemed to consider the irrevocable renunciation by Anjou of the French throne as genuine. Imperial Austria though was unwilling to accept the presence of the French prince in Madrid without further protest, and the Emperor Leopold had urged both England and Holland that they were paying far too little attention to the growing problem. Well, the interests of the three Allies were not quite the same: the Maritime Powers (England and Holland) were far more concerned with opening up trade with the Spanish empire and preventing France from established a monopoly of that trade for her own merchants, than in securing either Imperial Austrian expansion into northern Italy or the Spanish throne for an Austrian prince. However, these differing aims were not contradictory and there was enough common ground for the three countries to work together as Allies against Louis XIV with his perfectly understandable, but very troublesome, ambitions for his grandson. At the heart of the aims of the Alliance was the desire to partition the Spanish empire, the very same division envisaged under the Partition Treaties that had prompted

Carlos II to offer the throne and empire intact to Anjou. The added aim to place Archduke Charles on the throne would only really take shape and grow in importance in the councils of the Alliance as time went on.

Camille d'Hostun, Duc de Tallard, the French ambassador in London, was striving to mend diplomatic fences, but Louis XIV uncharacteristically continued to fumble in his dealings with this neighbours. He had caused great offence in England by declaring in that same month of September 1701 that the 'Pretender', the son of the exiled English King James II, was considered by France to be the rightful heir to the crowns of England and Scotland. Louis XIV had undoubtedly been overcome by emotion at his old friend's deathbed and spoken incautiously, but the declaration was a terrible diplomatic gaffe. Torcy attempted to explain the comment away as a simple anachronistic and historic form of speaking without real meaning, in the same fashion that monarchs of England at the time still claimed the Kingship of France. Few were convinced by this, and the French King had broken yet another important provision in the Partition Treaties. The resentment it caused added to the growing sense in London that something had to be done to challenge once again the burgeoning power of France.

It seemed plain in London, Vienna and the Hague, that Louis XIV was intent once again on interfering intolerably in the affairs of his neighbours, and Tallard was promptly expelled from England when news of the acknowledgement of the Pretender became known. This was unfortunate, for he was an astute diplomat and his calm influence had been useful to all parties. Before war could come again, however, William III died in March 1702 from the effects of a riding accident outside the palace of Hampton Court. His sister-in-law, the Princess Anne came to the throne in his stead, crowned on St George's Day. The new Queen was just as suspicious of Louis XIV, and proved to be as resolute as her dead Dutch brother-in-law had been. War was declared on France (and Spain in the form of the French claimant, Philip V), by the parties to the Grand Alliance on 15 May 1702.

This can almost be seen as war by timetable, in that the competing ambitions on each side, in their own way not unreasonable or illogical, led France and Spain into a war with England, Holland and Austria. Both sides could and did claim that they did not want to go to war, but neither side could achieve what they wanted and could not bear to relinquish to the other without war. The declaration of hostilities came as no great surprise to the French, for Louis XIV had been informed of the terms of the Grand Alliance almost as soon as they were agreed. He had already begun to increase the size of his armies, and took firm action to improve the French strategic posture in the north in preparation for a vigorous campaign in 1702. He intended to knock the Dutch out of the war straight away; if that could be accomplished the Grand Alliance would fall apart without further ado.

The Elector-Bishop of Cologne and Liège allied himself with the French, as his brother, the Elector of Bavaria would also do. French troops, in consequence, were permitted to occupy Liège and Huy and a number of other fortresses, including Bonn, in the Bishopric of Cologne. In this way, the Maas (Meuse) valley, and much of the lower Rhine, was occupied by the French and their allies right up to the borders of Holland. Dutch-held Maastricht, which had resisted the French campaign of seizure the previous year, was now rather isolated. This fragile posture for the Allies was partly countered by the doughty young Elector of Hanover (one day to be George I of Great Britain), who ignored superficially attractive approaches from the French King to conclude an alliance. Instead, he marched his troops into and seized the neighbouring Duchy of Brunswick-Wolfenbuttel, where the senior of the two joint-Electors (brothers) had recently sided with France. This swift operation was carried out neatly in a single day, and with hardly any bloodshed. It strengthened the Allied position east of the Rhine out of all proportion to the importance of the Duchy itself.

John Churchill, the 52-year-old Earl of Marlborough, had worked closely with William III to prepare both the Treaty of Grand Alliance (he was the signatory for England) and to restore the fighting capability of the armies on the English and Irish establishments.[7] These had seen a wholesale disbandment of regiments with the treaties of the late 1690s, which had for the time being seemed to promise peace. The Earl and his wife were the new Queen Anne's confidantes and close friends, and he was made the Captain-General of her land forces.

After some careful negotiation, Marlborough was also appointed to the field command of the Anglo-Dutch armies as 'A man of cool head and warm heart, proper to encounter the generals of France.'[8] Marlborough was well known to the Dutch as he had helped to negotiate the terms of the Grand Alliance with the States-General of Holland, and they both liked and trusted him. In the early summer of 1702, the Earl crossed to Holland to confer with them at the Hague. He then moved on to take command of the Anglo-Dutch forces, who by then were confronted by the French Marshal Boufflers and his army, along the lower Rhine and Maas rivers.

NOTES

1. The pro-French party at the Spanish court (after the death of Carlos II's first French-born wife) was centred on a small influential group of Grandees: Dons Medina-Sidonia, Villena, Villagarcias, Villafranca and San Eslavan. Their enthusiasm for France however was entirely based on their belief that only the military power of Louis XIV could maintain Spain's empire undivided.

2. B. St John, *Memoirs of Duc St Simon*, Vol I, 1876, p. 183. See also C. Martin, *Louis XIV*, 1975, p. 77.

3. See R. Hatton, *Louis XIV and His World*, 1972, pp 85–111, for an erudite and penetrating analysis of the threats that Louis XIV, perceived, with some justification, in the attitude of England and Holland at this time – a time when he was attempting, however imperfectly, to conciliate them – and of the renewed danger to France in apparently resurgent Habsburg encirclement. Hatton writes: 'Louis' aggressive acts have been put into better perspective as we have become more willing to admit that other nations, those that fought France, also had aggressive or acquisitive motives, as we are beginning to understand the extent to which fear is a driving force in relations between States and how difficult it is to keep the peace.' p. 111.

4. G.M. Trevelyan, *Blenheim*, 1933, p. 133.

5. M. De Langallerie, *Memoires*, 1710, p. 107.

6. See J. Falkner, *Great and Glorious Days*, 2002, p. 17, for details of the terms of the Treaty of Grand Alliance. Louis XIV learned the details of the Treaty from the Swedish Ambassador in London on 10 November 1701, see also G.M. Trevelyan, *Blenheim*, 1932, p. 149. Efforts to induce Prussia and Sweden to formally join the Grand Alliance proved unsuccessful, although large numbers of Prussian troops were provided for service with the armies of the Alliance. In return for this support, the Elector of Brandenburg was permitted by the Imperial court in Vienna to assume the title of King of Prussia. Due partly to the influence of Prince George of Denmark, Queen Anne's husband and consort, Danish troops in large numbers also served with, and were paid by, the Alliance.

As for Sweden, one of Marlborough's most significant, but often overlooked, strategic achievements was to persuade King Charles XII, mercurial and dangerous as he was, to stay out of the war for the throne of Spain. Instead the King turned his attention to the Baltic and to Russia. Such was Marlborough's confidence in the plenipotentiary powers he had, that he concluded the agreement with the Swedish King without reference to London.

7. In addition to the English and Irish army establishments, there was a Scottish establishment. Holland also employed considerable number of Scottish troops on contract.

8. H. Edwards, *A Life of Marlborough*, 1926, p. 108.

III

Troublesome Neighbours:
The Dutch Frontier, 1702–1703

The strongly garrisoned fortresses along the Meuse and much of the lower Rhine were a powerful strategic asset for the French, both as a shield for the heartland of the Spanish Netherlands and their own northern border region. They also provided a secure starting point from which to attack their opponents. Kaiserswerth, a small but well-fortified town on the Rhine about 25 miles north of Cologne, was potentially the most dangerous of these places for the Allies, as it barred easy communication between Holland and the Imperial armies which were gathering, albeit rather slowly, along the reaches of the middle and upper Rhine. The French garrison could also simultaneously threaten raids into the Imperial Circle of Westphalia, or against the rather neglected Dutch defences along their southern border.

The Alliance had already made an unfortunate strategic error, as Austria's lack of urgency in gathering her forces to confront the French (partly explained by Vienna's having to deal with a growing insurrection in Hungary), enabled Louis XIV to concentrate more troops in the Low Countries than would otherwise have been possible. The French were pursuing an active campaign in northern Italy, but with the middle and upper Rhine frontier untroubled so far, only Marshal Catinat, with about 20,000 French troops, was left to guard Alsace, which was under no real threat from Imperial forces. There was some surprise in Versailles when the elderly Prince of Nassau-Saarbruck was sent, early in April 1702, by the Dutch army commander, the Earl of Athlone, to begin a siege of Kaiserswerth. The trenches before the three ravelins which protected the bastions on the side of the town away from the Rhine were opened on 18 April. As hostilities with France had not yet commenced, the troops were considered to be in the service of the Emperor, acting against his wayward subject, the Elector-Bishop of Cologne and Liège. Despite this diplomatic nicety the actual fighting was fierce enough, with an early French counter-attack, led by the Marquis de Blainville, driving the Dutch infantry back as they prepared to break ground, and through their camp in some confusion, until cavalry came forward to support them and restore the situation.

The original French plan had been to move against Juliers, but on 21 April Boufflers crossed the Meuse and occupied Ruremonde instead. He then marched his troops into the Duchy of Cleves, as a response to the Allied moves against Kaiserswerth, early in May. In the meantime, Meinheer van Coehorn, the famed Dutch engineer, advanced against the Marquis de Bedmar near to Bruges and Middleburg in order to tie down the French troops in the west and prevent them being sent to reinforce Boufflers. Coehorn was not at first very successful, as the French opened the sluice-gates on the rivers and flooded much of the region, forcing the Dutch troops to pull back with the loss of a lot of their baggage. Still, the overall aim, that of keeping Bedmar and his army near to the Channel coast, was largely achieved. Meanwhile, war had been declared by the Grand Alliance on France and Spain on 15 May 1702, and open hostilities had begun.

Athlone had started his own operations against Marshal Boufflers before either of the main opposing field armies had properly concentrated their forces, and in this respect he was dictated to by events. The valuable fortress of Maastricht, lying between Liège and Ruremonde, neatly split the line of French-held fortresses along the Meuse into two component parts and had to be reinforced. This was undoubtedly prudent, but Athlone's field army was weakened in the process and he was for the time being able to field only 25,000 men, perhaps less than half the number that Boufflers had available. However, the Marshal in turn now sent Tallard with a force of 13,000 troops to interrupt the siege of Kaiserswerth, in response to a demand from Versailles that something be done to save the place. Tallard had orders not to cross the Rhine, for fear of aggravating the German princes who had yet to declare their allegiance. With that restriction on his movements, he could do little more than use his artillery to try – rather ineffectively as it turned out – to slow the Allied operations. Some round-shot was lobbed into the tented camp of the Prussian officers one night, causing a great deal of alarm but few casualties; Nassau-Saarbruck found that he could in fact just ignore Tallard and get on with his siege. The French garrison, ably commanded by de Blainville, were active, and several more sharp counter-attacks were mounted. Meanwhile, the two rival field armies, both reduced in numbers by the demands of the Kaiserswerth operations, settled down to watch each other – Boufflers moved forward to drive a Dutch detachment under Count Tilly away from Xanten. Tilly in turn marched northwards to join Athlone at Cranenburg, close to Cleves, with their main supply base five miles away at Nijmegen.

Although Boufflers was increasingly anxious about his lengthening lines of supply and communication, he had been obliged by instructions from Versailles to detach troops to support Bedmar; Coehorn had moved forward again in West Flanders and taken Middlesburg, before going on to threaten Bruges. Louis XIV was concerned that Boufflers had been deliberately drawn away towards the Rhine, so that Coehorn could achieve a numerical supremacy in West Flanders. As it happened, the Dutch general's operations ran out of steam soon enough, but in the meantime, Boufflers's army was stretched and reduced to a state where it could not really offer battle. His prospects brightened soon, as a large supply convoy made its way successfully from Brussels, past the Allied-held fortress of Maastricht, to the French camp now established at Xanten, arriving there on 26 May. A rumoured Dutch threat against Namur came to nothing, but Tallard soon found that his attempts to interrupt the siege of Kaiserswerth were having no effect, although he did manage to ferry some supplies across the river under cover of night to sustain the beleaguered garrison. Pointed instructions came from the King that he should go and attack Dusseldorf to distract the Allies from Kaiserswerth, but instead, Tallard moved to combine with Boufflers once again. Tactically this was likely to be more effective than a continued wasteful dispersal of French forces, and with this reinforcement and his army more or less at battle strength once again, the French commander marched rapidly to sever Ginkel's vital connection with his supply base at Nijmegen. If successful, the French might well pin the Anglo-Dutch army against the Rhine, starved of supplies and cut off from reinforcement; this would neatly conclude the war in northern Europe and give victory to Louis XIV.

At first light on 10 June 1702, Boufflers's men were on the road, and the French movement was only detected by Athlone that evening. His troops fell back in considerable haste and in some disorder towards Nijmegen, abandoning equipment at the roadside as they went. Captain Robert Parker, serving with the Royal Irish Regiment, wrote: 'Had they succeeded in this, not a man of our small army would have escaped. At the same time Nijmegen must have fallen into their hands. which would have opened them a way into the heart of the very province of Holland, and been a fatal blow.'[1] The forced march became a race that was only narrowly won by Athlone, and the Anglo-Dutch army got into the defences of Nijmegen just ahead of the French cavalry. The citizenry lined the walls and helped man the batteries. Frustrated of his prey, Boufflers had to draw off in the face of the guns of the town, taking up a position between Goch and Gennep. It had been a tantalisingly close thing, and James FitzJames, the Duke of Berwick (Marlborough's nephew), who was amongst the pursuers that day, wrote: 'It is a thing without example, that an army should have pursued another for two leagues, and should have driven it into the covered way of a fortification ... such strokes must be made on the instant, and without giving the enemy time to recollect themselves.'[2] Had disaster overtaken Athlone's army, the war would surely have ended there and then. The Earl had got away relatively unscathed; but with his dignity rather ruffled, hundreds of men and horses captured, and the abandonment of a lot of baggage. The morale of the Allied troops had also taken something of a knock, while Boufflers's own losses in the operation were hardly more than 100 killed and wounded.

As Berwick rather astutely remarked: 'Thus did the dash at Nijmegen hasten the fall of Kaiserswerth. An officer may be fair tactician and yet be a shallow strategist.' This thrusting pursuit of Athlone had drawn the French field army northwards, well away from any chance of a relief of Kaiserswerth, the retention of which place was of considerable value to the French. Kaiserswerth meanwhile had been left to its fate and on 9 June, after a bombardment with forty-eight big guns and twenty mortars, an Allied assault took one of the ravelins. Six days later a major part of the counterscarp was captured and the garrison submitted on 17 June. The Marquis de Blainville's troops had fought well and were granted the honours of war; the twelve battalions of French infantry were permitted to march away to Venlo without giving their parole or having to await exchange before resuming operations. The capture of Kaiserswerth had cost the Dutch and their allies the best part of 3,000 killed and wounded. Boufflers was by no means wrong, however, in trying to catch and overwhelm Athlone's army, and the attempt had very nearly been successful. Still, the French commander had in the process abandoned his efforts to relieve Kaiserswerth (which had been unsuccessful up to that point, of course) and then had not managed to engage Athlone before the Earl could get back to the defences of Nijmegen. By the time Tallard was sent back to Kaiserswerth, he found that the Dutch had pushed a strong detachment over the Rhine, too close for him to occupy his old camping ground, and there was little he could do but draw off and rejoin Boufflers once again. Despite his game efforts, the French commander had failed, both at Kaiserswerth and in trying to overwhelm Athlone, and might be said to have fallen between two stools.

On 2 July 1702, John Churchill, the Earl of Marlborough, left the Hague for Nijmegen to take field command of the Anglo-Dutch armies. The Earl of Athlone was inclined to be both resentful of the Englishman and reluctant to co-operate. This is not altogether surprising as the Dutch general had held the command up to then and Marlborough's appointment was widely regarded as political expediency. Athlone soon came to appreciate Marlborough's qualities, however, by the end of the year's campaign considering him to be an incomparable commander. Marlborough would soon have about 60,000 men under command (of whom just over 12,000 were Queen Anne's soldiers), almost equal to the force deployed by Boufflers. Although the contending forces had a rough equality in numbers, the recent performance of the French commanders had undoubtedly been more accomplished than that of their opponents. However, with his rapid advance towards Nijmegen, Boufflers had further overextended himself and stretched his lines of supply to an uncomfortable degree. The Marshal was well aware of this, and could repair the deficiencies in his supply arrangements, given enough time.

There was a week or so of cautious manoeuvring when the French let slip an opportunity to snatch an Allied convoy. On 15 July, Marlborough moved forward to Graves, but the pace of movement of the Dutch troops was slower than he hoped. The attention of Marshal Boufflers had been conveniently distracted from the operations of the Allied army, as Louis XIV sent directions that an advance should be made by Tallard's corps towards the middle Rhine as a diversion, preliminary to a concerted attack on Maastricht. In the event, the plan came to nothing, due in the main to Marlborough's own moves. The French troubles began to multiply, as the Imperial threat to Alsace was at last taking shape now, and the King wrote: 'Landau is besieged. The feebleness of the army [Catinat's] has always worried me, this increases daily as [the Margrave of] Baden's army grows ... You know the importance of this place which equally guards the entrance to Alsace and the approaches to the Saar.'[3] Reluctantly, Boufflers detached a substantial force southwards to support Catinat and in consequence had to assume the defensive in the Spanish Netherlands with his own reduced army.

News of this lessening of French strength spurred Marlborough on as his own forces steadily gathered in numbers. On 26 July the Allied army crossed three pontoon bridges to the west bank of the Meuse, moving rapidly in the direction of Eindhoven. The Earl, anxious to allay Dutch fears at such novel and bold moves, wrote to the States-General: 'Now, I shall soon rid you of your troublesome neighbours.'[4] As Marlborough advanced past Hamont, Boufflers took alarm and fell back past Venlo and Ruremonde on the Meuse, where garrisons were left to hold these important crossing places. A small French garrison was also left in Gravenbroeck, but the place was stormed by British troops commanded by Lord Cutts after a short bombardment on 30 July. By 2 August the weary French soldiers paused at Peer, while the Allied army in full battle array lay in wait on a heath only a couple of miles to the north, not far from the small town of Lille St Hubert. From there, Marlborough could easily fall on the exposed flank of the French columns as they marched past, but the Dutch felt that the risks were too high and would not agree to bringing on a general action. Boufflers hurried his troops away in great disorder to escape over the Demer river at Diest. The Earl had little choice but to be patient and try to persuade his allies to be more adventurous; but he could not resist taking the Dutch officers and the field deputies, who accompanied the army and refused to agree to the attack, to a vantage point from where they could watch the French army scurry past to safety. The Dutch openly admitted that they had been wrong, but it was small consolation for the lost opportunity, and Marlborough soon found that the lesson had not really been learned.

In the third week of August, another chance presented itself to maul the French army, near to the heaths of Helchteren. Boufflers once again tried to intercept an Allied convoy but Marlborough foiled his advance, although he had used the progress of the vulnerable wagons as an inviting bait to tempt the French commander out into the open. At the last moment Boufflers took alarm, and withdrew his advanced guard, under command of Marshal Berwick who, however, felt sure he could have captured the supply wagons if only he had been allowed to do so. Marlborough had then withdrawn towards the south (away from his own bases and lengthening his supply lines), thus luring the French farther on into a more exposed position. Dutch caution on 23 August, when an attack by Major-General Opdham miscarried, despite plain orders to get on with things, and again on the following day, enabled Boufflers to slip away. Opdham attempted to excuse his inaction by blaming the poor marshy ground he had to cross, but he had moved very slowly, allowing the French commander to pull back without much trouble. The Allied Camp Bulletin reported on 27 August 1702:

We had notice in the night that they were retired in great disorder ... the enemy were already so far advanced that it was
impossible to overtake them, only Brigadier [Cornelius] Wood
with some squadrons of the right [Wing] fell in with three or
four squadrons of the Household [cavalry] which had their
rearguard, and entirely broke them.[5]

Despite this, the French army got safely into an entrenched camp at
Beringen. Marlborough was understandably disappointed, and went
so far as to send a note to his opponent, explaining to Boufflers that
he had intended to attack him on several occasions, as duty required,
but that circumstances had prevented it happening.

The Earl could now fully turn his attention to the exposed French
fortresses along the Meuse. Boufflers had been charged by Louis XIV
to hold these places, although he had little choice for the time being
but to leave them to their fate. The same Camp Bulletin recorded
the move to invest the town of Venlo: 'Yesterday morning, M. de
Opdham marched away with the detachment for Venlo, and is to
invest the place on this side of the Meuse [the east] tomorrow night.'
A fortified post at Wert was stormed by a Dutch brigade under
Major-General Schultz after only a brief resistance. The town was
invested on 29 August by Nassau-Saarbruck and Opdham, with the
assistance of the Margrave of Brandenburg who covered the operation from the other side of the river. Marlborough was soon fretting
at the slow pace of the siege, even though van Coehorn had arrived
from West Flanders and went to take a hand. His allies preferred a
more sedate pace to the conduct of operations than the Earl, and he
wrote in understandable exasperation to London towards the end
of August:

It is now eight days since we made the detachment to Venlo,
and now we receive a letter from Monsrs Geldermalsen [Dutch
field-deputy] and Coehorn which says that for want of powder
and other necessaries they can't begin the siege till the beginning
of the next month.[6]

A week later Marlborough was still protesting at the lack of urgency
amongst the Dutch, but the trenches before the town were finally
opened on 7 September. The Earl appreciated that his generals had
been set a formidable target, and thirty-two infantry battalions and
thirty-six cavalry squadrons were employed in the operation, supported by ninety guns and mortars. In addition, 10,000 peasants were

conscripted from around Munster to dig the trenches. Opposed to them, the garrison was commanded by the very competent Marquis de Labardie, Comte de Varo, who had only a comparatively small force of six battalions and two squadrons of dismounted dragoons with thirty-eight guns.

The Allied Camp Bulletin for 11 September read: 'The siege of Venlo will be carried on by three different attacks; one on the castle, on this side, and the two others on the town, by the troops on the other side of the Meuse.'[7] The defences were strong, and a lengthy and expensive siege was expected; Marlborough having moved with the field army to Asche, to confront Boufflers and prevent him interfering with the siege. He also re-established contact with the garrison in Maastricht, with its amply stocked magazines and depots with which he could reprovision his army from close at hand, free from French interference with his long lines of supply back into Holland. From Asche, Marlborough could also move against the fortresses of Ruremonde and Stevensweert as he pleased, while Boufflers was unable to interpose his army without bringing on a general engagement. The Marshal did try to manoeuvre around Marlborough's left to threaten those same lines of supply and communication, but the Earl moved into a fresh position on 13 September, even closer as it happened to the valuable depots in Maastricht, in order to block the French in their new position near to Tongres. The Camp Bulletin the next day detailed the steady progress of the siege operations against Venlo:

> The trenches were opened on Monday night on both sides of the Meuse, without any loss, our men having covered themselves before the enemy perceived us; they likewise formed a battery of twenty guns and twenty mortars within 350 yards of the counterscarp.[8]

The Comte de Varo's soldiers were by no means inactive meanwhile, and did what they could, with their distinct lack of numbers, to hinder the progress of the Allies:

> The next morning the enemy fired very hard, especially on the Prussian attack ... The great battery against the fort will be ready to play this day; and to-morrow the Prussians will have two battalions ready; one to hinder the communications between the fort and the town, and the other to dismount the cannon in the town.

As it turned out, the garrison of Venlo would put up a fairly meagre resistance, but the siege operations were plagued by disputes between van Coehorn and the Dutch officers with whom he had to work. Arguments and delay were the inevitable results, to Marlborough's renewed frustration. In the meantime, Boufflers detached more troops to the Channel coast to attempt a diversion there, but their efforts to take Hulst failed as the Dutch copied Bedmar's tactics earlier in the campaign: opening the sluice gates and flooding the region.

A double assault on Venlo was mounted on 18 September. Prussian grenadiers seized an outwork on the right bank of the Meuse after a stiff fight, and British troops simultaneously captured the out-lying fort, which was known as St Michael. The fort was linked to the defences of the town by a bridge of boats. The assault was pressed so fast that the soldiers in their excitement carried right on over their intended target, the covered way and defensive ditch (although this was filled with water, the troops jumped in without hesitation and waded across), and onto the main defences of the fort itself. One participant, Robert Parker, wrote of the action:

> The Lord Cutts sent for all the officers, and told them, that the design of the attack was only to drive the enemy from the covert way, that they might not disturb the workmen [Allied pioneers] … About four in the afternoon, the signal was given, and according to our orders we rushed up to the covert-way; the enemy gave one scattering fire only, and away they ran … They that fled before us climbed up by the long grass that grew out of the fort, so we climbed after them. Here we were hard put to it, to pull out the palisades, which pointed down upon us from the parapet; and was it not for the great surprise and consternation of those within, we could not have surmounted this very point.[9]

The attackers had been unexpectedly helped by being able to clutch the grass, which they used for handholds in the assault on the fort; it was common practice to plant the slopes of a glacis and the forward faces of main defences with grass to bind the packed earth tightly, and prevent erosion by rain. Richard Kane, who also took part in the assault, wrote: 'We could never have climbed as we did, nor even as it was, had not the grass been long enough for us to hold by.'[10] A more prudent and alert garrison commander would certainly have kept the grass scythed short, and Marlborough noted with pleasure that it was the English grenadiers that had the honour of being the first to enter the fort, although Parker added rather waspishly that 'His Lordship [Cutts] had the glory of the whole action, though he never stirred out of the trenches till all was over.'

An artillery onslaught on the main defences of Venlo was now mounted with a massed battery of sixty-seven of the big 24-pounder siege guns supported by a large number of mortars of all calibres. Four days later a major breach in the main defences had begun to appear, and a series of artillery salvoes, fired in the Allied camp in celebration of the capture of Landau on the upper Rhine by the Margrave of Baden on 8 September, so alarmed the garrison that an immediate storm was feared. De Varo submitted after the citizenry and magistrates begged him to spare the town the possibility of a sack. 'The inhabitants,' Kane remembered, 'men, women and children, flocking to the ramparts with white clothes in their hands crying out "Mercy, Mercy, Quarter, Quarter".'[11] As time was pressing, terms were promptly granted on 25 September, and the Comte was permitted to march away with the survivors of his garrison to Antwerp without giving their parole.

Marlborough then moved on up the line of the Meuse. Stevensweert fell in just four days after a token resistance from the rather meagre garrison of 400 men, the Camp Bulletin of 2 October reading: 'Our batteries began to play … and continued firing without intermission till about ten last night, when, the besieged having abandoned the counterscarp, and our men being ready to mount the breach, they beat the chamade, and desired to capitulate.'[12] The garrison commander, the Marquis de Castellas, and his troops were granted good terms and allowed to go to Namur. While this was going on, Count Noyelles had moved with twelve cavalry squadrons to invest Ruremond by 29 September, and he was supported by nine infantry battalions commanded by George Hamilton, 1st Earl of Orkney. Marlborough's close friend, Johan Wigand van Goor, a robust Dutch engineer officer, was in command of the operations in the trenches. Under his vigorous direction, the digging of the parallels was begun on 2 October, and the bombardment commenced four days later. The garrison submitted and the town was occupied on 7 October after an artillery assault by sixty 24-pounder guns had opened a major breach in the defences. The governor, the Comte de Hornes, was permitted to march off with his troops, together with four pieces of artillery, to Louvain. Meanwhile, concerned that Marlborough would next turn his attention to the now vulnerable French-held fortresses on the Rhine, Louis XIV sent instructions that Tallard should take his corps back to cover Bonn and Cologne.

The King seemed to misjudge Marlborough's intentions and he was now dividing his forces – a risky thing to do at the best of times. It would soon have dire results. He had instructed Boufflers to cover Liège closely with the field army, but had then agreed to the Marshal's suggestion that he should manoeuvre against Marlborough while sending troops to create a diversion in West Flanders. Louis XIV had then weakened Boufflers by detaching Tallard and his troops to the Rhine, opting for the worst of all worlds. Landau on the upper Rhine had already fallen, so the King was plainly faced with some hard choices; but rather than seeking to regain the initiative on either the Rhine or the Meuse, he was reduced to trying to impose a measure of stability on to a campaign that showed every sign of running out of his control.

The apparently remorseless Allied advance would now be directed against Liège, thus threatening to turn the right flank of the entire French strategic posture covering Brabant. The Duke of Berwick wrote in sombre tones of the gloom that settled over the French court and army at this time: 'The King, seeing the ill turn affairs took in this campaign, recalled the Duke of Burgundy [his grandson] from the army to save him the mortification of being merely a spectator of the Earl of Marlborough's victories.'[13] Meanwhile, another stern note went to Boufflers from Versailles stressing that Liège had to be held. The Marshal however, having been reduced to splitting his army up into detachments to hold the minor fortresses in the region and already weakened by the sending away of Tallard at the King's insistence, was only able to put some 25,000 men in the field by this time. This was far too few to mount anything approaching a proper challenge to Marlborough, unable either to intimidate his opponents, deflect them from their purpose, or properly defend himself if confronted. 'The detachment we had sent into Germany' Berwick remembered 'had so weakened us, that we could not venture to risk an action.'

Boufflers took some comfort in that the season was getting to be late for active campaigning. The Dutch, who had been so reluctant to risk an open battle, nonetheless agreed that they should attempt to take Liège before winter came, so long as there was no major attempt to oppose them; Boufflers might well feel obliged to stand and fight, despite the long odds. The opportunity was too good to be missed: Liège was a mighty fortress, and it held a key position on the Meuse river. Boufflers had already inspected the defences of the citadel and sent in some reinforcements (two battalions of infantry) into the place before it was invested. For a while his army once again lay in a poor position, one from which it would have been ill-placed to resist any outright attack by Marlborough. The Dutch wanted to carefully reconnoitre the ground however, and on detecting the Allied approach the Marshal was able to fall back behind the Jaar river and avoid serious contact.

The French commander had now begun to entrench a new position along the Jaar near to Tongres, but this could easily be bypassed by the Allies in a direct advance on Liège. Despite urgings from Versailles to do so, Boufflers made no further active attempt to prevent a siege of the fortress other than to threaten an attempt on Marlborough's lines of supply. The Earl was not impressed and shouldered his opponent aside; the Marshal withdrew further to the west and left Liège to its fate. Marlborough hurried his army onwards, reaching the place late in the afternoon of 13 October 1702, with fifty squadrons of cavalry and dragoons. The unfortified town yielded to the Prince of Hesse-Cassell the following day, and on 18 October the trenches were opened by British and Dutch troops in front of the great citadel and a strong outwork on the other side of the Meuse, known as Fort Chartreuse. The Governor in Liège, Brigadier-General Marquis de Violaine, had under his command eleven battalions of infantry with two more in Fort Chartreuse. In a ruthless example of the kind of measures that might be taken to impede the beginning of a siege, he had the entire suburb of St Warburg set alight as the Allies approached, destroying over 100 houses in the process. The citizens of Liège, when submitting the keys of the place to Marlborough with great and elaborate ceremony, asked him not to mount an attack from the side of the town to avoid further damage and destruction as far as was possible.

The Allied siege train was brought up the Meuse on barges and the breaching bombardment proper, directed by van Coehorn, began two days after the trenches were opened. Forty-four cannons were employed in the artillery assault, supported by twelve large mortars, and many smaller coehorns were also brought into action. Success was soon achieved when a lucky shot sent a powder store in the citadel up in a huge explosion. The following evening, 21 October, another magazine blew up and almost all the French artillery had by this time been disabled, with only two pieces seriously attempting to reply to the Allied guns. 'Our mortars began to play ... and have since blown up several of the enemy's magazines of powder and grenades, which were dispersed in their works.'[14] The besieging troops could see the dazed defenders stumbling around in the flames and the smoke as they struggled to maintain some sort of resistance.

By 23 October, a practicable breach had been made in the walls of the citadel, and Marlborough had summoned the governor to surrender on good terms without putting the troops on either side to the trouble and expense of an attack. Despite the obvious difficulties of his position, the Marquis coolly and rather rashly replied that it would be time to think of discussing terms six weeks afterwards. This was to put the lives of his troops at considerable risk as a storm was now invited, and that very same afternoon at 4.00 p.m. the covered way was attacked by four battalions of British troops, led by 500 grenadiers. Donald McBane, serving with Orkney's Regiment, wrote:

> Every grenadier had three grenades, our password was God Be Foremost, we came with a loud huzza and fired our grenades amongst them, and small shot without number … we then made use of our swords and bayonets and made a sore slaughter amongst the French. [15]

So impetuous was the assault that the counterscarp was also taken after bitter hand-to-hand fighting. Driven back in disorder, the 1,700 survivors of the garrison surrendered as prisoners of war. Marlborough was able to write to London with news of the success:

> The post not being gone, I could not but open this letter to let you know that, by the extraordinary bravery of the officers and soldiers, the citadel has been carried by storm, and, for the honour of Her Majesty's subjects, the English were the first that got upon the breach and the Governor was taken by a lieutenant of Stewart's regiment. The necessary orders are given for hastening the attack of the Chartreuse. [16]

Fort Chartreuse across the river held out for another six days. The French troops there were helped by heavy rain which slowed the siege operations, but understandably they had been disheartened by the fall of the citadel. Lord Cutts accepted the submission of the governor, the Marquis de Millon on 29 October, and on this occasion, good terms were granted.

The Allied operations against Liège had been quite costly at 1,268 killed and wounded but the French loss, including those prisoners who gave their parole, was of the entire garrison of nearly 10,000 men. Many of these were veteran troops and this was a severe blow by any measure, regardless of the importance of Liège itself, sitting as it did on the route by which the French would hope to support their garrisons in places like Bonn and Limburg. By the terms of the capitulation, the defeated garrison troops were allowed to disperse at will; many simply absconded and did not rally to the colours. The Allies found a huge haul of money and notes of credit sufficient to pay their army for two months, military stores and provisions of all kinds, thirty-eight guns, powder and ammunition in the citadel. This was the last operation of the campaign for this year and the weary soldiers went off to their winter quarters.

As they did so Marlborough was almost snapped up by the French. The Camp Bulletin for 2 November 1702 reads: 'His Excellency intends to embark in a yacht at Maestricht, in order to visit Stevensweert, Ruremonde and Venloo, in his way to The Hague, when His Excellency hopes to be on Thursday next.'[17] However, on 8 November 1702 a patrol of French partisans, operating out of the small town of Guelders under the command of an Irish soldier of fortune named Captain Farewell, captured or drove off the escort and seized the Earl's boat. All the officers had passes of safe conduct (a common practice at the time) except for Marlborough who through some oversight was now in danger of being taken prisoner, with immeasurable consequences for the Allied cause. Luckily his clerk, Stephen Gell, had an old pass made out for Charles Churchill, the Earl's younger brother. This piece of paper was produced and Farewell accepted its validity even though it was plainly out of date; the Allied officers were allowed to proceed unhindered, although their baggage was rifled.

Meanwhile, the news of the escapade had reached the Allied camp and all was consternation and turmoil at the thought that Marlborough was now a prisoner of the French. Count Overkirk gave orders that the town of Guelders, Farewell's base, was to be stormed and put to the sack unless the Earl was released and messengers got ready to ride to Vienna to request that Marshal Villeroi, recently taken captive in Italy, should not on any account be set free unless it was by exchange with Marlborough. His party's safe arrival at the Hague, with the Earl's dignity only slightly ruffled, was greeted with an outburst of relief and public rejoicing that he was not in the hands of the French after all. Meanwhile, a galloper had reached Versailles with the glad tidings of the capture. Louis XIV was naturally delighted; he gave instructions that Marlborough was to be brought to him without delay and treated with the utmost courtesy and consideration.[18] Shortly afterwards though the unwelcome news was received that the Earl had been released after all, and Farewell, perhaps wisely, soon absented himself from the French camp.

In recognition of his success in the Low Countries in 1702, Marlborough was made a Duke by Queen Anne at the end of the year, soon after his return to London. While he had been clearing the French out of their fortified places along the Meuse valley however, French generals had been enjoying some significant successes elsewhere. The Margrave of Baden, Imperial commander on the upper Rhine, had, it is true, crossed that river and captured Landau in a generally very well-handled operation. The defection of the Elector of Bavaria to the French caused the Margrave to pull back across the river soon afterwards, and a promising opportunity was unavoidably let go. This did oblige Louis XIV though to begin to devote large numbers of troops to sustaining his new ally beyond the tangled passes of the Black Forest, when arguably they would have been better employed in the Low Countries.

A confused and inconclusive battle had been fought at Friedlingen on the upper Rhine in October 1702, when both the French infantry and the Imperial cavalry ran away at the same moment, but Claude-Louis-Hector Villars, the French commander, recovered his army's composure more quickly and was able, rather spuriously, to claim the victory. He received a Marshal's baton as reward, although the French King seems to have subsequently suspected that the award was rather premature. However, in the middle of January, despite bitter weather, Villars audaciously crossed the Rhine, slipped passed the Imperial garrison at Briesach in dense freezing fog, and laid siege to and took the fortress of Kehl in only twelve days. The way was laid open for French armies to move into southern Germany, when the moment was right, although Villars prudently pulled his troops back across the Rhine for the time being. The following May, the Marshal managed to manoeuvre his army past the Margrave of Baden and to combine with the Elector of Bavaria, although the two strong-willed men were soon at odds with each other. Meanwhile, the Duke of Vendôme was campaigning successfully in northern Italy, where even the undoubted skill of the Imperial commander there, Field-Marshal Guido von Stahremberg, seemed insufficient to stem the French tide.

The newly created Duke of Marlborough returned to the Hague, on 17 March 1703, to prepare for the new campaign season. The Earl of Athlone, unimaginative and brave, had died the previous month, but the reliable Henry of Nassau, Count Overkirk, had taken his place and been appointed Veldt-Marshal by the States-General. He was a good soldier and a staunch friend to Marlborough; their partnership was a significant asset for the Alliance. In the meantime, Louis XIV's armies had already begun their spring campaign along the middle and upper Rhine with some success, and Marlborough soon despaired of hearing good news from that theatre of operations. In the north, the opening Allied move in response to this new French offensive was to be made against the town of Bonn, strongly garrisoned with French troops under the Marquis d'Alègre. The French-held fortress of Rheinburg had been blockaded over the winter by Count Lottum with Prussian troops and this was given up without too great a struggle, with Lottum moving on to begin a blockade of Guelders. Bonn lay inconveniently on the route between the Low Countries and the upper Rhine just as with Kaiserswerth the previous year; an active French commander there could cause trouble for the Alliance and might even threaten a fresh move against the southern border of Holland. To capture the place would clear the line of the lower Rhine of all French troops, and would be well worthwhile.

Once again, Marlborough was frustrated at the lack of urgency among many of his colleagues, complaining on 24 April that Bonn should have been under attack by then. The Allied advanced guard did get there the following day. The Duke was all the more aggravated because Bonn had been the preferred choice of the Dutch when discussing the opening of the year's campaign, when he would rather have gone looking for the French field army; now, having got their way, they were slow to act. However, once Bonn was secured, the Allied plan was to move quickly against either Namur or Antwerp, and the impending loss of either of these important fortresses might tempt the French to stand and give battle in the open.

It was arranged that Overkirk with his Dutch corps and most of the British regiments would take position at Maastricht to shield the attack on Bonn from French interference. Marlborough with the Prussian, Hessian and Hanoverian troops would conduct the siege operations. One immediate problem for the Duke was that the Zell infantry battalions, provided by the Electress of Hanover, were found to be only half-trained and poorly equipped – they had to be stood down. Lieutenant-General von Bulow's Prussian regiments took their place in the trenches. The Camp Bulletin on 27 April reported: 'The great artillery from Holland is hastening up the Rhine, so that we expect to open the trenches in three or four days.'[19] However, the trenches were only opened on 3 May, and the bombardment began five days later. D'Alegre attempted to divert the fury of the assault by drawing the Duke's attention to an agreement made the previous year between the Elector Palatine, and the Elector-Bishop of Liège and Cologne, that the cities of Dusseldorf and Bonn should not be bombarded. Marlborough was not impressed by such a cosy arrangement, and replied to the French commander that it was not his custom or inclination to destroy cities or public buildings, provided that the enemy's conduct did not put him to such a stern necessity. Four days later, the Camp Bulletin commented on the numbers of workmen engaged in the entrenching, giving a good indication of the scale of the siege operations:

> At the chief attack were employed 1200 workmen, 800 at the second, and at the third 600, which will all be relieved at four this afternoon [4 May] by the like numbers. These workmen were covered by ten battalions of foot, four at the Prince of Hesse's attack [the first] and three at each of the others, who were likewise sustained by 300 horse at the prince of Hesse's attack, and at the others by 200 each, besides the picquets.[20]

So, no fewer than 5,200 labourers, in two shifts, covered by about 6,000 cavalry and infantry in addition to sentries and lookouts, and those engaged in the nearby woods cutting and making fascines, were engaged in the entrenching work.

The Duke at this time received the infuriating news that Louis XIV now expected an attack on Antwerp, just as soon as Bonn fell: 'I have seen a letter from Paris that the siege of Bonn is but a feint, but that the real design is Antwerp.'[21] He had cause on more than one occasion to bemoan the lack of security in the Allied camp, where officers discussed future operations freely, and often commented on them in letters to friends and relations. For the time being though, the French field army watched the Allied operations from their camp and did very little to interfere; plans were made to try and retake Liège, siege guns being brought down the Sambre river from Mauberge ready for the task but in the event their services were not called upon. Louis XIV had warned his commanders not to risk a general engagement at this time, feeling that as matters unfolded in southern Germany, the Alliance would in time be obliged to send troop reinforcements there to counter the threat to Austria. Then, when the Allied armies in the Low Countries were weakened, would be the moment to strike hard in the north.

On 9 May, a strong detachment of von Bulow's Prussian grenadiers stormed a breach in the walls of one of the ravelin outworks of Bonn, and the task of bringing forward the big guns into this new position began at once. D'Alegre was a dangerous opponent though, and after a number of probes the next day to feel for just where the besiegers' strength lay, he sent 1,600 troops into a sharp counter-attack. They did considerable damage to the works and the breaching battery;

ferocious bayonet fighting took place before the French withdrew as reinforcements hurried into the ravelin. Over eighty of the Prussians were killed and ten of the siege guns and six big mortars were spiked and the carriages smashed; the French loss in this well-handled affair was only thirty men. Despite this setback, the siege ground steadily onwards, and the gunners did their work in creating a breach in the fortress walls. A flying bridge that connected an adjoining ravelin with the main fortress was demolished by Allied artillery fire and the place was stormed shortly afterwards, with thirty of the garrison being taken prisoner. With his defences steadily battered down and the breaching batteries closed up to the main fortifications to do their work, d'Alegre beat for a parley on 15 May. 'The breach was large enough', Christian Davies recalled, 'for a regiment to mount at a time; we carried the covered way, made a lodgement on the palisades, and everything was ready for a general assault.'[22]

The Allied troops took possession of one of the gates, a formal sign of submission by the garrison, the following day. D'Alegre had endured for less time than might have been expected, but Bonn was not a first-class fortress, and he very sensibly wished to spare his men and the citizenry the rigours of a storm and a possible sack of the town. The garrison of 3,600 men was granted good terms and permitted to march away to Luxembourg. Had Marlborough the time, he might have forced a submission from the garrison as prisoners of war; but the Duke had already left the siege operations, for Boufflers, now joined by Marshal Villeroi, had moved forward with his army to threaten both Liège and Maastricht.[23] Overkirk was outnumbered and hastily moved into a position of defence to the north-east of Maastricht from which to meet the threat. The French did retake Tongres with its small Allied garrison, but this was a miserable place to have to defend, with dilapidated medieval walls and little artillery or stores. The two battalions there, one Scots-Dutch and one English, held out for over twenty-eight hours – generally thought to be a very creditable performance, everything considered – buying time for Overkirk to get into place.[24] Samuel Noyes, serving with Orkney's Regiment, wrote:

Tongres is a place fit enough for winter quarters but of no defence against an Army. The States [General] had two very fine regiments of foot in the place (one lately the Lord Portmore's, a scotch regiment) ... Those were so far surprised that they thought it was our army when they saw them [the French] from the walls of Tongres. They stood upon their guard at first, but the next day, after the French had made a breach in the wall sufficient to storm the place, yielded themselves prisoners at discretion.[25]

Marlborough had been concerned to hear that the French should have been allowed to achieve this minor success, writing on 12 May to Earl Orkney that he had received 'the surprising news of the enemy's having got into the camp at Tongres, and of their having taken two regiments of foot in that place ... I have sent to Lieut. General [Henry] Lumley an order for holding courts martial.'[26] The dilapidated state of the town's defences, the huge numerical superiority enjoyed by the French, and the stout day-long fight put up by the two belea-guered Allied battalions which, at least in part, enabled the Dutch corps to get off without a mauling on the line of march, seems to have escaped the Duke's attention at that point. Also, Overkirk, with only some 25,000 troops, could not afford to risk a pitched battle just to save such a relatively minor post as Tongres. The Allied troops in the town had done their best, but they had been set a hopeless task.

Although Boufflers then advanced to confront the Dutch, and even exchanged artillery fire with them at one point, he drew off with-out forcing a general engagement on learning that Bonn had fallen. As Marlborough gathered troops from the Rhine and advanced to combine with Overkirk, the French withdrawal became rather a scramble and their newly installed garrison in Tongres evacuated the town on 26 May before it even came under real threat. The Allies promptly re-occupied this welcome and unexpected windfall, although Marlborough's nephew, the Duke of Berwick, had pru-dently blown breaches in the walls and demolished the gates before giving the place up.

Marlborough now proceeded with the plan to surprise and capture the great port city of Antwerp. This was a complex and daring opera-tion, depending on several widely separated Allied columns march-ing at speed to combine close to the city before the French could react. Marlborough initially marched towards Huy on the Meuse laying a false trail for his opponents, who marched on a parallel course and watched his moves with care. On 9 June, the Allied army halted and began to gather forage, as if waiting for the siege train to come up before closing with Huy and commencing a siege there. The opposing armies then watched each other for some three weeks with very little activity, drawing criticism towards both commanders for their seeming inaction at the height of the campaign season. With commendable confidence in just who was dictating the pace of the campaign, the Camp Bulletin did however comment: 'The enemy have made several bridges on the Jaar, by which we might pass over them.'[27] Marlborough was actually waiting for the Dutch commanders in West Flanders to be ready to move, and on 27 June his army began a march westwards using both roads and waterways, heading to combine with his allies to threaten Antwerp.

In the event, the whole enterprise to capture Antwerp was too ambitious and complex, with the Allied columns coming together before their opponents could react. The operation did get off to a good start however, with the Dutch surprising the Marquis de Hussy, routing his large brigade of five newly recruited infantry battalions, and occupying part of the French lines. Opdham's Dutch corps then rather neglectfully occupied an exposed camp at Eckeren just to the north of Antwerp, while Coehorn's troops became engaged in a tactically irrelevant operation levying contributions (a nice euphemism for approved plundering) around Ghent and Bruges. Marlborough, who was rightly concerned at the risky dispersal of the various Dutch detachments, was marching to the scene with his own troops as fast as he could manage.

On 30 June 1703, Marshal Boufflers, after a 40-mile march from Diest to combine with Isidore Bedmar, got into position first and struck hard at Opdham. He drove the outnumbered Dutch troops headlong through their camp at Eckeren and off the field, in what became a bloody and messily fought battle. Opdham, rather ingloriously, got lost while scouting the advance of the French force and rode off to inform the States-General that their army had been caught and destroyed. On the field meanwhile, only the steadfastness of the Dutch infantry led by Freidrich van Slangenberg, under intolerable French pressure, prevented a complete disaster for the Allied cause. The French and their allies did their best to turn the left flank of the Dutch and so cut across their one available line of retreat, and they only narrowly failed in this attempt. The Dutch suffered over 4,000 casualties, including about 900 taken as unwounded prisoners (more than the casualties they inflicted). They drew off, badly battered but more or less intact, in the direction of Lillo, with the assistance of some Prussian cavalry brought forward by Graf Reynard van Hompesch. 'Yesterday Sire,' Boufflers wrote to Louis XIV, 'Your Majesty's army brought off the advantage and all the marks of victory, chasing the enemy from their camp, remaining the complete masters of the field of battle.'[28] Even so, many of the French regiments had such a hard time that they at first thought that it was it was not the Dutch who had lost the day at all, but themselves; Boufflers was not really in a position to mount a vigorous pursuit for several days. He decided not to do so, but moved instead into a position to cover Antwerp against any renewed Allied advance.

This defeat for the Dutch at Eckeren – although it could have been far worse had their beleaguered infantry not fought so valiantly – ruined Marlborough's plan to attack Antwerp. Still, later in the month he tried to trap a French corps under the command of Marshal Villeroi, which had moved into an advanced camp near to St Job. Although in a good position with several batteries in place to sweep the approaches to the camp, the Marshal burned his gear and stores and managed to slip away into defensive lines on 24 July. Slangenberg, who had done so well rallying the Dutch in the recent battle, was slow to come up to Marlborough's support and no attack with a real prospect of success could now be made. The Duke made a close reconnaissance of the area all the same, accompanied by an escort of six cavalry squadrons, and was warned by French officers not to come too close or he would be fired on.

Marlborough turned his attention instead back to the Meuse, his thoughts now fixed on the fortress of Huy, sitting on a hill above the river. Possession of this place would enable him both to shield Liège and exert a threat to French-held Namur, potentially opening the whole line of the Meuse to Allied supply convoys for much of its length – a strategic asset of real value given the appalling state of the roads at this period. Louis XIV foresaw this move, and warned his field commanders to be on their guard to protect Huy: 'You know its importance and the unfortunate effects its loss would entail; but I cannot believe the enemy will attempt it as long as the army you command is so close to them.'[29] Boufflers however was in a dilemma, as Marlborough had the capability to strike deep into Brabant or against the French-held fortresses on the Meuse, as he saw fit. Until his intentions became clear, the French commander found it difficult to commit substantial troops to reinforcing Huy or Namur. There was also some doubt in the Allied camp as to what would happen next. and, as the siege artillery had gone back downstream to Maastricht, it seemed obvious to everyone that no new siege operations were intended.

Coehorn was left with a strong detachment of Dutch troops to cover West Flanders while on 13 August, Marlborough's main army began its march to the Meuse, shadowed to the south by the French, cautiously watching his movements, but not coming close enough to risk an engagement. On 15 August Huy was invested by a detachment of cavalry under Prince Frederich of Anhalt-Dessau, while Marlborough moved to cover the operations against the fortress from a camp at Val Notre Dame near the Mehaigne river. The trenches were opened on 17 August and the undefended suburbs of Huy were occupied that evening, the French troops having withdrawn and broken down the bridge over the Meuse which linked the two parts of the town. Marshal Villeroi had now replaced the tired Boufflers, and he took up a position behind some sketchy lines of defence, stretching northwards from Namur towards Louvain, watching, in vain as it turned out, for Marlborough to make a mistake.

The Allied siege train was brought back up from Maastricht by way of the Meuse, and the big guns arrived at Huy on Tuesday, 20 August. The Marquis de Pracontal, who was occupying some high ground near the town with a strong detachment of French cavalry and dragoons, exchanging signals with the town, was driven off after some skirmishing and the bombardment began the following day. The garrison had already prudently withdrawn into the citadel and four out-lying forts, and the slow pace of earlier operations that had so frustrated Marlborough seemed to be a thing of the past. While the siege operations got underway, the Duke proposed to the Dutch that the field army should march out and confront Villeroi's army and try and bring on a battle. They could not be persuaded, fearing that the ground along the Mehaigne was not suitable for a successful action; the capture of Huy, a limited but undoubtedly useful objective, would be quite enough for them. Frustrated, Marlborough wrote of his disappointment to the States-General: 'If we do not attack the enemy in this place ... these lines they will make stronger every day.'[30] This of course the French did indeed do, and over the next few months the Lines of Brabant, as they became known, were greatly improved and extended. This series of flooded meadows, barricaded river crossings, entrenchments and fortified farms and hamlets eventually stretched in a great seventy mile-long sheltering curve from Namur, past Louvain and on round to Antwerp. The French would be able to manoeuvre in relative safety behind these defences, and defy Marlborough and his comrades to do their worst.

The siege took on a rather measured pace, perhaps unavoidable when faced with the strong defences of Huy, and this is well illustrated by the account given in the Camp Bulletin for 20 August, which described the commencement of the siege operations:

The disposition being made for the opening of the trenches against Fort St Joseph and Fort Picard [two outlying posts] on Friday [16 August] the Prince of Anhalt, major-general, who commanded the former attack with two hundred workmen, and one hundred and fifty men to cover them, began to break ground about eleven at night, and carried on the trench 190 paces, the ground being very rocky and difficult to work. The enemy soon discovered our men and made a continual fire, by which two soldiers were killed, and one captain and lieutenant, with three soldiers, slightly wounded. The same night the work against Fort Joseph advanced twenty-six paces, and only one man killed.[31]

The protecting cloak of night also evidently had a detrimental effect on the laborious operations, resulting in an element of confusion and delay:

The engineer who was to have conducted Brigadier Hamilton to Fort Picard missed his way through the darkness of the night and the difficulty of the passage, which hindered the beginning there for that night, whereupon the Brigadier with his men marched to the assistance of the Prince of Anhalt in carrying on his approaches … On Saturday night the trenches were opened against Fort Picard, as was designed the night before; the work was carried on about sixty-six paces, of which thirty-six is intended for a bomb [mortar] battery, and is within 400 paces of the fort. The enemy fired continually all night.[32]

The two out-lying forts were subjected to a massive bombardment from 116 guns and mortars. It was essential to reduce these places before the main assault could begin, and the report of the operations in the Camp Bulletin on 23 August 1703 ran:

On Tuesday night the trenches against Fort St Joseph were advanced about two hundred and ten paces; the same day the bomb battery of six mortars began to play against Fort St Joseph, and at night the battery against Fort Picard was quite finished, and we had thirteen cannon mounted, six 12 and seven 24 pounders, which began to play early on Wednesday morning … We look down into the castle and can annoy them with small shot.[33]

At least one of the French magazines, and possibly a second, blew up under the Allied bombardment, causing great confusion amongst the defenders in Fort Joseph. The garrison commander submitted rather than face storm, and the Allied batteries could be dragged forward to engage Fort Picard. Chaplain Samuel Noyes, present at the siege with Orkney's Regiment, wrote on 24 August:

> Our cannon and bombs from all the batteries, but especially from the English field train which was now planted on Fort Joseph (which overlooked the castle and flanked them) murdered them so cruelly that within less than two hours they [Fort Picard] cried quarter ... At six of the clock exactly, all firing ceased ... The Great Fort, viz; Fort Joseph, had surrendered shamefully the day before without being attacked, articling only to go into the castle but the governor refused it. Its seems the commander [of Fort Joseph] was a merchant's son who had lately bought his commission to a company, and not being used to these things was frightened out of his wits by cannon and bombs.[34]

The outlying posts (which also included Fort Rouge) having now been given up or abandoned in the face of the Allied bombardment, preparations began for a storm of the citadel. The ostentatious preparation of scaling ladders, in full view of the garrison, made it appear that the besiegers would not wait for a practicable breach to be created, but intended to carry the place by storm. The chief of engineers in the besieging force, the Baron de Trogne, led a party of grenadiers forward to lay the ladders at the foot of the glacis, as if an attack was imminent.

Rather than face an assault, and with his defences crumbling in front of the powerful Allied artillery, the garrison commander, the Marquis de Millon, asked for terms that evening, 25 August. Samuel Noyes again:

> Colonel Dunnell was sent to order the guns to begin to fire at nine [o'clock], but a quarter before that the governor beat the chamade the 2nd time, and Colonel Ranleigh being sent to know his mind. He agreed to deliver up the garrison as prisoners of war ... Thus the castle was taken by strength of cannon and bombs, and t'was mighty well that t'was so, for t'was hardly possible for men to mount the breach [it being high up on a slope].

The report of this success, in the Camp Bulletin for 27 August ran 'The enemy thought we were coming to the assault, and thereupon about six in the afternoon, beat a parley, and offered to surrender upon conditions to march out to Namur with the usual signs of honour.'[35]

At first this request for terms was refused, and negotiations continued until a fresh assault was well ahead in preparation. The Marquis could do no more, except at the cost of his soldiers' lives, and the fortress could not stand much longer. The Camp Bulletin went on: 'Orders were thereupon given for beginning the attack upon yesterday morning, which the Governor perceiving, he accepted the terms offered him, and a detachment of our troops took possession.' A substantial quantity of stores and ammunition was found in the place, enough, it was said, to sustain the garrison for another two weeks. The 900 or so survivors of the garrison were eventually exchanged for the two Allied battalions, taken when Tongres was lost earlier in the campaign. 'My Lord Marlborough', Noyes reported, 'refusing them any other conditions but to be prisoners at discretion, which he does to get again the two Regiments taken at Tongres.'[36] The cost to the Allied army of this success at Huy was remarkably small, at just forty-three men killed, proof, it seems, of the efficient and intimidating use of their artillery.

Marlborough once more urged the Dutch to join in an advance on Villeroi's field army but to no avail – even though he assured the States-General that the French commanders were nervous, intent on preparing the defence of Namur before anything else, and could be beaten wherever he found them.[37] Instead, they insisted that the minor fortress of Limburg be attacked, but the Duke led his cavalry escort on a bold feint towards the French lines at Avennes on 5 September as if scouting the ground before an attack was mounted. 'My Lord Duke of Marlborough advanced before the army with ten squadrons of horse to view the enemy's lines, which he did within little more than musket shot. They fired several shots with their carabines, but did no manner of harm.'[38] In this way he had hoped to entice Villeroi to give battle, but without success. The Duke then turned away, to lead the siege operations against Limburg, determined to have no one engaged in the siege who was not willing to do his bidding.

The investment of Limburg by von Bulow was completed by 10 September and the siege train came up from Liège without the usual delays a week or so later. Marlborough supervised the work in the trenches himself, siting the big guns and encouraging the labouring soldiers as they crept forward in wet weather across difficult, slippery, ground. A storming party soon occupied the lower part of the town against slight resistance, and the siege batteries were set up on 23 September, commencing the bombardment of the upper town and citadel two days later, with twenty-four guns and eight mortars. The defences were generally acknowledged to be inadequate; although sited on rising ground, and protected by flooded meadows on two sides, there was just a single line of small modern bastions and ravelins, and no real depth to the defence. In addition, the citadel was small, and could be dominated from the town once that had fallen. The narrow frontage between the inundations did offer limited scope for the besiegers, but meant that only five Allied battalions were required to carry out the siege operations. The rest of the army, under Overkirk, could manoeuvre to foil any attempt by the French, however unlikely that might be, at a relief of the garrison.

The Marquis de Reignac, the governor, had permission to yield the place at the right moment to avoid unnecessary bloodshed. It was widely rumoured in the Allied camp that he had intended to demolish the defences and withdraw once they approached and that von Bulow's march had been so swift that the opportunity to do so had been lost. Despite the poor position in which he found himself, the Marquis mounted two spirited and very well-handled sorties, although these were stopped in the forward trenches, and soon driven back. Better terms not being granted, he surrendered the 1,400-strong garrison on 27 September as prisoners of war as soon as a breach was been made in one of the bastion walls. In the position he faced, De Reignac had little alternative but to yield, yet he did so rather sooner than might have been expected and Marlborough's refusal to grant better terms reflects this. 'However, all the French officers were handsomely treated and nothing was taken from them', Christian Davies remembered.[39]

While Marlborough was stripping away the French-held fortresses on the borders of Brabant and Limburg, the fortunes of the Grand Alliance were not prospering elsewhere. In particular, Imperial Austria was under growing attack by a combined French and Bavarian army in the Danube valley. Here, on 20 September 1703, Marshal Villars and the Elector of Bavaria had defeated an Imperial army commanded by Count von Styrum on the plain of Höchstädt. Soon afterwards, taking advantage of Imperial disarray, Tallard began to lay siege to Landau on the upper Rhine. If this town should fall, as seemed quite likely, then the French would have free use of the passes through the Black Forest to resupply Villars and his troops in Bavaria. Whatever threat was posed to Vienna would be strengthened, although Louis XIV was being drawn into an expensive campaign on the far side of the Rhine in the process. The Prince of Hesse-Cassell was sent with an Allied force to try and relieve Landau, but Tallard routed him in battle at Spire (Speyerbach) in November, and gained his Marshal's baton by doing so. Landau was left without support, and submitted to the French soon afterwards.

With the weather deteriorating the Allied campaign drew to a close. Count Lottum had gone with a detachment of Prussian troops to maintain a blockade of the town of Guelders; this was a rather overlooked operation that had been in progress, off and on, since the spring. The small garrison in the town, despairing of a relief effort which was plainly beyond Villeroi's capability to attempt, submitted early in December but not before the Allied bombardment had reduced much of the place to ruins. The States-General minted a medal to mark the successes achieved by Marlborough that year, in particular the capture of Bonn, Huy and Limburg. *'Sine Clade Victor'* was the motto the medal bore (Victorious Without Slaughter), and this was all very gratifying, but the Duke looked for greater things which were apparently not achievable with cautious allies constantly at his elbow. It was not difficult to see that, while the Duke was steadily capturing French-held fortresses in the Low Countries, France was winning the war elsewhere.

The Allied soldiers went to their winter quarters once again, and Marlborough returned to London. There, plans for a fresh campaign, not wholly new or unexpected (other than in the Hague), were put to him by the Imperial Ambassador in London, Count Wratislaw. This plan, in its essentials, was that the Duke should take his army away from the defence of the Dutch frontier – an undoubtedly important, but not war-winning, effort – and march southwards to combine with the Imperial forces and destroy the French in Bavaria.[40]

NOTES

1. D.G. Chandler, *Captain Robert Parker and Comte de Merode-Westerloo*, 1968, p. 16. See also G.M. Trevelyan, *Blenheim*, 1932, p. 236.

2. C. Petrie, *The Marshal Duke of Berwick*, 1953, p. 152. See also J. Falkner, *Marlborough's Wars*, 2005, p. 18.

3. D.G. Chandler, *Marlborough as Military Commander*, 1973, p. 100.

4. J. Fortescue, *History of the British Army*, Vol I, 1899, p. 405.

5. G. Murray, *Letters and Dispatches of the Duke of Marlborough*, Vol I, 1845, pp. 25–26.

6. W.S. Churchill, *Marlborough, His Life and Times*, Vol I, 1947, p. 592.

7. Murray, *Letters and Dispatches*, p. 35.

8. *Ibid.*

9. Chandler, *Captain Robert Parker*, pp. 22–23.

10. R. Kane, *Campaigns of King William and Queen Anne*, 1745, p. 39.

11. *Ibid.*, p. 40.

12. Murray, *Letters and Dispatches*, p. 43.

13. Petrie, *The Marshal Duke of Berwick*, p. 154.

14. Murray, *Letters and Dispatches*, (Camp Bulletin for 23 October 1702), p. 49.

15. D. McBane, *The Expert Swordsman's Companion*, 1728, p. 107.

16. Murray, *Letters and Dispatches*, pp. 48–49. The picked volunteers leading such an assault, known as the 'Forlorn Hope', would typically be paid a bounty of two shillings and sixpence in the currency of the time for their hazardous service. However, it was usual for this bounty money to be pooled and paid out to the survivors of the action. This was known as enjoying the dead man's wage. The Allied Camp Bulletin for the day described the exciting incident: 'It was intended only to make lodgement, yet our men went on with so much courage, that being masters of the breach, they entered the citadel and took it sword in hand, having after the first fury been very merciful to the enemy.' The impetuous and unexpectedly successful assault at Liège, is sometimes confused with a similar occasion at Venlo earlier in the campaign, when the uncut grass on the glacis helped the attackers scramble up.

17. Murray, *Letters and Dispatches*, p. 53.

18. Marlborough granted Stephen Gell a pension for this valuable service in this exploit, but, always careful with money, rather

regretted his generosity in later years. The Irishman, Captain Farewell, subsequently absconded to the Allies, and was granted a captaincy in the Dutch army. He had served in their army previously, but had been suspected of attempting to set fire to the magazines in Maastricht and had deserted to the French. Rumours abounded that Farewell had in fact recognised Marlborough from the start, but had accepted a bribe to let him go, with the further promise of sinecure in the Dutch service and forgiveness for past misdeeds. It was generally reported that, had the French managed to get their hands on Farewell, he would have been broken on the wheel in return for his treachery.

19. Murray, *Letters and Dispatches*, p. 88.

20. *Ibid.*, (Camp Bulletin for 4 May 1703), p. 90.

21. Chandler, *Marlborough as Military Commander*, p. 114.

22. J. Fortescue, (ed.), *Life and Adventures of Mother Ross*, 1929, p. 50.

23. Boufflers was arguably a more capable tactician than Villeroi, and was a resilient, if rather uninspired, field commander. However, his inability to handle Marlborough in the opening campaigns in the war led the French king to lose faith in his abilities. His later operational record, particularly in 1708 (at Lille) and 1709 (at Malplaquet), was distinguished and Louis XIV came, once again, to hold him in high regard, although he denied Boufflers the appointment of Constable of France in 1711, which apparently left the veteran commander broken-hearted. Villeroi enjoyed the enormous advantage of being a close confidante of Louis XIV (they had been friends in childhood). However, the King's regard for the Marshal may have done him a disservice, sustaining Villeroi in a position of high authority and heavy responsibility which his rather limited qualities did not merit. He was, all the same, a brave soldier and an honourable opponent.

24. Portmore's Scots Regiment in Dutch service was joined by the English Queen Dowager's (Catherine of Braganza) Regiment in the hopeless defence of Tongres.

25. S. Johnston, *Letters of Samuel Noyes 1702–1704*, 1959, p. 35.

26. Murray, *Letters and Dispatches*, p. 96.

27. *Ibid.*, (Camp Bulletin for 4 June 1703), p. 111.

28. Chandler, *Marlborough as Military Commander*, p. 116. See also T. Lediard, *Life of John, Duke of Marlborough*, Vol II, 1736, p. 241 for Slangenberg's interesting, if partial, account of the battle at Eckeren.

29. Chandler, *Marlborough as Military Commander*, p. 118.

30. Murray, *Letters and Dispatches*, p. 166.

31. *Ibid.*, p. 162.

32. *Ibid.*, pp. 162–163.

33. *Ibid.*, p. 164.

34. Johnston, *Letters of Samuel Noyes*, p. 70.

35. Murray, *Letters and Dispatches*, p. 169.

36. Johnston, *Letters of Samuel Noyes*, p. 69.

37. It is too easy to scoff at excessive Dutch caution at a time of almost unbroken successes for their army, but the near calamity at Eckeren had been a shock and the years had taught them to be careful. Good officers like Overkirk, Oxenstiern and Albemarle all argued that to attack the French lines was too risky at this moment, and their views cannot just be dismissed as nonsense.

38. Murray, *Letters and Dispatches*, p. 174.

39. Fortescue, *Life and Adventures of Mother Ross*, p. 53.

40. Marlborough had for some time considered the merits of a campaign in southern Germany. This was a plan with a long gestation period for on 8 June 1703 he wrote: 'If the French be not some way or other checked there (in Bavaria) we shall run great risk of losing the Empire.' See Murray, *Letters and Dispatches*, pp. 73–74. Marlborough was hatching several plans which might

enable him to operate away from the constraints of the Dutch. The Moselle valley in particular caught his attention, and he had written on 11 August 1703 to London: 'It might tender very much to the service of the public if we could send a good body of troops to winter on the Moselle, who might in the meantime take Trarbach and possess themselves of Trèves [Trier] the better to enable us to begin the campaign [in 1704] early on that side.' See Murray, *Letters and Dispatches*, p. 15. Louis XIV had been unable to resist the lure of an alliance with Maximilien-Emmanuel Wittelsbach, the rather erratic Elector of Bavaria. Although owing personal allegiance to the Emperor in Vienna, the Elector took advantage of Imperial weakness and a current concern with rebellion in Hungary, to invade the Tyrol and seize, by deception, the Imperial free city of Ulm of the Danube. Louis XIV was drawn in to southern Germany to support his ally, initially with troops commanded by Claude-Louis-Hector Villars, who found the Elector impossible to work with, and then under Ferdinand Marsin. Although superficially attractive and offering the lure of a strike at Vienna itself, this campaign was a distraction, the far-off army expensive and laborious to maintain through the tangled passes of the Black Forest. On the face of things, a French army operating with their Bavarian allies in southern Germany and threatening the capital of one of the main parties to the Grand Alliance was an encouraging prospect. The passes through the Black Forest, on the whole, were undefended or could be forced by a resolute commander as Tallard proved twice in 1704. Still, Marsin was out on something of a limb and having to depend upon the Elector for the subsistence of his army. In fact, large numbers of French troops were tied up in this campaign, when they could have been more productively employed elsewhere. Prince Eugene of Savoy, the President of the Imperial War Council, had spent some time engaging the attention of the whole Grand Alliance towards the perceived threat to Vienna, posed by the French and Bavarian armies operating in the Danube valley. By so doing, the aim was to destroy Marsin's force while at the same time dealing with the faithless Elector of Bavaria. Austria could not do this alone (and, in fact, was losing that particular part of the war), and her allies had to be drawn southwards if anything was to come of the scheme. See also J. Falkner, *Blenheim 1704*, 2004, pp. 20–21.

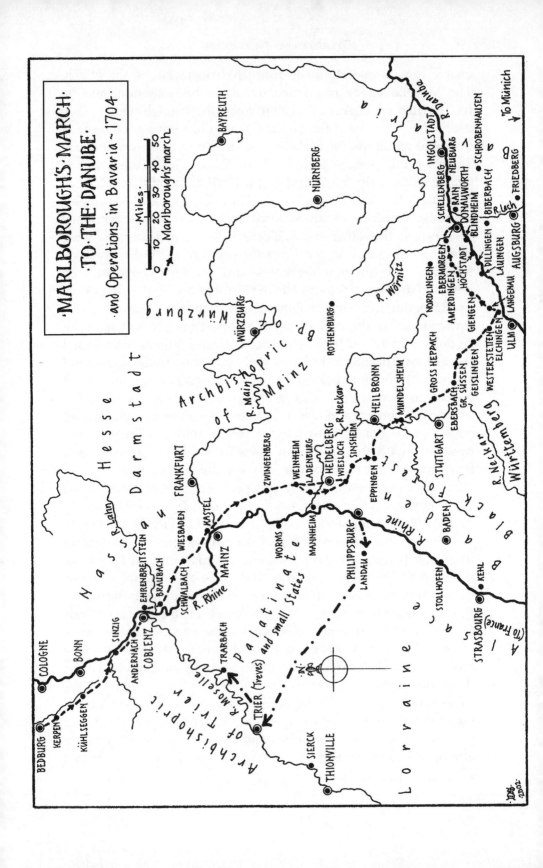

·MARLBOROUGH'S·MARCH·
·TO·THE·DANUBE·
and Operations in Bavaria ~ 1704·

·Miles·

0 10 20 30 40 50

Marlborough's march

IV

Over the Hills and Far Away: The Danube, the Rhine and the Moselle, 1704–1705

The alliance between Louis XIV of France and the Elector of Bavaria posed a persistent and growing threat to Imperial Austria throughout 1703. First Marshal Villars, and then Marshal Marsin, commanded a French army in Bavaria and southern Germany in co-operation with the Elector, and their opponents proved incapable of holding them. The occupation of Imperial lands and cities such as Augsburg and Ulm was serious enough, but should Vienna fall to a French and Bavarian raid even for a short time then so too might the Grand Alliance, with Austria driven out of the conflict. Louis XIV would then be triumphant in the war for Spain. However, the trouble and expense of maintaining a field army in Bavaria, separated from its bases, depots and magazines by the barrier of the Black Forest, was a considerable effort and strategic distraction for France. The Elector himself, capable and brave enough but unreliable, was not an ideal ally; assurances that he would supply and sustain the French forces in southern Germany soon proved worthless. In the long run, Louis XIV's involvement in Bavaria might prove to be just as much a wasteful drain on his war effort as the Spanish peninsula was to become to the Grand Alliance in later years, as they allowed themselves to be drawn into that troublesome theatre of war.

The growing threat to Vienna coincided neatly with the moment when the Duke of Marlborough had thoroughly tired of Dutch caution and obstruction of his plans in the north. Even if his allies' attitude had been very different, the constricted nature of the terrain in the Southern Netherlands – the marshy rivers and many fortified places there – laid wearisome obstacles in the path of the Duke when pursuing his goal of an aggressive campaign. Chaplain Samuel Noyes, serving still with Orkney's Regiment, wrote: 'Flanders, says he, was, at the beginning of the war, a very bad part to attack France in; it was covered with so strong a frontier. It was for this reason the Duke of Marlborough looked out for another scene of action, and did all he could on his part towards it.'[1] The threat to Vienna – however real or imagined – was in effect a very convenient reason, valid in part if not the whole, enabling the Duke to switch the main Allied campaign from the Low Countries to southern Germany. Once there he could operate, to a large degree, as he saw fit.

In March 1704, Queen Anne gave Marlborough permission to take his army up the Rhine and to campaign in the south that summer. The States-General in the Hague were offered the chance to decide whether or not to approve the plan, for the Duke only intended to take the troops in British pay with him. The Camp Bulletin on 2 May 1704 ran: 'This afternoon the Deputies of the States-General were in conference with the Duke of Marlborough, at which his Grace declared to them his resolution of going to the Moselle.'[2] The Duke made it clear that the Dutch troops, commanded by Veldt-Marshal Overkirk, would remain to guard their borders in the meantime. With some reluctance, the States-General made the best of things and agreed to his plan with good grace. They had of course only been told a part of the plan, believing that Marlborough only intended to go to the Moselle valley and that he could quickly return to support Overkirk if he suddenly came under French attack.

Marlborough's audacious march up the Rhine began on 19 May 1704. He by-passed the army of Isidore Bedmar in the Moselle valley and that of Marshal Tallard in Alsace (either of whom might have been the intended target, for all the French knew), and took his steadily-growing force into the valley of the Danube, to combine with the Imperial armies under Prince Eugene of Savoy and the Margrave of Baden. This was a masterpiece strategic stroke: transferring the whole centre of gravity of the war from the border of Holland to southern Germany. Although the Duke's preparations for a march up the Rhine were plain enough to see, the French were taken by surprise by its utter audacity when it actually happened, and they proved unable to prevent this major shift in the Allied war effort.

Louis XIV was not so innocent that he was unable to see that the Allied main campaign might switch all the way to the relief of Vienna, as the threat to that city and to Imperial Austria as an active partner in the Grand Alliance, steadily grew. Still, the King could not be sure where the blow would eventually fall, and, wrong-footed, he lost the initiative and never really regained it through all the years of war that stretched ahead. His army commanders, baffled by Marlborough's rapid moves, proved incapable of interrupting his progress, and Marshal Villeroi, who trailed along in the Duke's dusty footsteps on the road leading to the Danube, struggled in vain to catch up with the Allied army, and at last gave up and concentrated his army with that of Tallard in Alsace. Because Marlborough's march southwards took the main Allied effort away from the Low Countries, and the French had to go with him or be outflanked strategically, the threat to Holland faded away for the time being. The States-General, after some initial misgivings about the wisdom of the whole enterprise, soon gave Marlborough authority to employ a detached corps of their own troops, under command of Johan-Wigand van Goor, which had been operating for some time past with the Imperial armies on the upper Rhine. This suited the Duke very well as he knew Goor to be a good, aggressive commander who would not put difficulties in the way of an active campaign.

On 2 July 1704 Marlborough and the Margrave of Baden defeated a 12,000-strong French and Bavarian corps under command of Comte d'Arco on the Schellenberg hill near to Donauwörth, at the confluence of the Wörntiz river with the Danube. Baden protested that the cost of attacking such a strong position would be prohibitively expensive, but Marlborough pressed on and the result was a bloody but complete victory with d'Arco's troops shattered and in complete rout. This gave the Duke a crossing place over the Danube and a convenient forward base. The defeated Bavarians also left their very useful pontoon bridge train lying at the river's edge in the hastiness of their flight. This was a resounding success, with the Allied army now interposed between Vienna and the French and Bavarians. If the city had been under threat it was now safe. However, Marlborough could not progress with an advance into Bavaria in order to bring the Elector to terms while the small fortified town of Rain, standing beside the river Lech, lay on his line of advance.

The immediate practical difficulty was that Marlborough had no proper siege train with him with which to batter the walls of even such a minor place. He wrote on 9 July: 'The enemy have left a garrison of about a thousand men in Rain, a small town on the other side the river, which we shall attack tomorrow as soon as the great artillery comes up.'[3] It had not been possible to bring the big guns on the march south; they had taken a more roundabout route through central Germany to be safe from French interference. Baden had assured the Duke that this artillery would be made available on arrival beside the Danube, but this was not the case. The Duke's impatience at the enforced delay in the pace of his operations after the Schellenberg victory is evident in his letters at this time, as when writing on 13 July to the Secretary of State, Robert Harley:

Nine 24-pounders came up yesterday and we are hourly expecting three more, so that this night we shall break ground and hope to have the batteries fixed tomorrow; in the meantime we are repairing the bridge the enemy destroyed on the Lech, and likewise that at Nieuburg, and are making another bridge over the Danube between that place and Donauwörth.[4]

Rain was not a strong fortress of modern design by any means, but it was held by tough troops under resourceful commanders, and the operations to subdue the place, under command of the Count of Ost-Friese, went forward rather slowly.

Colonel Jean-Martin De La Colonie, who had narrowly escaped with his regiment from the Schellenberg hill, was tasked with the defence of Rain, commanding a rather scratch force of 500 troops and some partly-trained local militia. The Allies, however, were at first under the impression that the garrison was much stronger. De La Colonie recalled in his memoirs:

> I was in the town of Rain, occupied in rallying my grenadiers. This little town, which lies beyond Donauwörth on the edge of the Bavarian Lowlands, was a much-exposed position, and there could be no doubt but that the enemy having captured Donauwörth would presently seize it ... The town itself was by no means in a position to offer resistance, having only an old brick enceinte [curtain wall], very thick, with towers at intervals, and a dry ditch ... it needed an extraordinary combination of circumstances, such as had just occurred to us at Schellenberg, to cause Rain to be regarded as a fit position to cover the rest of the country.[5]

In the difficult circumstances in which the Elector of Bavaria found himself, he was obliged to rely on the dubious protection of the smaller river Lech, now that he had lost the line of the Danube. Rain, feeble though it was, had to be held as long as could be, to allow his army to recover its composure:

> Orders had been given in the neighbouring districts for the constant supply of peasants to work under my direction at the construction of such defences as time would permit, and, with every faith placed in my efforts, I was requested to take the work in hand at once. By this time I had about four hundred grenadiers, who had managed to save themselves and the colours.

My grenadiers, and the detachment with six small pieces of cannon, gave a thousand men for the defence of the worst place in Europe against two powerful armies. Nevertheless, it was absolutely necessary to check the enemy's advance with this handful of men, the policy of the State demanded this, a thousand men were exposed to sacrifice in order to bring salvation to a much larger number.[6]

The colonel very neatly illustrates the core purpose of the fortress in warfare. The tactical success gained in its capture can be an illusion, for a breathing space will have been gained for the defender's field armies in which to recover, manoeuvre for a better position, and in that way seek to regain the advantage that had been temporarily lost in battle.

So it proved at Rain, for Marlborough was forced to employ both time and effort at reducing this 'worst place in Europe' as the French colonel so succinctly put it, and the Duke's operations were made more difficult by the absence of the siege train. Everything can be recovered on operations with careful management except time, that most precious commodity for military commanders. Marlborough was at last able to open trenches and begin to bombard the defences of the place on 15 July, using eighteen guns and six mortars. John Deane recalled: 'Our great guns began to play at the town of Rain about one o'clock and quickly set fire to their houses with some of our mortars.'[7] De La Colonie goes on to describe the Allied assault:

> The enemy did not seem to think much of our town, for without opening a regular trench, they merely traced a small parallel in which they mounted a battery of ten pieces of cannon, for they believed that it would prove but a simple matter to level our old ramparts to the ground. For three days they treated us to a leisurely cannonade … I amused myself with my six pieces of cannon, moving them from one place to another to disconcert their gunners, who were never certain where to aim in order to dismount them, and who suffered much discomfort in their battery from our fire. At last, finding their efforts were no nearer finality at the end of these three days, this fine army, to do us the honour of laying siege to us in a regular fashion, began the construction of trenches after nightfall.[8]

The garrison of Rain held out for a further two days, when De La Colonie and the governor of the town, Count Mercy, fearing that a sudden Allied assault would overwhelm the small, weary garrison, asked for terms. The Allied Camp Bulletin recorded on 20 July: 'On Thursday [17 July] the garrison of Rain, consisting of about 400 foot, with Brigadier Mercy, the governor, marched out with their arms, and were conducted by a party of horse to the Elector of Bavaria's camp near Augsburg.'[9] Samuel Noyes recalled with some feeling the inefficient performance of Baden's artillery train at this point in the campaign. 'The German Gunners are good for nothing. The time they did fire on the wall [of Rain] they made no work of it, and after all, I believe we were glad to have the place at any rate that we might go forward.'[10] The defence of Rain had detained Marlborough in an unproductive operation, when he was eager to press on with his campaign. However, his quartermasters were able to lay hands on a substantial supply of grain left in the storehouses when the place was vacated by the French garrison.

The Elector of Bavaria in the meantime was anxiously awaiting the arrival of a fresh French army. Marshal Tallard had once already that spring brought a massive reinforcement for Marsin through the mountain passes of the Black Forest and returned safely to Alsace, despite the clumsy efforts of the Imperial commanders to stop him. Now he had avoided a blocking force commanded by Prince Eugene at the Lines of Stollhofen on the Rhine and was drawing closer to the Danube. The Elector began negotiations with Marlborough, but quite evidently, he was just hoping to deflect the fury of the Duke's increasingly ruthless campaign across Bavaria and to see what inducements were on offer if he were to switch his allegiance to Vienna once more. The Elector's insincerity was soon recognised by the Duke for what it was and the campaign of destruction by the Allied cavalry was extended, with even the suburbs of Munich being raided. Christian Davies, who served with Hay's Dragoons in the campaign, remembered:

Even the Electress of Bavaria did not think herself in safety in Munich, though she had 8,000 men of regular troops; but desired the Archbishop of Salzburg to give her shelter. Her fear was not groundless, for, after the taking of Rain and Aiche [a small town stormed by Marlborough] the Allies sent parties on every hand to ravage the country.[11]

On 8 August 1704, Tallard combined his army with that of Marshal Marsin and those Bavarian troops not otherwise wastefully dispersed protecting the Elector's own estates from Allied raids. Five days after the junction of the French and Bavarian armies, they were attacked in their camp on the plain of Höchstädt (near to the village of Blindheim/Blenheim) by the combined army of Marlborough and Prince Eugene. After a hard fight, which ranked as one of the greatest military triumphs in all history, Tallard's army was completely destroyed, and Marsin and the Elector hurried their own battered troops off the field to avoid annihilation.[12] Vienna, never really under serious threat, but a cast-iron excuse for Marlborough to use in getting away from the cautious Dutch, could now truly be said to have been saved. The Grand Alliance, as a result, had taken the initiative in the war, and would continue to hold it, never quite letting it slip, until the closing months leading to peace nine years later.

Despite the magnitude of their success on the plain of Höchstädt, the Allied armies, worn out from their exertions that day, could only follow-up their defeated opponents at a measured pace. As a result, Marsin and the Elector got their forces away, but the city of Ulm was left to the Allies:

> The enemy have left in garrison here four French battalions and five of Bavaria. We shall block up the place till it should be settled what troops shall carry on the siege, and then the rest of the army will advance through the country of Wurttemberg, towards the Rhine.[13]

Baron Thungen's batteries opened fire on the defences of the city on 8 September and the governor yielded two days later. There was plainly no hope of a relief, and he had quite possibly been left without instructions in the turmoil after the sudden defeat at Blenheim. There was also the extraordinary sense of shock and despair that engulfed the French and Bavarians after the battle. Amongst the munitions which now fell into Allied hands were 1,200 barrels of gunpowder; these were soon on their way to sustain the Duke's operations on the Rhine. Four hundred and thirty Imperial German prisoners, taken from Eugene's army early on in the Danube campaign, were released and returned to their units.

Marshal Villeroi had been left to guard France's frontier on the Rhine. He now came forward with his troops to shepherd the broken French and Bavarian armies back across the river. By the second week of September, the Allied army had also crossed over, using pontoon bridges that they had laid earlier in the summer on Marlborough's orders, to make the French believe that his intentions were to attack Alsace and not go to the Danube valley at all. Eugene had drawn all the Imperial troops away from their watch on the Lines of Stollhofen and some siege artillery was provided by the Landgrave of Hesse. Marlborough, drawing his forces together, could deploy ninety-three battalions of infantry and 181 cavalry squadrons in all. Although many of these units were under-strength after the expensive actions at the Schellenberg and Blenheim, the Allies could deploy significantly greater numbers than their rather disheartened opponents. Villeroi could muster just eighty-nine battalions and 112 squadrons (many also under-strength) to defend Alsace. On 9 September, as Marlborough's troops prepared to cross the Queich, Villeroi decided against making a fight for the line of that river (Marsin had injured his leg, and was now recovering in Strasbourg). With his inferior bayonet strength, the French commander fell back in good order to the Lauter river, some 20 miles to the south, moving on to the shelter of the Moder at Hagenau shortly afterwards. The Allies could now turn to the siege of Landau, which had been left exposed as a result of the French withdrawal.

Although it might seem that Villeroi was ingloriously giving ground without attempting to make a stand, his chosen course was prudent, necessary, and correct in the circumstances; having lost Tallard's field army entirely, Louis XIV could not afford to lose another. The French Minister of War, Michel de Chamillart, wrote to Marsin at this time 'I should never have believed that the consequences of the day of Hochstadt would be so disastrous ... the enemy terrify Alsace and have it in their choice [power] to besiege this place or that, as they judge proper.'[14] Marlborough now learned that Ulm had surrendered to Thungen, and the Camp Bulletin on 15 September gave the details:

My Lord Duke of Marlborough received an express from General Thungen dated the 10th instant, with advice that the garrison of Ulm had that day desired to capitulate, and this morning his Grace had another express from him with the Articles of surrender, by which the garrison was to march out the next day with two pieces of cannon and all other marks of honour in order to be conducted to Strasburg.[15]

The same Bulletin described an attempt to reinforce the garrison in Landau before the place was properly invested:

A party of Imperial horse met some squadrons of the enemy who had been conducting four battalions and a considerable sum of money into Landau. The Imperialists immediately charged them and put them to the rout; they killed upwards of a hundred men upon the spot, and took several prisoners. The enemy were commanded by the Duc de Montfort, a major-general, who is since dead of his wounds.

The Duc de Simon wrote that de Montfort, who was a close friend, had been very depressed in the aftermath of the defeat in Bavaria, when his whole regiment had been amongst those forced to surrender in Blindheim village. St Simon felt that his involvement in this relatively minor cavalry action was tantamount to suicide: 'A convoy of money was to be sent to Landau. Twice he asked to be allowed to take charge of the convoy and twice he was told it was too insignificant a charge for a camp-marshal [Maitre de Camp] to undertake.'[16]

The Margrave of Baden smarted with indignation at having missed the glory of the victory at Blenheim, where he felt (with some justification) he had been deliberately excluded by Marlborough and Eugene. He now oversaw the siege operations against Landau, investing the town on 19 September, but he suffered from a wound to his foot received at the Schellenberg and his troops failed to make much progress. The suspicion that he was sulking cannot easily be dismissed and Marlborough might have done well to have had him replaced, but, in the interest of harmony amongst the Allies, he did not do so. Prince Eugene commanded the covering army from a camp at Weissenburg, together with the Emperor's eldest son Joseph (King of the Romans). With all these arrangements in place and no sign that Villeroi would seriously challenge the siege of Landau, Marlborough felt able to look northwards to the Moselle valley. The region was now ill garrisoned by the French, so many of their troops having been drafted to counter the growing threat to Alsace. The Allies, for the moment, had troops to spare even if many of their units were still under strength. The capture of Landau, when it came, would certainly be welcome, but an Allied army rampaging through the Moselle valley would pose a potentially fatal strategic blow against France – bypassing the formidable natural defences of the mountainous regions in Alsace and Saar-land, while neatly outflanking the man-made fortress belt along the low-lying northern border of France. For the first time, Marlborough was able to move into this potentially valuable region in some strength.

The season for campaigning was growing late and the troops were tired; many officers felt that with so much having been achieved in this year there was no need to risk more. There was also the pressing need to rest and reconstitute some regiments after such a demanding campaign; Richard Pope, a subaltern serving with Marlborough's cavalry, remembered that they had no more than twenty horses left in each troop (only about half their normal strength), and probably not more than ten of those were really able to march any distance. Despite such considerations, Marlborough characteristically wanted more from his army; what could be had cheaply this year, with his opponents still shocked and reeling after Blenheim, would cost dear in years to come.

Villeroi meanwhile had been commended by Louis XIV for the prudent way in which he had fallen back before the renewed Allied advance and avoided giving battle in what must have been disadvantageous, even disastrous, circumstances. With his numerical inferiority, the Marshal had little option but to trade ground for time, although he was concerned that the King suspected him of cravenly avoiding a battle. On 19 September, Louis XIV wrote in reassuring terms to his old friend:

> You have done your duty as a true man ... In disregard of a false pride which would have been ill-founded, you have been more concerned in preserving my army and my state than with your personal reputation. Nothing could convince me more of your devotion to me.[17]

The King astutely foresaw what Marlborough would next attempt in this audacious season of campaigning, and went on:

> It looks very much as if M. de Marlborough will send at the same time cavalry, and perhaps even infantry, to strengthen this corps to occupy Trèves [Trier] if they can, and even to attack Trarbach in order to develop their plans and besiege Thionville at the beginning of the next campaign.

His instincts were soon to be proved right, but in the meantime the operation against Landau went on very slowly; some of Baden's troops were ill equipped, and seemed reluctant to engage in a serious siege. The defences of the fortress were well laid out and the garrison resisted stoutly, with frequent well-directed counter-attacks to regain any lost ground. Marlborough wrote on 13 October: 'The Germans possessed themselves, again, after an obstinate dispute of the redoubt they had taken, and were obliged to quit the night before.' He added that the soldiers 'discovered one of the enemy's mines, wherein was about eight hundred weight of powder.'[18]

Later that same day, as if response to the French King's prediction of his next course of action, Marlborough sent a detachment of 12,000 troops marching northwards. The Duke left the weakened British, Hessian and Prussian regiments at Landau. He soon joined the troops heading for the Moselle valley, marching in rapidly deteriorating weather through the appallingly rough country of the Hunsruck. It was learned from local people that Fort St Martin, an important outwork of the defences of Trèves, was only weakly held by French troops. On 28 October, as Marlborough's advanced guard approached, the garrison rather prematurely burned their stores and the bridge beside the fort, then withdrew in haste to the town. It was reported that the Marquis d'Alegre was now on the march northwards with fresh troops, but on 1 November 1704 Marlborough established his operating base at Consaarbruck, masking Trèves while he pressed onwards to Trarbach further down the valley. Two days later Bernkastel was reached and the Prince of Hesse-Cassell began the siege of Trarbach. A very welcome reinforcement of twelve Dutch infantry battalions, under command of Count Overkirk, arrived that same day from the Low Countries. The Camp Bulletin reported: 'The artillery which is to be employed in the siege is coming up the Moselle from Coblenz ... his Grace intends to give out his necessary orders this evening for attacking the place.'[19]

Confident that Hesse-Casselle and Overkirk could push the siege of Trarbach forward without supervision, Marlborough then went back to the Rhine to attend to the ponderous operations against Landau. He was not at all impressed by what he found there, and wrote to Hesse-Cassell on Friday, 7 November:

> I have arrived here last evening but I do not find our arrangements are as advanced as those involved would wish. We are masters of the counter-scarp, and tomorrow all the batteries begin to fire on the breach which should be wide enough by Wednesday [12 November].[20]

The siege operations against the town eventually made better progress under the Duke's firm direction. John Deane of the 1st English Foot Guards recalled the Allied batteries beginning their bombardment and 'killing abundance of the besieged, particularly the governor, and blinded the deputy governor … the French [having] made the town vast strong since they took it last year.'[21] The defences had been improved with a stout earthen bank and deep water obstacle and Deane wrote: 'The besiegers were obliged to cross with floats before they come to scale the walls.' Still, some parts of the fortress were defective due to the mortar not being properly set in the newly constructed defences. These were rather vulnerable to artillery fire and the Camp Bulletin issued on 10 November ran:

> The batteries continue to fire at the breaches, having already made one practicable, in the face of the counter-guard on the right: and the miners likewise continue the sap under the covered way both on the right and the left, for the passages into the ditch, for the filling of which great part of the materials are already provided, and the rest expected tomorrow.[22]

The garrison resisted doggedly, even with their crumbling walls, but several breaches were being widened out by now, and a general assault was ordered for 24 November, with 5,000 stormers detailed for the task. The now-blind deputy governor, the Marquis de Laubanie, had done all he could and prudently beat for a parley at 10.00 a.m. the next day. The twenty-eight articles of capitulation were signed that same afternoon.

The 3,400 survivors of the garrison were granted good terms in recognition of their fine performance in holding out for over seventy days. By this time though, Marlborough had been called away to diplomatic duties. After arranging for the British regiments, very reduced in strength, to return to Holland, he went rattling off in his coach along the road to Berlin to confer with the Prussian King and ensure he remained staunch for the Alliance in 1705. After a very good defence, Trarbach on the Moselle surrendered to the Prince of Hesse-Cassell on 20 December. The Dutch chief of engineers at the siege, Baron Trogne, had been killed right at the side of Hesse-Cassell as he directed the last assault on the covered way. The Allies had suffered nearly 1,000 killed and wounded in taking Trarbach, while the governor of the town had been mortally wounded in the fighting and over half of his small garrison, who had fought well, became casualties. With Trarbach now secure, the Duke could leave a substantial force in the Moselle valley over the winter months, securing the region for the Grand Alliance, ready for a mortal thrust deep into France in the next campaign season.

After his visit to Berlin, Marlborough went to Hanover to see the Electress Sophia and her son George, and then to the Hague to receive the acclaim of the Dutch States-General after his triumphant summer on the Danube, the Rhine and the Moselle. By mid-December he was back in London, together with the captive Marshal Tallard and other prominent French prisoners, with piles of captured colours, standards and drums. Replying to an address from the House of Lords which wobbled at times on the verge of adulation, Marlborough paid a neat compliment to his troops, without whom all his efforts would have been for nothing:

> I must beg on this occasion to do right to all the officers and soldiers I had the honour of having under my command. Next to the blessing of God, the good success of this campaign is owing to their extraordinary courage. I am sure it will be a great satisfaction as well as encouragement to the whole army, to find their services so favourably accepted.[23]

Louis XIV was well aware that after the awful reverses suffered by his generals in 1704, time and patience had to be devoted to rebuilding his military strength and recovering the initiative for France in the war. Fresh regiments were raised from amongst the militia, new drafts of horses were acquired from Switzerland and orders went out to the French commanders in the field to remain firmly on the defensive in the Low Countries and along the Rhine frontier. Marshal Villeroi and the Governor-General of the Spanish Netherlands, the fugitive Elector of Bavaria, would hold the line in Brabant. Meanwhile, Villars would command in the Moselle valley and Marsin cover Alsace and what stretches of the upper Rhine remained in French hands. The instructions from Versailles were clear: these commanders were to co-operate together to an unprecedented degree, shifting forces from one theatre of war to another as the Allied threats developed. The King had no intention, however, of slowing the pace of operations in Spain and Northern Italy, where Marshals Tesse and Berwick, and the Duke of Vendôme, were active.

The Dutch, unaware that Villeroi was instructed to act on the defensive, remained particularly concerned at the French threat to their borders. The success in Bavaria had heartened and impressed them, but they insisted still that the bulk of their own troops remain in place near to Maastricht, to watch for any new aggressive moves by the French. Marlborough on the other hand wanted to get on with a renewed campaign in the Moselle valley without delay, and on 21

April 1705 he wrote to London with rare impatience that the Dutch 'Desire of keeping fifty battalions and ninety squadrons on the Meuse is very unreasonable; for if this should be complied with, I should have on the Moselle but sixty battalions and seventy-nine squadrons to act offensively.'[24] It was clear that even so astute a commander as Veldt-Marshal Overkirk, reliable in all things but this, had not learned one of the main lessons of the previous year – if Marlborough marched southwards with enough bayonet strength to impose his will elsewhere, and pose a real threat in the Moselle valley, then the French would have to march south also. By contrast, it would soon be seen that the French generals, so often derided for their apparent lack of awareness, had learned this particular lesson. They would show just how to exert pressure, oblique certainly but powerful enough, on the most sensitive nerve of the Grand Alliance.

It is one thing to make grand plans and quite another to bring them to fruition. Marlborough returned to the Moselle on 26 May 1705 with fewer troops than he had hoped for. He was dismayed to find not only that the Margrave of Baden was not yet ready to begin the campaign as arranged, but the well-stocked magazines and depots established in the valley the previous year were now empty. Baden was certainly very unwell, not having recovered from the gun-shot wound he received at the assault on the Schellenberg. Marlborough's secretary, Adam Cardonnel, wrote of him: 'The prince was pretty well when we arrived yesterday in the afternoon, but has kept his bed most part of this day for his lameness.'[25] Far worse news, without doubt, was that the army contractor, in whose charge the stores had been left, had sold them and promptly defected to the French to avoid the retribution he deserved. Promised detachments of German and Imperial troops did not appear and there was no reliable information as to when they would arrive. 'Our General's chief care at present is to subsist his Army, and second to press the German Princes to be punctual to their promises.'[26]

Marlborough was now out on something of a limb, far from his own depots but eager to begin a campaign that promised high rewards in return for some risk. He wrote to London on 27 May: 'We have no more hay, and on this side of the river there is very little corn in the fields … it would be very happy for us if the Marshal de Villars would venture a battle.'[27] If his army stood still it might well go hungry and would certainly achieve nothing. If they advanced there was a chance they would be successful even if hungry, and news was coming in that that Villars, further up the valley, was daily receiving reinforcements. On 3 June at first light, Marlborough advanced with his troops up the Moselle, moving across a countryside swept clean of provisions by French cavalry to confront Villars at Sierck that same evening. The position the French held was strong and Marlborough rightly decided not to sacrifice his men in a fruitless assault, for he could only field some 42,000 British, Danish, Prussian, Palatine and Hessian troops against the 55,000 men Villars had under command. The Marshal, despite his numerical advantage, could see that hunger and want would defeat his opponents just as well as musketry and cannon fire, and was content to wait.

Marlborough soon received worrying news from the Meuse, where Marshal Villeroi suddenly moved out from his defensive lines, and on 10 June had surprised the Allied-held fortress of Huy, so hard won by the Duke's troops two years previously. Colonel De La Colonie wrote of the affair:

> The assault was of a different character to that which usually obtained in such cases, because it was necessary to employ escalading [ladders], and I lost many men who were thrown from the tops of the ladders ... The outwork carried, the town capitulated the next day.[28]

The French had then gone on to occupy the city of Liège and were threatening to storm the citadel, where the Dutch garrison was too weak to hold out for long. Overkirk had insufficient strength to counter the French offensive, which was very well timed while Marlborough was engaged on the Moselle. The Veldt-Marshal was outnumbered by Villeroi and had little alternative for the time being but to put his troops into an entrenched camp at St Peter's Hill, near to Maastricht, while summoning Marlborough to come to his support.

All this was no mere coincidence, with Marlborough and his troops away to the south. Louis XIV's strategy of having the commander on one front operate in such a way to foil the enemy threat on another was plainly having some effect. The States-General's written appeal to Marlborough recounted the new and increased dangers they faced: 'The loss of Huy; the siege of Liège, which was begun, the threats of the Elector [of Bavaria] and Marshal de Villeroi, that they would recover the former conquests of the Allies; the necessity, which there was, to make a powerful diversion to oppose their enterprises.'[29] De La Colonie's perceptive comment on all this was: 'France ... desired to draw them back in the direction of Flanders, where the country was covered by a chain of fortified towns suitable to ward off reverses.'[30] The Moselle valley was France's weak point, and Villeroi's limited offensive in Brabant had the desired effect, drawing Marlborough northwards once again.

Although Imperial German troops and much needed supplies were at last on the way to reinforce Marlborough, he had little choice but to abandon his Moselle campaign and hurry to support Overkirk at Maastricht. Faced with the impasse of Villars's solid defence at Sierck, Marlborough had in any case – even before the news came of the loss of Huy – laid plans for a tactical withdrawal towards Coblenz if it were necessary. He was now concerned that, with the Dutch in such a state of alarm, they might even be tempted to conclude a separate peace with the French: 'The alarm is so great in Holland that I am apprehensive they may be frightened so as to harken to a proposition of peace before I get thither, so that I make all the diligence possible.'[31] Breaking contact with as skilled an opponent as Villars was a risky business, for the French commander could well try to take advantage of any slip on Marlborough's part and harry the Allied rearguard as it moved off. Villars made no move however, having no need to attack Marlborough to achieve what was intended. The Allied troops broke camp and marched off without being molested.

By 18 June, the Duke's army was well on its way down the valley, and he wrote to the Emperor in Vienna that evening:

> The enemy have had the time and the occasion to alarm the Dutch, and this has been so great that they have sent me requests one upon the other to ask me to march will all due despatch to their rescue with a corps of troops … Tomorrow I will march the troops towards the Meuse. This disruption in our affairs, I assure your Imperial Majesty, leaves me in despair.[32]

Count d'Aubach commanded the rearguard with a strong detachment of 10,000 cavalry and infantry. He had orders to screen Trèves and the lower Moselle against any French advance, and the Count's force was well able to handle itself in anything other than a major engagement. Marlborough did not move away in so much haste that the rearguard was in any danger of being cut-off before it could get into place to defend itself, and rain helped to conceal the movement: 'M. de Villars might have sent some troops to observe our march, but nothing appeared; the weather indeed, was so rainy and misty all day that if he had designed any such thing, it would have been very difficult.'[33] A force of Palatine and Westphalian troops were to garrison Trèves and the lower Moselle valley, in the hope that a fresh campaign there might be undertaken in the future.

The marching pace the Duke set his troops was fast with only brief pauses, both to put distance between his army and any pursuit Villars might attempt, and so that Overkirk should be reassured that help was on the way. Marlborough had received information that the Marquis d'Alegre had been sent by Villeroi with a detachment of 13,000 infantry and dragoons to threaten the Bishopric of Cologne. If that were so, then the Duke's own line of march would soon cut across him. Marlborough added a postscript to a letter he sent to London on 21 June: 'We shall know in two or three days whether this be his intention, which our march will make very difficult for them to execute.'[34] The forced pace, quite unusual for the time, called on the Allied troops to march both night and day with only short periods for rest.

The Duke's army combined with the Dutch corps at Haneffe on 2 July. The Allies had superiority in numbers once again and Dutch resolve stiffened as Marlborough approached. Villeroi now had to abandon the operations against the citadel of Liège, falling back to Tongres, while the Elector of Bavaria took his own troops to Tirlemont. As a result, any opportunity to harass the Allied army as it moved forward to regain lost ground was missed by the French commander. However, although he apparently gave way rather too meekly as soon as Marlborough arrived on the scene, Villeroi could be pleased with what had been achieved. The Duke had been drawn away from the Moselle, the most promising theatre of war for his plans, and very reluctantly had once again to campaign in the confines of the Low Countries. Whatever lay ahead, the French commander had obliged Marlborough to comply – for the time being at any rate – to his own moves, and this was success to a limited degree. Villeroi had no desire or particular need to stand and fight a general engagement with Marlborough.

By his capture of Huy and then making the threat against Liège, Villeroi had drawn Marlborough away from the Moselle, back into the fortress belt of the Low Countries. The Duke's campaign in the south had of course got off to a poor start, but he might well have recovered once supplies and reinforcements joined him on the Moselle; Villeroi's offensive against Overkirk, nipping at the most sensitive nerve in the Alliance, had neatly spoiled Marlborough's plans for the campaign season beyond hope of recovery. In this respect it was a significant achievement for the French, made even better when the officer Marlborough had left behind in the Moselle valley, Count d'Aubach, took alarm at a fresh French advance – not actually very serious in itself – burned or abandoned all the stores left in his care, and withdrew to Coblenz at the end of June. 'Thus', Richard Kane wrote, 'was the Duke of Marlborough disappointed in the noble scheme he had formed for carrying the war through Lorraine into the heart of France.'[35] The loss of stores was made all the more galling because forty cannon were also left in Coblenz and these were gleefully seized by Villars when he moved forward to occupy the town.

By 6 July, operations to retake Huy were underway and Fort Picard, which the Allies had stormed two years earlier, once again received the attention of Marlborough's gunners: 'A battery of twelve pieces of cannon and six mortars began to play this morning upon Fort Picard, and tomorrow another battery will be ready to fire.'[36] Within a week, Danish troops under Count Scholten had retaken both the fort and town in a well-handled assault and at the cost of little more than a dozen casualties. The 450-strong garrison commanded by Brigadier-General St Pierre was taken to Maastricht as prisoners of war. At this, Villeroi fell back once more behind his defences, divided his army, and posted them by brigades along the length of the lines. In the process he lapsed into a passive, defensive posture in his campaign once more. With careful management, the French and their allies could manoeuvre behind the Lines of Brabant to foil any attempt by Marlborough to suddenly storm across and engage them in open battle.[37]

Marlborough swallowed his disappointment and turned to his maps. Determined that the summer campaign season should still not be wasted, he prepared a plan to force Villeroi away from the defensive Lines. The point he chose was exactly that at which the Dutch had refused to attack during the siege of Huy two years earlier. This time they made no complaint, and the scheme swung into action on the night of 18 July when Overkirk's corps was sent marching southwards towards Namur, using bridges ostentatiously laid over the Mehaigne river on the way. Villeroi was immediately alerted to the move and took the bait; he moved his own army to the south to cover the city. Marlborough then set his own British, German and Danish troops marching northwards through the night to breach the almost-deserted Lines beside the villages of Elixheim and Wanghe.

Marlborough's troops were almost immediately attacked by a powerful French and Bavarian force as soon as they got across the Lines, but he drove these away with heavy loss after a hectic battle in which he was almost sabred by a Bavarian trooper. Villeroi was too far off to the south to intervene. Having lost the protection of the lines of defence, he had little choice but to hurriedly withdraw behind the comforting protection of the Dyle river, leaving several of his guns and quite a large number of stragglers as prisoners behind him. The Duke's success was plain to all and the Elector of Bavaria, whose troops had behaved very well but been roughly handled at Elixheim, wrote resignedly to an acquaintance about the retreat of Villeroi's army: 'God forgive those that suffered themselves to be surprised. The whole army is here [Louvain] and the evil is not so great as to be past remedy. The country of Brabant may be saved, as well as Antwerp, if it please God.'[38] The Allied pursuit was less rapid than might have been expected, as the Dutch troops, who had performed the valuable but unglamorous role of decoy to the south, were tired after their march, having covered twenty-seven miles in thirty hours over poor roads. Villeroi wrote to Versailles with his explanation of the sorry affair:

> They caused part of their army to pass the Mehaigne, which pre- sented them before our lines near the Meuse, as if they really had a design to force them there. Monsieur the Elector and I being so persuaded, caused the greatest part of our troops to march towards that part, and we thereby weakened our guard about Elixheim, which they were advised of by their spies. However, the troops which we had left there under the command of the Marquis d'Alegre and Count Horn, seeing themselves attacked by the great numbers of the enemy, were, after they had a long time disputed their passage, obliged at last to give ground.[39]

Having broken through the supposedly formidable French Lines with only small loss, Marlborough moved forward in full force ten days later towards the Dyle river, and pushed a strong advanced guard of Dutch and British troops across on pontoon bridges near to Neideryssche (Neerysche). Villeroi had his army in position slightly to the north to cover Louvain from a direct approach, and he was in danger of being outflanked by the Allied movement. Instead, the Dutch deputies decided that a battle would be too risky and Villeroi had time to side-step and close up to the Allied bridge-heads over the river. With the Dutch determined to recall their troops even though their artillery was already in action, Marlborough had no choice but to abandon what had seemed an otherwise promising move. He wrote from Meldert on 30 July: 'It was not thought fit to pursue the attempt; so we withdrew our men and marched to this camp with very little loss but we are told that our cannon did the enemy consid- erable mischief.'[40]

Within a couple of weeks the Duke was ready to try and get at Villeroi again. Loading his wagons with four days' supply of bread, he cut loose from his supply lines and struck westwards, turning the right flank of the French position covering Brabant completely. Villeroi hesitated, uncertain where Marlborough's blow would fall, and the Marquis de Grimaldi, commanding a French detachment on the Yssche river to the south of Brussels (in the forest of Soignes, not far from Waterloo), suddenly found the whole Allied army bearing down on him. On 18 August, all seemed set for a successful Allied attack, and Grimaldi, heavily outnumbered although in a fair defensive position, faced defeat:

> Our army was formed in order of battle, and my lord Duke of Marlborough having with M. de Overkirk visited the posts they had resolved to attack, were giving orders accordingly to the troops to advance; but the Deputies of the States, having consulted with their generals, would not give their consent.[41]

Grimaldi and his isolated detachment would have been overwhelmed had the Dutch not intervened and demanded a council of war to discuss the risks of such an operation. When the talking had finished, the evening had gone by and any attack had to be deferred. The following morning, it was seen that Villeroi had closed his main army up to Grimaldi and their position had been fortified in the night. The opportunity was lost, and, fuming with frustration, Marlborough drew his army off to resupply the now emptying wagons. He wrote the next day: 'After four days' continued march through a difficult country and many defiles we came yesterday in the presence of the enemy, and were all afternoon drawn up in order of battle; but our friends could not be persuaded to attack them.'[42] The Dutch deputies, stung by the Duke's anger with them, defended themselves, writing to the Hague: 'The attacking the enemy in their posts would be attended with the greatest difficulty and hazard.'[43] They also complained that Marlborough did not discuss his plans with them, but it was widely known that they had difficulty keeping things in confidence. The Duke meanwhile made it plain to the States-General and to Queen Anne that he would not continue to serve with such intolerable restrictions on his ability to command the army as he saw fit. This had the desired effect, and at the end of the campaign the more obstructive of the Dutch deputies and Dutch generals were quietly posted elsewhere.

Foiled by Dutch caution at both the Dyle and Yssche, Marlborough turned aside to attack the small French-held fortress of Leau

(Saint-Loewe) – 'A little strong town and castle … it stands in a morass almost inaccessible'[44] – which covered the now-abandoned defensive Lines of Brabant. Lieutenant-General Dedem was sent on 27 August to invest the place, which was done two days later. After some careful negotiation, Brigadier-General Du Mont, the governor, yielded the town and citadel without very much fighting – if in fact there was any at all. The 400-strong garrison who, the Duke recalled in a letter written on 7 September, had surrendered without obliging his troops to fire one gun, was conducted to Maastricht to await exchange as prisoners of war. The rich haul of booty in the citadel was found to include eighteen pieces of cannon, two brass mortars, 10,000 grenades, 2,000 muskets, 100 barrels of small-shot and 18,000 sacks of meal: a very welcome increment indeed to the Allied war-stocks and all gained for remarkably little effort. The work of levelling the Lines of Brabant now commenced in earnest; 3,000 soldiers and labourers being employed in the work, which was completed by the end of September.

Marlborough's army began moving again in the second week of October, heading towards the small fortress of Santvliet on the Scheldt. On 24 October, Count Noyelles was sent with a detachment of fifteen infantry battalions and eight cavalry squadrons to invest the place. He was joined shortly afterwards by six more battalions from the garrison in Bergen op Zoom. Soon, the Duke left the army in Overkirk's capable hands, and went to Vienna where discussions on preparations for the campaign the next year were to take place. By 29 October, Noyelles's guns had made two breaches in the walls and a storm by the assembled grenadiers of the army was ordered for the following day. The governor promptly surrendered the place – plainly the correct decision in the circumstances – and he and the garrison were marched away as prisoners of war.

In the meantime, on 24 October the Marquis de Grimaldi moved out and captured the small Allied-held town of Diest on the Demer river. The garrison was commanded by Brigadier-General Gaudecker and they were apparently taken by surprise. Once an outwork had been stormed with the loss of thirty men in a sharp little engagement, Gaudecker yielded the place and was refused good terms by Grimaldi. He and the garrison of four Hessian, Hanoverian and Saxon infantry battalions and some dragoons were marched off to Brussels as prisoners of war. The distraught Gaudecker wrote shortly afterwards: 'He was extremely concerned, that, after thirty-four years' service, performed without the least disgrace or stain to his reputation, he should be put into a place where a man of honour was not capable of defending himself.'[45] Gaudecker had a perfectly valid point for if the fortifications – as in this case – were feeble and unable to resist an early storm, to fight on with the aim of simply maintaining his professional reputation would be to risk a sack and butchering of the garrison. So, such weak places had either to yield quickly, as happened with Leau and Diest with attendant risk to reputations, or be prudently abandoned beforehand.

This minor French success at Diest was really was of no great importance to either army. However, it came soon after the failure to press on with the river crossing at Neeryssche and the decision not to attack Grimaldi in good time at the Yssche river. Villeroi was impressed to an unwise degree with his apparent ability to get the better of Marlborough when he chose to do so. This series of missed opportunities by the Allies reinforced the Marshal's growing, comforting delusion that he had after all handled the autumn campaign rather well. Villeroi chose to overlook the salient feature: that Dutch caution and obstructiveness, more than anything the French commander had done, had foiled Marlborough's plans. The French were beginning to suspect that Marlborough's successes at the Schellenberg and Blenheim in 1704 had all been due to luck. They were nurturing a disdain for the Duke's capabilities and that was foolish. It fatally coincided with a decision taken in Versailles, that the French commanders on all fronts should move out and vigorously attack their opponents in the forthcoming campaigns.

NOTES

1. N. Tindal, *History of England*, 1738, pp. 39–40

2. G. Murray, *Letters and Dispatches of the Duke of Marlborough*, (Allied Camp Bulletin, 2 May 1704), Vol I, 1845, p. 152.

3. *Ibid.*, p. 348.

4. *Ibid.*, p. 351.

5. W. Horsley, (ed.), *Chronicles of an Old Campaigner*, 1904, p. 198.

6. *Ibid.*, p. 199.

7. D.G. Chandler, (ed.), *Journal of John Deane*, 1984, p. 9.

8. Horsley, *Chronicles of an Old Campaigner*, pp. 200–201.

9. Murray, *Letters and Dispatches*, p. 361.

10.S. Johnston, (ed.), *Letters of Samuel Noyes*, 1959, p. 145.

11.J. Fortescue,(ed.), *Adventures of Mother Ross*, 1929, p. 57.

12.The French and Bavarian armies, under command of Marshals Marsin and Tallard and the Elector of Bavaria, had moved north of the Danube on 10 August 1704. This was an attempt to destroy Prince Eugene's small army before it could combine with that of the Duke of Marlborough, who at that point was still at Rain to the south of the river. They failed to catch Eugene and instead went into an encampment on the plain of Höchstädt, near to the small village of Blindheim (Blenheim), while the next Allied moves in the campaign were awaited. This was a good spot for a camp but not ideal terrain on which to fight a pitched battle. Marlborough and Eugene combined their armies in the evening on 11 August and two days later they closed up to the French and Bavarians and attacked them in place. Eugene had a particularly hard fight at Lutzingen on the right of the Allied attack where the Bavarians drove his soldiers back several times. Marlborough meanwhile engaged the French cavalry under Marshal Tallard on the open plain of Höchstädt and by evening had defeated them and driven them off the field in complete rout. Tallard was taken prisoner, as were most of his French infantry who became trapped in Blindheim village. The Elector of Bavaria went almost as a fugitive to resume the governorship of the Spanish Netherlands while his wife was left to negotiate a settlement of sorts with Vienna. She was able to reside with her children in Munich with a pension and a guard of honour but all Bavarian troops (other than those already behind the Rhine or in the Low Countries and still commanded by the Elector) were to be disbanded. Imperial forces also took control of Bavarian fortresses while the war lasted.

13.Murray, *Letters and Dispatches*, p. 423.

14.W.S. Churchill, *Marlborough, His Life and Times*, Vol I, 1947, p. 894.

15.Murray, *Letters and Dispatches*, p. 465.

16. *Ibid.*, p. 471.

17. B. St John, (ed.), *Memoirs of the Duc de St Simon*, Vol I, 1889, p. 291.

18. W.S. Churchill, *Marlborough*, p. 900.

19. Murray, *Letters and Dispatches*, p. 527.

20. *Ibid.*, pp. 527–528.

21. *Ibid.*, p. 15.

22. *Ibid.*, p. 531.

23. E. Edwards, *Life of Marlborough*, 1932, p. 170.

24. W. Coxe, *Memoirs of the Duke of Marlborough*, Vol I, 1847, pp. 266–267. Not quoted, however, by Murray in *Letters and Dispatches*.

25. Murray, *Letters and Dispatches*, Vol II, p. 51.

26. D.G. Chandler, *Marlborough as Military Commander*, 1973, p. 156.

27. Coxe, *Memoirs*, p. 275.

28. Horsley, *Chronicles*, p. 292.

29. Tindal, *History of England*, p. 135.

30. Horsley, *Chronicles*, p. 293.

31. J. Reid, *John and Sarah*, 1914, p. 234.

32. Murray, *Letters and Dispatches*, pp. 109–110, and facsimile of original letter in the author's possession.

33. *Ibid.*, p. 113.

34. *Ibid.*, p. 123.

35. R. Kane, *Campaigns of King William and Queen Anne*, 1745, p. 59.

36. Murray, *Letters and Dispatches*, p. 159.

37. John Deane described the Lines of Brabant as 'Of a most prodigious strength, being eighteen feet deep and sixteen feet broad ... So thick that four men might have walked abreast upon it and fired upon the enemy that should approach.' See *Journal of John Deane*, p. 30.

38. Tindal, *History of England*, p. 142.

30. M. Langallerie, *Memoirs*, 1710, p. 282.

40. Murray, *Letters and Dispatches*, p. 495.

41. Murray, *Letters and Dispatches*, Vol II, p. 224.

42. *Ibid.*, p. 225.

43. Tindal, *History of England*, p. 144.

44. *Ibid.*, p. 145.

45. *Ibid.*, p. 147. See also J.L. Vial, *Garnison de la ville de Diest prise par les Francais*, (Nec Pluribus Impar website, 2001.) The decision on occasions such as that faced by Brigadier-General Gaudecker at Diest was often finely balanced, and a tough choice had to be made. The commander of a fortified place was plainly expected to do his best and his duty and hold out – the 'rules' of siege warfare set out what was expected in all but the most unusual circumstances. To yield a place in a significantly lesser period of time might be construed as incompetence or cowardice, possibly even treachery with all the awful consequences that would entail. However, to expect an officer to defend an inadequately strong place, with a garrison too small, or too ill equipped, for the task was plainly an unreasonable demand. The professional reputation of the commander would unfairly be at risk, hence Gaudecker's plaintive letter. He had been given a task that, other than at the expense of the lives of his soldiers gratuitously thrown away, he had no hope of carrying out. Still, the garrison had been taken completely by surprise, as Gaudecker wrote in his letter: 'At break of day we realised that the enemy was posted on all sides.' This awareness of the French approach seems to have come rather late to the garrison.

V

Glorious News of Success: Ostend, Menin, Dendermonde and Ath, 1706

Encouraged by the lack of any major Allied success in 1705, Louis XIV attempted to open negotiations with the Grand Alliance to gain an advantageous peace. Broad hints were even dropped to Marlborough that should he use his influence to secure a settlement, a large gift of money would be his as a token of appreciation from the King. The French proposals at this point were broadly that Philip V should have Spain, the Milanese in northern Italy, and the empire in the Americas. Archduke Charles (the Austrian claimant) would receive Bavaria, while Maximilien Wittelsbach, the Elector would become King of the Two Sicilies (which included at that time Naples, Sardinia and much of southern Italy). Holland would receive Guelders and Limburg as recompense for the costs of the war, while the Duke of Lorraine would become ruler of what remained of the Spanish Netherlands. This complicated and rather impractical arrangement was plainly in France's interests, at a moment when her fortunes had not recovered from the shocks sustained in 1704. It fell far short of the aspirations of the Grand Alliance as they existed at the time and so nothing came of the approach.

On the morning of Sunday 23 May 1706, the Duke of Marlborough came upon Marshal Villeroi's French and Bavarian army at the Ramillies watershed, stretching between the Mehaigne and Petite Gheete rivers a few miles to the south of Louvain. The French commander, a naturally cautious man, had not been expected by Marlborough to fight at all but Louis XIV wanted to show his enemies that his war effort was as vibrant as ever. Accordingly, his Marshals had been instructed to take the field on all fronts and the French Minister of War, Michel de Chamillart, was impatiently urging them to get on with their campaigns; Villeroi was moving forward in obedient response to these commands. At about 1.00 p.m. the artillery duel began. Two hours later, the Allied attack went in and late in the afternoon a combined Danish and Dutch cavalry attack crumpled the French army on the wide plain to the south of Ramillies – it broke and fled. Virtually all Villeroi's artillery and equipment was abandoned on the field of battle, and Marlborough's troops pursued the defeated Marshal and what was left of his army through the night.[1]

The city of Louvain was abandoned by the French the following day, with the line of the Dyle river given up without a fight. Marlborough's troops occupied the city on 25 May and the Duke sent a summons to the governor of Brussels, the Marquis de Deynse, and the city magistrates to submit. This they did three days later, along with the States of Brabant, declaring their allegiance to Charles III and at the same time prudently expressing their thanks to Marlborough for delivering them from the unwelcome rigours of French occupation. The magistrates handed the keys of the city to Marlborough on a golden platter that evening and entertained the Duke and his staff to a lavish civic banquet. He was at pains to assure the citizens of both cities that the 'Joyous Entry of Brabant', by which their ancient civic rights and privileges had been guaranteed many years before, would be maintained under the rule of Archduke Charles.

Villeroi's army was in tatters and within a few days it had withdrawn, first behind the river Dender and then the Scheldt, to try and recover. Marlborough's advance was too rapid; there was no respite for the Marshal and the Allied advanced guard under command of the Duke of Württemberg crossed the Scheldt at Gavre just downstream from Oudenarde on 31 May. Fearing that he would be cut off from France by this move, Villeroi abandoned any attempt to hold on to Ghent and Bruges in the north and withdrew with his troops to Courtrai on the Lys, close to the protective fortress belt along the French border. He had evidently given up any hope of holding most of the towns, fortified or otherwise, in the Spanish Netherlands and Marlborough was free to conduct a triumphant campaign, meeting little opposition. The French and Bavarian troops were demoralised for the time being and the soldiers in Spanish service were, quite understandably, in some doubt quite where their loyalty should lie. On the day he passed the Scheldt, the Duke wrote to Sidney Godolphin:

We should have cut the French army from their old lines; but they rather chose to abandon Ghent, which they did this morning at break of day, so that I have camped the left of my army at Gavre and the right at this place [Merlebeck]. I shall send tomorrow a detachment to Bruges, they have already abandoned that town. As soon as we have the cannon, and what is necessary, we shall attack Antwerp; after which I should be glad the next place might be Ostend; for unless they draw the greater part of their army from Germany, they will not be able to hinder us from doing what we please.[2]

1 June was declared by Marlborough as a Day of Thanksgiving in the Allied army, for the outstanding victory gained at Ramillies.

Meanwhile, the French Minister of War had hurried from Versailles to confer with Villeroi. The two men met at Courtrai, where the Marshal was attempting to gather his shaken troops together and put them back into some kind of fighting order. Aghast at the scale of disarray and more significantly the despair in the French army, de Chamillart approved Villeroi's plan to fall back into the fortress belt along the border, in effect abandoning all of northern Flanders, Brabant and much of Hainault in the process. There was nothing else to be done. Ground had to sacrificed on a huge scale to save the field army and only Dendermonde, Ath and Mortagne would be held as forward posts. Louis XIV did send the elderly Marshal Vauban with a hastily-gathered force of twenty-four battalions of infantry and nine cavalry squadrons to cover Dunkirk, Gravelines and Calais on the Channel coast and provide some measure of support for Villeroi's left flank. The Elector of Bavaria, who shared the command and the disgrace with Villeroi in the recent battle, had already fallen back to Mons with the battered remnants of his own troops – he would hold the French flank in the east as best he could. Marshal Marsin was hurrying troops northwards from the Moselle valley, and before long reinforcements would be summoned from Spain and Italy to hold the line along France's northern borders. Such were the effects of Ramillies and in the time taken for the French to gather themselves, Marlborough would be free to do almost what he wished in the Spanish Netherlands. The pace of his advance was really only slowed by the speed, or otherwise, with which his artillery and supply trains could be brought forward.

This became a campaign of conquest, and the Duke would write to his wife: 'So many towns have submitted since the battle, that it really looks more like a dream than the truth.'[3] The port of Antwerp was the great prize, second only to Brussels in terms of prestige – a mark of the abject defeat of the French in this campaign. The city had withstood a lengthy siege during the wars of Dutch independence; Marlborough could in other circumstances rightly have expected to mount a complex and costly operation lasting many months to secure such an important place. On Thursday 3 June he reported the progress of the campaign to the Lord Treasurer, Sidney Godolphin:

> I have sent Brigadier Cadogan with six squadrons of horse, to offer terms to the town and citadel of Antwerp. If I can have the place without a siege it will gain us a month. I am doing all I can to gain the governor of Dendermonde, which place would be of great consequence. They have let out the waters, so that we cannot attack it.[4]

Marlborough's comment was significant – water obstacles are always a serious hindrance to military operations. Later that day, the Duke wrote to William Cadogan:

> The capitulation you say the Baron du Whitefield is willing to accept comprehends both the town and citadel. In that case ... I would have you lose no time in concluding [terms] with them for their evacuating both upon the conditions you mention, or easier of you can bring them to it ... I send you here the power to sign the articles [of capitulation] ... The publishing at the head of the Spanish [Walloon] battalions that those who are willing to serve King Charles, or to remain at home in the country, are at liberty to do it, is a very good article, and I hope may have its effect. You may assure then that we are taking measures with the States of Brabant and Flanders for the pay and subsistence of all such as will come over to King Charles III.[5]

Two days later, the Duke wrote again to his Quartermaster-General giving him in effect *carte blanche* to conclude what terms he thought best, in what was developing into a very fast-moving tactical situation as the Allied forces pressed onwards. Marlborough could not supervise the negotiations in person, even when such an significant prize as Antwerp was concerned.

There was also a gentle reproof in his tone, implying that Cadogan should not look to him quite so readily for approval:

> [Colonel] Armstrong will have told you that Lord Orkney is to be tomorrow night with a thousand horse on the other side of Antwerp, where he will be joined on Monday [7 June] by seven or eight battalions of foot. We are now at too great a distance to be consulted on every little nicety that may occur, therefore I must rely on your discretion to make an end of this business.[6]

In case agreement was not to be had, preparations for a siege were pushed forward with as much speed as possible, but Antwerp yielded to Cadogan and Overkirk on 6 June. The six battalions of Walloon troops amongst the garrison immediately declared their allegiance for Archduke Charles, as did the governor, the Marquis de Tarazena, who understandably saw an advantage in switching to the victorious side at the earliest opportunity. The 3,000 French troops there, commanded by the Marquis de Pontis, were granted terms and permitted to march away to Le Quesnoy and Landrecies. The keys of the city were presented to Marlborough by the magistrates on 11 June, and given the size and importance of Antwerp, this was an astonishing and cheaply won success.

As always the Duke was concerned about the heavy guns of the Allied siege train, trundling laboriously along the bad roads of the day: 'We march tomorrow to Deynse, and the French are retired behind Menin, by which you see we are at liberty to attack Ostend and Nieuport, if we had our artillery.'[7] This pressing need dictated that Marlborough temporarily suspend the hectic pace of pursuit – until both Antwerp and Dendermonde were in his hands he could not use the Scheldt and Dender for transportation. Dendermonde in particular would prove to be a problem for some time. However, the strong and well-equipped modern fortress of Oudenarde on the Scheldt was given up without a fight. The two Walloon battalions there declared for the Archduke, while the French troops in the garrison were permitted to march off to their own lines. Keen as always to find out whatever he could about his opponent's intentions and abilities, Marlborough wrote to Colonel de Voght, who had been appointed as the the temporary governor in Oudenarde: 'I would like to receive an exact account of all that you have found in the town appertaining to the enemy.'[8]

Marlborough's army was soon reinforced by Hanoverian, Hessian and Prussian troops, which had previously been held back in camp while arguments over arrears of pay and terms of service were settled. Villeroi by comparison was dispersing what was left of his army to garrison the now all-important fortress belt along France's border. A Royal Navy cruising squadron under Sir Stafford Fairborne appeared off Ostend and was in contact with Marlborough by 14 June, ready to give gunfire support when it was needed. Overkirk had moved forward from Antwerp and on 18 June became engaged in the operations against Ostend, possession of which would give Marlborough a valuable entry port for men and supplies direct from England. The Veldt-Marshal also attempted to seize Nieuport further along the coast, but the French garrison opening the sluice gates of the local waterways made this operation impractical. So, Overkirk left a force of dragoons and infantry to screen that town and moved on to Ostend, an operation hampered by the many dikes, canals and streams in the area, all of which were picketed by Vauban's troops. The outpost at Plas Endael was secured by Baron Fagel on 28 June, as was a defended bridge at Sandwort, and five days later the breaching artillery, forty-six guns in all, began their work against the defences of Ostend. That evening, the trenches were opened before the south-western side of the town without incurring any casualties. Marlborough covered the siege with the field army from Rosselaer, sending detachments under command of Brigadier-General van Pallandt to Oudenarde and Courtrai to guard against any sudden counter moves by Villeroi. These did not come, but the French still stubbornly held on to Nieuport and could, whenever they chose to do so, move against the exposed left flank of the Allied troops besieging Ostend. Overkirk probed the defences and captured the outpost at Nieuendein, but he was not strong enough to try and storm Nieuport itself and so just continued to mask the place.

While the siege of Ostend went forward, operations against Dendermonde, at the confluence of the Dender and the Scheldt and sitting across Marlborough's lines of supply and communication, had not got off to a promising start. The Marquis de Tarazena, until recently the Spanish Governor of Antwerp, was preparing to bombard the place but he had insufficient troops to even properly blockade the garrison. Brigadier-General Meredith, who accompanied Tarazena, was unable to exert much influence and the obstinate Marquis was reluctant to ask for help. Marlborough understood the degree of tact that was required with someone as proud and prickly as Tarazena, particularly when that officer had taken the arguably controversial step of changing allegiance mid-way through a campaign, and felt he might be open to criticism. The Duke wrote to Meredith:

> It would not be amiss that you make him a compliment as soon as this comes to your hands, to acquaint him with the orders you have, and that you are very ambitious to receive his commands; and when he comes, you must take care to humour him in every thing you do.[9]

This was all very understandable but Meredith and Tarazena made heavy weather of working together. On 21 June, the Elector of Bavaria, perhaps aware of the Allied lack of numbers before Dendermonde, took the chance to send in 400 infantry and dragoons together with a section of field guns as reinforcements to the garrison, elbowing aside Meredith's half-hearted attempts to prevent him.

Marlborough's rather sarcastic comment when he heard of this failure was 'Brigadier Meredith was upon his guard, but had not the strength to prevent it; he had five or six men killed, and as many, with a captain, taken prisoner.'[10] Meredith had in fact asked that more troops be sent, but the Duke refused, having too many other commitments to attend to at that time. The bombardment of Dendermonde began on the following day, although Tarazena soon expressed his concern at a lack of ammunition for sustained firing. Peasants were being conscripted locally to work on the trenches at this time; they were quite understandably inclined to avoid this service if they could and to shirk the labouring work if they could not. Marlborough had to send William Cadogan from Oudenarde with a strong reinforcement of cavalry and infantry to oversee, if not actually take charge of, the siege. The investment of the garrison was still not really complete and Marlborough wrote to Cadogan at the end of the month: 'The blockade, since M. Delvalle [the governor] is so obstinate, must be put in execution with all the diligence possible … I would hope you stay with Meredith three or four days, by which time I hope everything may be in good order.'[11]

At Ostend meanwhile, the entrenching was proving to be a slow business, due partly to the high water-table which flooded the works almost as soon as the spades went into the ground. Extensive use had to be made of fascines and gabions to erect barricades and breastworks instead and the soldiers were working in miserable, sodden conditions. Despite these difficulties, the bombardment by land and sea began on 3 July; the Royal Navy squadron commanded by Stafford Fairborne, which included the bomb-ketches HMS *Blast* and HMS *Salamander*, supported the operations from offshore. The fire from these vessels quickly subdued the already rather dilapidated seaward defences and began a number of fires in the town itself. This destruction would certainly have unsettled both populace and garrison, but may not have been deliberate: it was generally considered bad form to fire into a town rather than at the defensive works themselves.[12]

The Duke of Marlborough was amongst those who watched the bombardment of Ostend. The covered way and counter-scarp was secured by a Dutch assault, led by a mere fifty British grenadiers, on 4 July. The governor, Comte de la Motte, had sent an appeal to Vauban to come forward with some of the 12,000 infantry he had under command near to Dunkirk, but this met with no response. So, the Comte sent in a sharp sortie against the besiegers, but this was quickly repulsed. Some of the garrison were unreliable and dispirited, particularly the Walloons in Spanish service. The citizenry were pleading with de la Motte to submit and he asked for terms on 6 July. The French garrison gave their parole not to serve again for six months and marched away to Dunkirk, while the two battalions of Walloon infantry promptly declared for Archduke Charles and joined Marlborough's army. The valuable port was now in the Duke's hands, guaranteeing direct and easy access to the Channel coast for the cost of fewer than 500 casualties. The booty taken included two French ships of the line (one of eighty and the other of fifty guns), whose commanders through some neglect failed to scuttle in time to avoid capture, as well as ninety cannon, and a huge quantity of powder and shot to supplement the hungry magazines of the allied armies.[13]

At this time, the Emperor Joseph in Vienna offered the governorship of the Spanish Netherlands, on behalf of his younger brother, to the Duke of Marlborough. The previous Governor-General was the Elector of Bavaria, who was once again after Ramillies – just as after Blenheim – almost a fugitive. The offer was very tempting, both in terms of prestige and the enormous stipend that went with the post (no less than £60,000 per annum). Marlborough appeared to be the ideal choice given his prestige as victor and the high regard in which he was held by the Dutch. To Vienna, it seemed that the Duke would be robust enough to withstand any encroachment by the States-General into the region. After consideration and consultation with London, Marlborough politely declined the offer – he was aware that such an appointment would be unwelcome to the Dutch, despite their respect and affection for him. There was already predictable friction between the Hague and Vienna over the whole issue, as the Emperor viewed the region as his brother's legitimate domains to do with more or less what he pleased, while the Dutch looked on it as providing their Barrier against the French. The victory at Ramillies, which had delivered the Spanish Netherlands into Allied hands had in large measure been achieved by the efforts of the Dutch troops when no Imperial forces at all were engaged. These two positions were hardly reconcilable. The offer to Marlborough, for all its apparent logic, caused great offence amongst the States-General, who suspected the Emperor of trying to steal a march on them. The offer had been promptly declined, but the Duke's relations with the Dutch were put under some strain and never entirely recovered.

As soon as it was seen that Ostend would fall, Marlborough had the option to move against Ypres, Tournai, or even Menin on the very edge of French soil. The Duke was aware that with several widely separated columns operating simultaneously, there was the chance that his opponents might stir themselves and attempt to fall on one or other of his detachments before it could be supported. He wrote to his brother, Charles Churchill: 'I have taken the best care I can to be informed when they assemble any body of troops, and you may be sure will immediately march to your relief.'[14] In any case, Villeroi's troops were widely dispersed amongst garrisons and reinforcements hurriedly brought from the Rhine and the Moselle were sent straight to join them. Vauban's detachment on the coast posed no real threat, although it did hold the otherwise vulnerable French flank there reasonably secure. Marlborough prudently kept his opponents in doubts of his intentions as long as he could, going first to Courtrai, which had been occupied by the Prince of Holstein-Beck, and on 11 July to Helchin. The Allied columns then closed quickly up to invest Menin, the powerful Vauban-designed fortress on the Lys, well garrisoned with 5,000 veteran troops under the command of the very able Comte de Caraman, and the governor, the Marquis de Bully.

As the preparations for the siege of Menin steadily developed, just as on earlier occasions, the Duke's nimble mind did not fit very well with the habits and procedures of those around him. Finding that he had to wait for Dutch troops to come up at a steady pace, he wrote with a hint of irritation to Sidney Godolphin on 14 July:

> Now that the siege of Ostend is over, I was in hopes we might have lost no time in attacking Menin, but M. Geldermaison sends word that they have not the preparations ready. But as soon as they come to Ghent he will let me know it. I am afraid we shall find at last that some of our friends are of the opinion that we have already done too much.[15]

The fortress of Menin was 'a small place', Colonel De La Colonie remembered, 'but it is one of the strongest in the kingdom. Its fortifications are constructed in the most perfect manner.'[16] The defences were certainly well planned, making careful use of the course of the Lys river as it ran through the town, enabling complex water defences to be constructed on the southern and eastern sides. Unusually, there was no separate citadel; the immensely strong defences that encircled the 'small place' seeming to fulfil that purpose. Advanced redoubts and lunettes, also with water-filled ditches to protect them, provided a forward measure of defence. Added to all this, the main gate of Courtrai on the north side of the town, had a substantial reserve

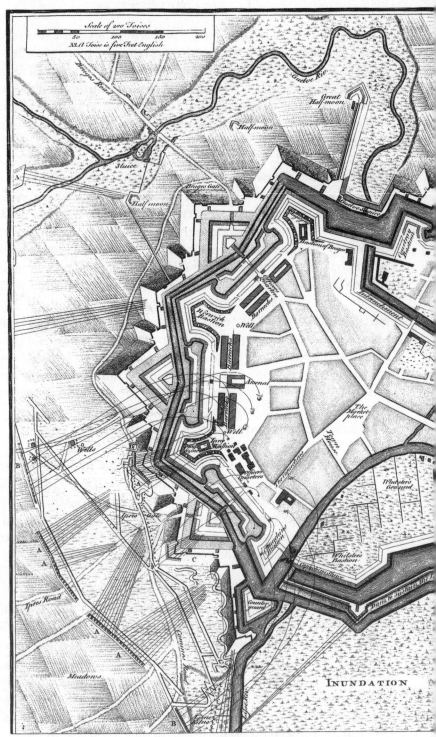

Scale of 200 Toises

50   100   150   200

N.B. A Toise is five Feet English.

Gueive Riv.

Great Half-moon

Half-moon

Bruges Road

Sluice

A

Bruges Gate

Half moon

Bastion of Bruges

Intrenchment

Berwick Bastion

Barracks

Well

Arsenal

The Market place

B

Wells

Well

D

A
A

Officers Quarters

Ypres Gate

Entrenchment

C

Whister's Ground

Whister's Bastion

Dam to sustain the

Counter guard

Ypres Road

A

A

B

Meadows

INUNDATION

A.A.A. Batteries of Cannon.
B.B.B. Batteries of Mortars.

MENIN

For Mr. Tindal's Continuation of Mr. Rapin's History of England.

MENIN
A very Strong Town
in the Earldom, of
FLANDERS
Taken by y Allies
in the Year 1706,
and retaken
by y French
in 1744.

I.Basire Sculp.

Lisse Riv.

Mill

Courtray Road

Drain

Redoubt

INUNDATION

Drain

Castle of Halluin

Redoubt

Tree

Sluice to Sustain the Inundation

standing Water of the Lisle

Friton

Redoubt

Bastion of the Mills

Sluice under Halluin Dike

Redoubt

Intrenchment

Hornwork of Halluin

Lisle Gate

Redoubt

Lisle Road

Village of
Halluin

C. Places undermined to blow up the Ravelin.
D. Place where the enemy sprung a Mine.

water obstacle, behind which the garrison could regroup if the gate itself was carried by assault.

Marlborough wrote on 15 July that, as always, the nimble operations of the field army were held back by the logistical difficulty of getting the siege train in place in good time:

> I find we must not expect all our cannon till the end of the month; but on the 22nd I think to invest Menin, and employ the first six or seven days in covering some of the quarters; for we cannot spare more than thirty-two battalions for the siege. There will remain with me seventy-two, which I hope will be a sufficient strength to oppose whatever they can bring ... I neither think it their interest nor their inclinations to venture a battle, for our men are in heart, and theirs are cowed.[17]

The Duke sent detachments to break down the sluice-gates on the waterways around Armentières, Menin and Wavrechain, to prevent the French from further varying the water levels and by this means impeding the Allied operations. He was too late however, the French having already broken them open, and the prevailing state of low water prevented him bringing up his siege train by either the Scheldt or the Lys. The French hold on Dendermonde still guarded the junction of the Dender and the Scheldt. Instead, the guns of the Allied siege train had to be dragged with great labour and expense of time over the rutted roads. Overkirk joined Marlborough at Courtrai with his Dutch corps on 17 July and five days later Menin was invested by Lieutenant-General Salisch with thirty-two infantry battalions and twenty-five squadrons of cavalry. The Allied field army, now reinforced by the previously absent German contingents, covered the operations against Menin from a camp established at Helchin. The siege batteries made slow progress on the road from Ghent and were not established until 4 August, but that night the trenches were opened opposite the massive Bastion of the Capuchins on the western side and the bombardment began in earnest.

The Duke of Vendôme had been summoned from northern Italy by Louis XIV to restore the calamitous situation in the Spanish Netherlands. A formidable and bruising campaigner, he replaced Villeroi as army commander in the region and arrived at Valenciennes on the same day that the allied trenches were opened before Menin. Villeroi left the army to return to Versailles on 5 August, it having been given out at Court that he had asked to be relieved – although this was not the case – and the Marshal had stubbornly held on to the command as long as he could. Vendôme's great energy enabled him to gather together a more-or-less respectably sized field army, comprising 163 squadrons of cavalry and 63 infantry battalions (perhaps 50,000 troops). He rather scornfully noted that everyone in the French camp seemed entirely in awe of Marlborough after the recent defeat at Ramillies. Vendôme would still be out-gunned by Marlborough in open battle, but with the Allied army split into several besieging forces at this time, an opportunity to spring a surprise on one or the other of the Duke's detachments might occur. Louis XIV however was concerned at the chance of a further disaster to his armies and urged caution on Vendôme. However, this French field army 'in being' posed a threat that Marlborough could not ignore and he could no longer march about at will, attacking this town and that with near impunity.

The trench works against Menin were supervised by two Huguenot engineers, Colonel de Roques and Colonel Hertel, who soon had 12,000 pioneers and labourers preparing the lines of contravallation. Caraman's artillery fired briskly at the working parties who were rather careless at first about their cover, but the men soon learned caution after several of their number were wounded. The preparations for the siege were made more difficult by the extensive flooding over meadows to the east of the town, where the banks of the Lys river had been broken down by the garrison. Caraman proved to be an active and dangerous opponent, and at mid-morning on 6 August a grand sortie was made by the garrison on the besieger's lengthening trenches. The effort was driven off after stiff fighting which cost Caraman the French Major-General who led the attack, together with sixty of his men. 'The governor disputed every inch of ground with us', Robert Parker remembered, 'Until we carried our approaches to the foot of the glacis.'[18] Two days later the bombardment of the fortress began in earnest, with seventy-two guns and forty-four howitzers and mortars taking part. Almost immediately, the Hotel de Ville was set alight and burned to the ground. On 14 August Marlborough felt it necessary to reinforce the besiegers, sending an additional 6,000 troops, under Baron Fagel, to add weight to the operations.

The following day, 15 August, a misfortune befell William Cadogan when a foraging party he was accompanying was surprised by some French cavalry who seemed at least to have recovered some of their spirits after the Ramillies debacle. Peter Drake, an Irish Jacobite in French service, took part in the affray and remembered that the governor of Tournai had 'Directed the grenadiers and pickets, as well as the cavalry to attack the enemy, and an obstinate engagement ensued several being killed and wounded on both sides; but at last we prevailed and got a considerable booty of horses, besides many prisoners, some of note.'[19] In the scrambling skirmish the Quartermaster-General was tipped off his horse and taken captive. Marlborough was greatly concerned for his safety, but apart from having his purse stolen, Cadogan was unharmed and generally treated well, although 'I was thrust into a ditch [but] we met with quarter and civility, saving their taking my watch and money' he remembered indignantly.[20] A few days later, on 18 August, Cadogan was exchanged for Count Pallavacini, who had been taken prisoner in the recent battle; the Duke of Vendôme, although often described as a boorish man, gallantly expedited the exchange as he knew how much Marlborough appreciated the Quartermaster-General's services.

A major assault on the defences of Menin was made that same evening and Marlborough observed the operations from the forward trenches. Just after at 7.00 p.m., two mines were blown under the defenders in the salient angles of the covered-way, along the major hornwork feature known as the 'Half-moon of Ypres'. There were two main efforts: Earl Orkney led the attack on the left, while Count Scholten had command of that on the right. Each commander had 600 stormers in the front line supported by 300 pioneers carrying fascines and spades, able to 'turn' the defences as soon as they were taken. In immediate support were nine battalions of Dutch, Prussian and British infantry and four more battalions stood ready to move forward and exploit any success at the right moment. The whole operation was very effectively carried out, even though the defenders also blew defensive mines in the faces of the attackers. After two hours of bitter fighting the covered-way at the half-moon was in Allied hands, at a cost of more than 1,400 of the assailants killed and wounded; Ingoldsby's Regiment alone had fifteen officers killed or wounded in the attack. Many of those that fell did so while standing exposed to the French musketry before the Allied pioneers could get their fascines into place to give them cover.

Robert Parker, who took part in the assault with the Royal Irish and was amongst the wounded, remembered: 'Our entire regiment was engaged in this attack, and we paid for our looking on at Ramillies, having had two captains and five subalterns killed.'[21] Parker got a long-awaited promotion to captain of grenadiers as a result. Marlborough's own report of the action ran:

Yesterday in the evening we attacked the covered-way before Menin, and our men were soon masters of the counterscarp, but being some time before they could cover themselves, and being exposed in the meantime to the enemy's fire from their ravelins and other works, it is computed we have lost about seven or eight hundred killed and wounded.[22]

The Duke's figure was a considerable under-estimate, as he subsequently acknowledged, and based on inaccurate early reports of the action. With the huge hornwork in Allied hands though, the defence of Menin could not be sustained for long. The big guns had done their work and on 22 August, a breach having been made, Caraman capitulated; the garrison, whose own loss was 1,101 men killed and wounded, were permitted to march away to Douai on 25 August with the honours of war, taking four pieces of artillery with them in recognition of their fine resistance. However, 'I saw the garrison of Menin march out yesterday', Marlborough wrote from Helchin, 'The fear they had of being made prisoners of war made them give up the place five or six days sooner than, in decency, they ought to have done.'[23]

Marlborough's casualties had not been light all the same: at 2,628 they were well over twice those suffered by the French garrison. The booty taken in Menin included sixty-five field guns, of which four were found to be stamped with the royal arms of England. These had been captured by the French at the battle of Landen thirteen years before and they were now sent in triumph back to London. Marlborough went on in his report: 'My brother will be to-morrow before Dendermonde, and I hope the cannon may fire by Monday, and if we have no rain five or six days may make us masters of the place.' With Menin safely out of the way, Charles Churchill had been sent with six battalions of infantry, six cavalry squadrons and sixty guns from the Allied siege train to bolster the effort against the fortress, which had so far been rather ineffective. It seems likely that Marlborough granted Caraman good terms to bring the siege at Menin to a close as soon as the opportunity arose, so that he could turn his full attention to the rather more pressing problems that had developed at Dendermonde. Vendôme had drawn quite close to Menin using the shelter of the Lys and Deule (Dyle) rivers, and this caused Marlborough some concern as he had begun on 22 August to shift troops away to support the siege at Dendermonde. In the end, the French army commander drew off again without risking an engagement; with his lack of numbers he could really do little more, for all his manoeuvring.

During this time, negotiations had been carried on with the governor of Dendermonde, the Marquis de Delvalle (sometimes given as de Vallé), to persuade him to surrender the place. These proved fruit-less, even though a substantial portion of his garrison were comprised of Walloon troops whose reliability was in some doubt after recent events. The blockade of the town had been slow to be put into effect, with neither Tarazena nor Meredith really getting a grip on the opera-tions; and there were insufficient guns to mount a proper breaching bombardment while Menin was still under attack. The operations as a result had been reduced to little more than a blockade and the siege only really began in earnest on 29 August, after Cadogan took a hand and the investment of the town was at last complete. Matters then came under the direct command of Charles Churchill; and his brother, the Duke, arranged for a substantial amount of ammunition to be gathered at Ghent, ready to move forward to Dendermonde as soon as Menin fell. Although Churchill soon got a better grip on mat-ters, the siege was hampered by the extensive inundations around the town and the garrison had even managed to increase the depth of the water by two feet by careful manipulation of the sluices in the area. Louis XIV, aware of the natural strength of the place (having once spent six weeks trying without success to take it), scornfully commented that only with an army of ducks could the Allies hope to succeed.

Frances Hare, Marlborough's chaplain, wrote rather dismissively that the Dendermonde garrison was: 'Inconsiderable, sickly and half starved, and the fortifications in very ill condition, but its strength is water, which, though lessened by the extremely dry season we have had, we are afraid is still too much to be mastered.'[24] The weather had certainly been dry (seven weeks without a drop of rain falling), which helped Churchill's troops. 'We have ordered some cannon, with a detachment, to attack Dendermonde', Marlborough wrote, 'My brother Churchill is appointed to command the siege, and if the dry weather holds, I hope we shall in a few days be masters of the town.'[25]

The Allied bombardment was initially undertaken with only nine artillery pieces, but the defences of the Brussels and Mechlin gates very soon began to crumble. On the evening of Sunday 5 September, an outwork at the Brussels gate was surprised and captured by a storming party led by Lord John Dalprymple and the fleeing French soldiers were pursued into the town by the elated Allied infantry. With his defence falling apart, de Delvalle was given two hours to submit his garrison as prisoners of war or face a storm of the place. The rather haughty reply, according to Frances Hare in a letter written on 9 September, was: 'He would sooner be cut into thousand pieces

1. John Churchill, 1st Duke of Marlborough. The Captain-General 1702–1711.

Above **2.** Sebastian le Prestre, Marshal Vauban. Louis XIV's engineer genius.

Opposite **3.** Diagram of trench layouts from Vauban's manual of siege warfare *Le Triomphe de la Méthode.*

LES TRAVERSES.

Fossé.

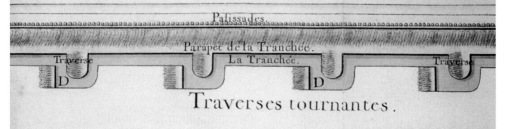

Chemin couvert.

Palissades

Parapet de la Tranchée.

Traverse   La Tranchée.   Traverse

D   D

Traverses tournantes.

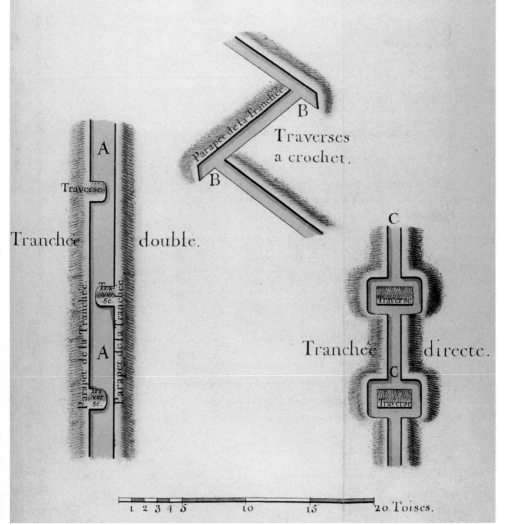

Parapet de la Tranchée

B

Traverses a crochet.

B

A

Traverse

Tranchée   double.

Tra-ver-se.

Parapet de la Tranchée.

Parapet de la Tranchée.

A

Tra-ver-se.

C

Traverse

Tranchée   directe.

C

Traverse

1 2 3 4 5   10   15   20 Toises.

BATERIES DE MORTIERS.

Profil d'une Baterie representant un Mortier qui tire.

Parapet.

Plateforme.
Affust du Mortier.
Le Mortier.

Plan d'une Baterie telle, qu'elles doivent estre construites

Parapet.

18 a 20 pi.

Plateforme droite.

Plateforme imparfaite.

Plateforme biaise

..15. a 16. pieds...

Plateformes achevées avec
les Mortiers dessus.
Plateforme qui fait voir de quelle-
façon, les Gistes doivent estre disposez.
Madriers qui couvrent les Gistes.

1   2   3   4   5   10. Tois

Above **5.** Queen Anne of Great Britain. Her friendship and support of Marlborough was a great asset while it lasted.

Opposite **4.** Illustration of a mortar battery from Vauban's *Le Triomphe de la Méthode*.

6. King Louis XIV of France, *c.* 1670. He extended his northern border and gave Vauban the task to fortify the region.

7. John Churchill, 1st Duke of Marlborough with John Armstrong, his chief of engineers. Armstrong is holding a plan of Bouchain. *By kind permission of His Grace the Duke of Marlborough.*

8. Prince Eugene of Savoy. Imperial Field Commander and close friend of Marlborough.

9. Henry of Nassau, Count Overkirk. Dutch Veldt-Marshal. Died at the Siege of Lille, 1708.

10. Godart Rede van Ginkel, Earl of Athlone. Dutch general. Resented Marlborough's appointment, but came to admire his abilities.

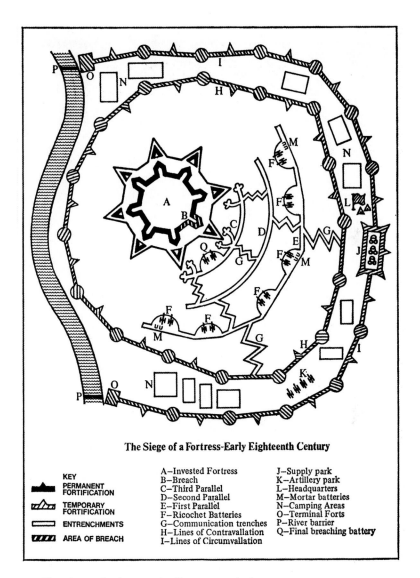

The Siege of a Fortress-Early Eighteenth Century

KEY

PERMANENT FORTIFICATION

TEMPORARY FORTIFICATION

ENTRENCHMENTS

AREA OF BREACH

A—Invested Fortress
B—Breach
C—Third Parallel
D—Second Parallel
E—First Parallel
F—Ricochet Batteries
G—Communication trenches
H—Lines of Contravallation
I—Lines of Circumvallation

J—Supply park
K—Artillery park
L—Headquarters
M—Mortar batteries
N—Camping Areas
O—Terminal Forts
P—River barrier
Q—Final breaching battery

11. The siege of a fortress in diagrammatic form.

12. Siege battery layout *c.* 1710.

13. Philippe, Duke of Anjou. Youngest grandson of Louis XIV and the French claimant to the throne of Spain, (Felipe/Philip V).

14. Francois de Neufville, Marshal Villeroi. Defeated by Marlborough at Ramillies, 1706, he lost the Spanish Netherlands.

15. Maximilien-Emmanuel Wittelsbach, Elector of Bavaria. Shared the defeats at Blenheim and Ramillies.

16. Louis-Guillaume, Margrave of Baden. His slow siege operations exasperated Marlborough, 1704.

17. Lord John Cutts of Gowran. Led the storming party at Venlo, 1702.

18. Jean (John) Ligonier. Led the storming party at Menin, 1706, as
Captain with North and Grey's Regiment. Became Field-Marshal and
Commander of the British Army.

19. Siege operations against a major fortress *c.* 1706.

20. Louis, Duke of Burgundy. Louis XIV's grandson, heir to the throne of France. Nominal army commander in the Low Countries, 1702–1703 and 1707–1708.

21. James Fitzjames, Marshal Berwick. Marlborough's nephew. One of Louis XIV's best field commanders.

22. Louis-Joseph de Bourbon, Duke of Vendôme. Beaten at Oudenarde by Marlborough, and failed to save Lille, 1708.

23. The massive main gate to the citadel of Lille. Captured by Marlborough and Eugene, December 1708.

24. The Battle of Wynendael, September 1708. Fought to ensure the re-supply of Marlborough's army at the siege of Lille.
Wynendael Tapestry, Blenheim Palace. By kind permission of His Grace the Duke of Marlborough.

25. The surrender of Lille by Boufflers to Marlborough, December 1708.
Lille Tapestry, Blenheim Palace. By kind permission of His Grace the Duke of Marlborough.

26. Louis-Francois, Marshal Boufflers. Conducted epic defence of Lille, August–December 1708.

27. Claude-Louis-Hector, Marshal Villars. French army commander in Flanders, 1709–1713. Gravely wounded at Malplaquet (1709).

28. Arnold Joost van Keppel, 1st Earl of Albemarle. Highly capable Dutch cavalry commander and close friend of Marlborough.

29. Major-General John Armstrong. Marlborough's chief of engineers.

30 George Hamilton, 1st Earl of Orkney. Marlborough's aggressive British infantry commander.

31. The siege of Tournai, 1709.

than surrender on such terms.'[26] Despite such bravado, Marlborough was unyielding and he allowed de Delvalle an hour more in which to consult the town council and his own senior officers. These worthies did not share the rather misplaced confidence of the Marquis, and Dendermonde capitulated that evening, the Mechlin gate being given up as a sign of submission. The following day, while the garrison marched out as prisoners of war, heavy rain began to fall and the meadows and trenches were quickly flooded, driving the soldiers out to stand in the open, but just too late to save the place. Frances Hare went on: 'It has rained every day since Dendermonde capitulated and the wet season seems to be set in, a week of which would have made the enterprise impracticable.' The French were sent to Bergen op Zoom to await exchange, although the Walloon troops in the garrison (like their compatriots in Antwerp and Ostend) volunteered for service in the Allied army instead.

The line of the Scheldt was now largely clear for Allied transports to use. Although Vendôme attempted to break down the river sluices on the Dender, he found them to be too securely watched by Allied cavalry. As soon as the fall of Dendermonde was assured, Marlborough moved up the line of the Dender against the fortress of Ath, the seizure of which should lay open the road to Mons. He took care to secure the flanks of his army, allowing time for the troops who had been engaged in levelling the siege works at Menin and Dendermonde to close up, before moving forward. Ath was held by 2,000 French troops under command of Brigadier-General de St Pierre. It was invested by Veldt-Marshal Overkirk on 16 September, work beginning on the trenches four days later. John Millner wrote:

General Ingoldsby, at night, with a competent number of the besiegers, with and without arms, opened their trenches with little loss on the south-side of the town, by the strategem, in first attempting to open them on the north-side, to which the enemy drew most of their strength; so that before the enemy could discover them, they got under good cover. [27]

The ruse was all the more effective as the defences on the northern side had been only partially repaired after a French assault during the wars of the 1690s, and they seemed as a result to be the most likely part to be attacked. Instead, Overkirk wrong-footed the garrison by going for the strongest part. Meanwhile, welcome news came in to the Allied camp that a great victory had been secured over the French by Prince Eugene at Turin, although the details were still sketchy.

The Allied siege train came up the Scheldt to Oudenarde and were then dragged along the roads through Lessines to Ath. Marlborough covered the operations from near to Leuze and he wrote to the Secretary of State, Robert Harley, on 20 September: 'I hope it will not be many days before I shall be able to give you an account of being masters of the counterscarp, beyond which the French have not yet defended any place in these parts.'[28] The bombardment of Ath began on 26 September, but the next day the French garrison sprang into action, in the shape of two dashing sorties that did considerable damage in the trenches and battery positions before they were repulsed. The Duke of Vendôme was nearby and exchanged signals with the garrison, which may have prompted the sorties. He had only managed to scrape together his slim army by denuding other garrisons and Louis XIV, writing from Versailles on 24 September 1706, had forbidden him to attempt to relieve the town: 'You know that the Duke of Marlborough is only seeking an opportunity for a battle, he attacks places in the hope of enticing you thither.'[29]

The French troops in Ath fought well, and Marlborough acknowledged that the resistance had been stiffer than he expected. The closeness of the opposing trenches was remarked on by John Deane, who wrote: 'They could easily call to each other and throw their grenades into each other's works.'[30] The covered way was taken by storm by 1 October, when a breaching battery could be brought right forward, and the French commander prudently asked for terms soon afterwards. The garrison submitted the next day as prisoners of war and were, Millner recalled, conducted to Mons: 'The besieged had about sixty men killed and wounded, and the besiegers about two hundred men killed and wounded.'[31] John Deane, however, recorded that the Allied loss was much greater.[32] The garrison, which comprised four French infantry battalions and one battalion of Swiss, actually marched out on the way to Mons, on 4 October.

The campaign season for the year, which had seen such success for the Allied armies, was coming to a close, but Marlborough wanted to go on to take Mons; such a move would lay open the French frontier to attack in the following spring. The weather was turning bad, with frequent heavy rains as Francis Hare had remarked early in the month and the Dutch were reluctant to do more. Marlborough was also aware that the garrisons in both Mons and Valenciennes were being reinforced. The Allied army had achieved much that year: virtually the whole of the Spanish Netherlands had been captured in a matter of a few victorious weeks when an expensive campaign of many months, perhaps even years, might have been expected and justified. The Dutch really felt that they had risked a lot and come happily through with success. 'Our friends', Frances Hare wrote, 'think we have done enough.'[33] Marlborough suspended the operations reluctantly, although Vendôme came forward again in mid-October, apparently to challenge the Allied deployment. The Duke wrote of his opponent: 'He has neither will nor power to do it, which we shall see very quickly, for we are now camped in open country that, if he marches to us, we cannot refuse fighting.'[34] Louis XIV had forbidden the French commander to fight an open battle and finding no isolated Allied detachment to pounce on, he soon drew off. Marlborough continued to look for one more opportunity before closing the campaign, writing on 19 October: 'I just now have an account from Tournai, that the garrison consisted yesterday of only ten weak battalions, one regiment of horse, and a troop of dragoons.'[35] If the Duke was really tempted nothing came of it and after a grand review of his victorious army on 25 October, he sent the troops off the their winter quarters early in November, leaving 50,000 men under Overkirk to garrison the army's conquests.

This had been an extraordinary year for the Grand Alliance, with the wholesale capture of the Spanish Netherlands by Marlborough's armies in the summer and the deliverance of Savoy by Prince Eugene from almost certain defeat at the battle of Turin in September. At a time when little success had been expected after the disappointment of 1705, an astonishing amount had been gained. French commanders with heavy responsibilities in far-off theatres of war were stripped of their best troops to restore the now shattered French army on the northern border. Louis XIV though, astute as ever, did not take very many troops away from Spain, where the fortunes of his grandson, after a rather dismal period, were beginning to revive in the competent hands of Marshal Berwick.

Marlborough's complete victory at Ramillies – a triumph, which with Blenheim two years earlier secured his place as one of the great captains in history – drew the Duke into the very kind of positional warfare which he most disliked. In such operations, his daring, judgement and quick thinking could be put to lesser effect than in open battle. He undoubtedly began very well with the capture of such notable places as Antwerp, Ostend, and Menin; some of these had held out for years in past wars (admittedly at times when a garrison could not expect to receive mercy from their attackers, and therefore would be inclined to hold out for longer). Towns and fortresses fell to the Allied armies with gratifying regularity and speed, and the territories seized in this dazzling campaign yielded huge revenues to help fund both the war and pay for Archduke Charles's growing expenses as King of Spain. Still, for all his success in the 'Year of Miracles' for the Allied cause, Marlborough was stepping forward into an a region artfully prepared for defence by Vauban over twenty years before and quite how this formidable obstacle might to be overcome had yet to be seen.

NOTES

1. The Duke of Marlborough deployed 62,000 troops for battle at Ramillies, just slightly more than the 60,000 French, Walloon and Bavarian soldiers that Marshal Villeroi had under command. The French commander, although first on the ground, instantly deployed into a defensive position, whereas Marlborough moved sharply into the attack as soon as his troops got into position. The main cavalry action took place on the wide open plain to the south of Ramillies, while the difficult marshy country between that village and Autre-Eglise in the north saw mostly infantry action. Dutch troops stormed into the small villages of Franquenay and Taviers on the extreme right of the French line, driving out the Swiss brigade placed there. A hasty and rather ill-judged counter-attack by French dragoons and infantry went wrong and was broken up by Danish cavalry working their way around the French flank. Meanwhile, Dutch and German infantry fought their way into Ramillies in the centre of Villeroi's line, while British infantry attacked the ridge-line leading from the north of the village to Offuz and Autre-Eglise. As pressure mounted on the French commander he moved his reserves towards his left, leaving his cavalry on the other flank without proper infantry support: 'The Elector and Villeroi were startled; whereupon they in a great hurry sent off from the plain a great many of those troops which put the rest on the plain in some disorder.' See R. Kane, *Campaigns of King William and Queen Anne*, 1745, p. 65. The Allied infantry attacks went forward with such violence against Ramillies and across the Mehaigne stream to the north that Villeroi drew away the French infantry reserves from the support of his cavalry. Marlborough meanwhile reinforced his own cavalry in the south. Too late the Marshal realised the danger and his exhausted cavalry was outflanked and routed by Marlborough's more numerous horsemen. The French army broke and fled from the field, and the way lay open for the Allies to conquer in a few short weeks the whole of the Spanish Netherlands.

2. W.S. Churchill, *Marlborough, His Life and Times*, Vol II, 1947, p. 125.

3. *Ibid.*

4. *Ibid.*, p. 126.

5. G. Murray, *Letters and Dispatches of the Duke of Marlborough*, Vol II, 1845, p. 555.

6. Murray, *Letters and Dispatches*, pp. 565–566.

7. Churchill, *Marlborough*, p. 126.

8. Murray, *Letters and Dispatches*, p. 562.

9. *Ibid.*, p. 584.

10. *Ibid.*, p. 628.

11. *Ibid.*, p. 659.

12. A French officer who watched the bombardment of Brussels in 1695, wrote: 'We can see most of the houses of Brussels are on fire. The neighbouring hills are crowded with troops, both French and the enemy, who are watching this wonderful spectacle … I have never seen before such a blaze or such destruction.' The bombardment was widely criticised and had uncertain military value. See C. Duffy, *Fire & Stone*, 1975, p. 100. However, Marlborough at times undertook such grim work, as when the Royal Navy's bomb vessels set light to Ostend in 1706.

13. John Millner wrote that the garrison suffered 800 killed and wounded during the short siege of Ostend. He added, rather ambiguously, that there were: 'About 1,600 men, officers, included on both sides.' This implies that the total loss, besiegers and besieged, was this figure. See J.A. Millner, *A Compendious Journal*, 1736, p. 184.

14. Murray, *Letters and Dispatches*, p. 605.

15. Churchill, *Marlborough*, p. 142.

16.W. Horsley, (ed.), *Chronicles of an Old Campaigner*, 1904, p. 318.

17.Churchill, *Marlborough*, p. 143.

18.D.G. Chandler, *Captain Robert Parker and Comte de Merode-Westerloo*, 1968, p. 64.

19.C. Sturgill, *Amiable Renegade*, 1962, p. 82.

20.D.G. Chandler, *Marlborough as Military Commander*, 1973, p. 182.

21.Chandler, *Captain Robert Parker*, p.64. The forlorn hope in this attack was led by a French-born officer, Jean Ligonier, who had come to England as Huguenot refugee. He would rise to become a Field-Marshal and commander of the British Army. See R. Whitworth, *Field Marshal Lord Ligonier*, 1958.

22.Murray, *Letters and Dispatches*, Vol IV, p. 92.

23.Churchill, *Marlborough*, p. 181.

24.F. Taylor, *The Wars of Marlborough*, 1921, p. 407.

25.*Ibid.*, p. 409.

26.*Ibid.*, p. 410.

27.Millner, *A Compendious Journal*, pp. 191–192. Veldt-Marshal Overkirk however, quoted in T. Lediard, *Life of John, Duke of Marlborough*, Vol II, 1736, p. 115, gives the scale of losses as being smaller than this.

28.Murray, *Letters and Dispatches*, p. 141.

29.Taylor, *The Wars of Marlborough*, p. 411.

30.D.G. Chandler, (ed.), *Journal of John Deane*, 1984, p. 43.

31.Millner, *A Compendious Journal*, pp. 101–102.

32.Chandler, p. 44.

33. Taylor, *The Wars of Marlborough*, p. 418.

34. *Ibid.*, p. 419.

35. Murray, *Letters and Dispatches*, pp. 179–180.

VI

The Great Campaign:
The Siege of Lille, 1708

The French gradually recovered their strategic poise after the dread-ful events of 1706, a year which had seen the crushing Allied victories at Ramillies and Turin, and the loss of almost the entire Spanish Netherlands to the armies of the Duke of Marlborough. Undoubtedly, the two defeats and recent setbacks in Spain, coming as they did hard on the heels of the Allied triumph at Blenheim, had shocked Louis XIV. The King, with lofty understatement, wrote to his grandson in Madrid that his generals had not been fortunate in Flanders. There was little doubt now that peace was what was required.

One way this might be achieved was to divide his opponents and Louis XIV increasingly sought to drive a wedge between the Allies. In particular, one of the main aims of the Grand Alliance had always been to restore the Barrier Towns unwisely taken away from the Dutch in 1701. Now Louis XIV offered, in effect, to divide the Southern Netherlands with them, giving the Dutch even more fortresses than before, 'that they may serve as a rampart and barrier to separate and keep France at a distance from the United Netherlands.'[1] Not surpris-ingly, this interested the States-General, particularly as the Austrians were not keen to ensure the restoration of the Barrier in a region they regarded as their own terrritory. The Dutch were cautious men all the same and inclined to be wary of the French King and his offers. In any case, success on the stunning scale of Ramillies made all the Allies ambitious, and terms that they would have hurried to accept in 1702 were now regarded with thinly veiled contempt. The Allies did however try to detach the Elector of Bavaria from his own alliance with the French, offering him attractive terms for the restoration of his estates.

With negotiations producing nothing – at least for the moment – Louis XIV needed to gain time. The area of greatest threat to France was in the Low Countries and a cautious campaign against the Duke of Marlborough was to be pursued there. Elsewhere, in Spain and on the Rhine frontier, a more aggressive approach could be taken. The new campaigning season in 1707 would, as it turned out, be almost entirely without positive results for the Grand Alliance, while the French strengthened their position nearly everywhere. Perhaps most significantly, Austria and France concluded their own agreement to suspend hostilities in northern Italy and this enabled Louis XIV to redeploy his troops elsewhere, more or less as he wished. Marshal Berwick defeated the Allies in Spain at Almanza in April and Archduke Charles's campaign in the peninsula never fully recovered, despite the occasional false dawn.

Meanwhile, on the upper Rhine, the Margrave of Baden had died from the long-lasting effects of the wound to his foot. His successors proved no more capable than the Margrave had been in dealing with the freshly aggressive Marshal Villars, who began mounting raids into central and southern Germany. The French cavalry reached the Danube at certain points, visiting the old battlefields at the Schellenberg and on the plain of Höchstädt and Blindheim village, and caused fresh alarm in Vienna. It was soon evident, however, that Villars's main intention was to intimidate the small German princely states that provided such excellent troops for the armies of the Grand Alliance.

Marlborough remained in the Low Countries, impatient with the lack of opportunities for action. The Dutch were seized with caution once again, now so much had been achieved after the French disaster at Ramillies; having gained much, they feared to lose much. The Duke felt obliged to look further afield for fresh opportunities as he had done in previous years and considered, albeit briefly, going with his army on campaign in the Moselle valley again. He continued to see this region, rather wistfully, as the best route into the heart of France, well away from the heavily fortified belt along her northern border. The Dutch would not hear of it and the plans came to nothing. Marlborough turned his attention to holding the French army under the command of the astute and dangerous Duke of Vendôme long enough to force a general action. Meanwhile, a plan was formed for Prince Eugene to lead an Allied offensive against the great French naval port of Toulon, in southern France, in conjunction with the cruising squadrons of the Royal Navy. Neither Eugene, or Victor-Amadeus, Duke of Savoy, with whom he shared the command, really seemed convinced of the merits of the plan. After a promising start it all came to nothing, with the Allied army being obliged to hurry away from Toulon in some confusion. Although this was a major disappointment, this operation did draw much of the French army away from Spain, preventing a full exploitation of Berwick's recent victory at Almanza. The French Mediterranean Fleet had also been destroyed; beached or burned at anchor in Toulon harbour to prevent capture.

Vendôme had his problems also, for the nominal commander of the French army in the Spanish Netherlands was the Duke of Burgundy (Bourgogne), eldest grandson of Louis XIV and after the Dauphin, heir to the throne of France. The young prince had no real talent for war or taste for the role of commander, but his grandfather was keen that his armies should know their future king better. The real flaw in the arrangement was that Burgundy was on the very worst of terms with Vendôme, a hard-bitten soldier whose coarse personal habits were very much at odds with those of the fastidious and studious younger man. It was not unknown for contradictory orders to be issued simultaneously by the staff of the two men, even though Burgundy was, in theory at least, supposed to defer to the experience and skill of Vendôme; and they sometimes went for days on end without exchanging a word other than when absolutely necessary. Despite this handicap, which might be very dangerous indeed when in close proximity to Marlborough, Vendôme conducted his campaign in the summer of 1707 with care and skill, keeping just enough out of reach to avoid a battle, but never so far that the road to the French border was laid bare. However, the room for maneouvre was quite literally limited and at times he had to fall back well inside the fortress belt to evade Marlborough.

On 23 May 1707, Marlborough wrote to the Earl of Sunderland: 'In three or four days we shall make a march forward nearer the enemy and then may guess whether they design to come out of their lines.'[2] Only a week later he had reason to complain once again of Dutch intransigence, writing to London at the end of the month: 'I would have marched yesterday to Nivelles, but the [Dutch] Deputies would not consent to it, telling me very plainly that they feared the consequences of that march might be a battle.'[3] When the Allied army did march, Vendôme proved elusive and Marlborough was unable to fix him long enough to force a battle other than minor clashes and skirmishing: 'They continually retired before us ... they have lost two thousand men from desertion, besides what they suffered by the fatigues of their march.'[4] In mid-August however, Marlborough was in hot pursuit of the withdrawing French rearguard near to Soignies and a promising opportunity seemed to beckon. The French army had abandoned its camp and a lot of stores and began to pull back, but time had been lost on the crowded roads and the Allies were steadily closing the gap between them. Count Tilly, the Dutch cavalry commander, was sent on ahead of the main army with forty squadrons of cavalry and 6,000 grenadiers, under command of Count Scholten. They failed to make serious contact and the French escaped by a hair's breadth.

Tilly could plead with some truth that Marlborough's message reached him after nightfall, that a light could not be found in the rain with which to read the note, and that at any rate the French were by then almost out of reach. Their pioneers had been felling trees across the roads to try and impede the Allied pursuit, but Tilly did move forward at first light and managed several damaging skirmishes with the rearguard. The incident was just one example of the frustrations and missed chances that Marlborough and his generals suffered during that campaign season, and foul weather added to the misery of the armies: 'The rain continued to fall with a violence so that the infantry could not keep their arms dry, nor come up to assist the cavalry.'[5] Despite strenuous efforts, the French were not to be caught on this occasion, and they fell back in good order to take up a position covering Mons and Mauberge. Vendôme then moved to stand between Tournai and Mortagne, as Marlborough edged his own army to the westwards, looking to get around the flank of the French position.

The Duke crossed the Scheldt, near to Allied-held Oudenarde, and by the second week of September Vendôme had to fall back to Lille, inside France itself. 'The enemy', Marlborough wrote, 'is encamped almost under the cannon of Lille, with the River Marque before them, so that you can expect little news from these parts.'[6] The Duke did lead a force of 15,000 cavalry and infantry forward on 15 September, to drive off the French foraging parties near the city and take the opportunity to gather in the provisions for his own army. The early autumn weather was still foul and before long it was decided to bring the unproductive campaign to a halt; in the first week of October, Marlborough began to disperse his army to winter quarters. At the close of this frustrating year, the Duke, usually so urbane in manner, was observed to be ill tempered and impatient. His peace of mind was made no easier by the conduct of Duchess Sarah, choosing as she did to pursue pointless quarrels with the Queen, who was rapidly becoming tired of her belligerent friend. Anne was increasingly relying on others for advice and support, those who had no great liking for the powerful Duke and his fiery Duchess, and Marlborough's position at Court was being undermined.

In the early part of 1708, an attempt was made to launch an invasion of Britain, with the Chevalier de St George, the Jacobite Pretender to the British throne, supported by French troops. Marlborough had to send temporarily ten infantry battalions from the army in Flanders to northern England and Scotland, but bad weather and the ships of the Royal Navy intervened and nothing very much came of the enterprise in the end. On 12 April, Marlborough, Eugene and Hiensius (the Grand Pensionary of Holland) met at the Hague to consider their strategy for the forthcoming campaign season. Eugene requested that his army on the Rhine be reinforced from the Low Countries, so that a fresh advance through the Moselle valley could be attempted. On this occasion, Marlborough would not agree; he had tried that route twice before (in 1704 and 1705). He knew what difficult country had to be traversed and how awkward the Dutch could be if large numbers of troops were seen to leave their borders to campaign elsewhere. Also, the Duke stressed that the destruction of the French army in the Spanish Netherlands should be seen, for the time being, as the most important objective. It is also difficult to shake off the thought that Marlborough, who had been an ardent advocate of a Moselle campaign in the past, did not now relish the Prince leading one in 1708 while he was once again limited to trying to fix the French long enough to get them to stand and fight in Flanders. Eugene was not inclined to insist, and so the project was shelved.

Vendôme would be able to deploy just over 100,000 troops; significantly more than Marlborough who had only about 90,000. The French commander had proved remarkably adept at avoiding open battle the previous year, tying the Duke down in frustratingly unproductive marches while the war went well for France elsewhere. The Grand Alliance was growing weary with the effort and expense, apparently all for nothing; another campaign with no real result might just be too much. After lengthy discussions, the plan at last agreed at the Hague was that Eugene would march northwards from the Moselle with 40,000 troops to combine with Marlborough and then crush Vendôme's outnumbered army before it too could be reinforced from elsewhere. The plan was good, but not at all subtle; in fact it was so obvious that the French were aware of the possibility and made plans to counter any such move by Eugene. They could not start to substantially reinforce their own forces in the Low Countries, however, until the Prince began his march from the Moselle, for fear of being wrong-footed in that region in consequence.

With his superiority in numbers, Vendôme had his own plans for the new campaign: he could strike at Ostend and cut Marlborough's direct communications with England, or move against the Meuse fortresses of Liège and Huy to the east. The more open country in that region would suit the deployment of his numerous cavalry very well and draw Marlborough away from the French border. Vendôme would also be moving closer to reinforcements from the Moselle if, as anticipated, Eugene marched north. Burgundy had a preference for a straightforward advance on Brussels, although this would almost inevitably bring on an early clash with Marlborough on ground of his own choosing. Vendôme tried to ignore this suggestion, although it had the merit for the French of bringing on a confrontation with Marlborough while they still had the larger force. The matter had to be referred to Versailles for the King's considered opinion. In the meantime, after a period of inactivity due to persistent heavy rain, the French army advanced across the Haine river as if intending to turn the left of the Allied posture and threaten Brabant. Marlborough shifted his army to the east to cover both Brussels and Louvain, but by 3 June Vendôme's army had reached Braine L'Alleud and Genappe where he halted, as if foiled by the Duke's confident counter-moves. This was just sparring, with each commander looking for the other to make a mistake, and there was now a pause in operations as both armies watched each other and waited for reinforcements to come from the Moselle. At last, Louis XIV sent instructions against making any attempt on Huy or Liège, as a much more enticing possibility had now arisen in northern Flanders.

Many Imperial German troops had to be left to watch the Rhine under the command of George, the Elector of Hanover, who had been rather offended to find that he was to be largely left out of things by Marlborough and Eugene.[7] Eugene took longer than Marlborough expected to begin his move north, and when he did come, starting out from the Moselle on 29 June, it was with only some 15,000 troops – not the 40,000 intended when the plan was made. Three days later the Duke wrote to London with hardly concealed impatience:

> Prince Eugene began his march with his army on Friday last, in order to join us, and I hope he will make so much diligence as to prevent the enemy, upon which the whole depends; for, though we have no account yet of their motions, it is not to be doubted but they are likewise hastening this way.[8]

The Duke learned that Eugene was on the march on 1 July, but close on the Prince's heels were about 27,000 French troops under the command of Berwick, striving to intercept the line of march and throw the Allied plans into disarray. He was in actual fact moving on a straighter line than Eugene, but was 48 hours later starting his march. The competing timetable for this strategic shift in the dispositions of the opposing armies was extremely tight. As Marlborough feared, if Berwick could just once get to grips with Eugene's rearguard and make it stand and fight, or if he could get his own cavalry across the Prince's line of march and force an engagement, the whole Allied plan would fall to pieces.

Vendôme had apparently been inactive for several weeks, but he had by no means been idle. The French had become aware that many citizens in the Spanish Netherlands had quickly tired of Dutch occupation in the wake of Ramillies, and in particular they resented the heavy rates of taxation demanded of them in order (to some degree) to fund the war effort. The French War Minister in the region, Count Bergeryck, came to Vendôme with an old plan intended originally to surprise Brussels or Antwerp but now modified to fit present circumstances. This was put into dramatic effect on the evening of 4 July 1708. The French army suddenly moved westwards through a rainy night to the crossing places over the Senne and Dender rivers, while cavalry detachments spurred ahead to summon the citizenry of Bruges and Ghent to return to their allegiance to Philip V. This they did with remarkable promptness, and at this bold stroke Vendôme had command not only of these two important towns but of the useful waterways of the region. Marlborough had plainly and very publicly been wrong-footed by the French commander, who had pulled off a considerable and very creditable coup. The Duke's embarrassment was the greater because he had recently been warned by the Comte de Merode-Westerloo of just such a possibility but had abruptly discounted the advice as being unreliable. This was despite his having been alerted to a possible French attempt against Antwerp only two months earlier, which caused him to write and warn the Allied commanders in northern Flanders to be on the alert.

Marlborough learned of Vendôme's march late in the evening that it began. The response was swift, and Count Bothmar was sent with a strong cavalry detachment to shield Dendermonde (which had taken the Allies such effort and expense to capture two years previously), while reinforcements were also rushed into Oudenarde on the Scheldt. At 2.00 a.m. on 5 July the Duke wrote to Major-General Murray, whose detachment was posted near to Ghent, 'Their whole army is marched, of which we only expect the confirmation to begin ... I desire that immediately upon receipt of this, you cause Sir

Thomas Prendergast to march with his regiment to Oudenarde, there to remain until further orders.'[9] The warnings to Murray and other local commanders near Ghent and Bruges were too late to have any effect, due to the speed with which the magistrates and citizenry of the towns opened their gates to the French. Marlborough soon had his army moving forward to overtake their rearguard as it marched westwards but was unable to make up the lost ground, although there was an inconclusive and brief clash at the Dender river crossings. The weather continued to be bad and misfortune dogged the Duke's efforts, for Vendôme was playing his hand well. By 8 July, the French army had drawn up behind the Dender, in a good position to cover the conquests in northern Flanders and to attack Oudenarde on the Scheldt. Burgundy wanted to move to attack Allied-held Menin rather than Oudenarde, as this would close the gap between the French army and their supply bases in northern France, while maintaining pressure on Marlborough at the same time. The two men could not agree – Oudenarde or Menin? – and so the matter had to be referred to Versailles for a decision; Vendôme's campaign began to lose some of its sparkle in the resulting delay.

Marlborough was suffering with a severe headache at this time, and without doubt his performance suffered accordingly. On 6 July, the Duke put his army into camp at Assche, to the west of Brussels, and the following day felt so unwell that he did not come out from his tent, the orders being issued by Overkirk on his behalf. However, Eugene had hurried ahead of his marching troops, and that evening he came to the Allied camp to confer with Marlborough. The Prince was entirely unconcerned at the loss of Ghent and Bruges, for a victory in open battle would immediately set everything right for the Allies again. The Duke's spirits revived instantly, and the two friends set to plotting how to bring Vendôme to battle at the earliest possible moment before Berwick came, even though it meant fighting the French without the reinforcement of Eugene's troops, who were still trudging along the roads from the Moselle.

First, the Allies had to get across the Dender, and Vendôme would be sure to dispute the river crossings if he realised what his opponents intended. Early on 9 July, William Cadogan was sent marching southwards with an advanced guard through the small town of Herfelingen and on to Lessines which offered a convenient and so far undefended crossing place. The main army followed, with Earl Albemarle covering the trains with his Dutch cavalry. Earl Orkney, in command of a strong brigade of infantry, was tasked to shield Brussels against any sudden French raid – there was to be no unwelcome repetition of the surprise of Ghent and Bruges. By midnight on 10 July, Cadogan and his troops were firmly across the Dender and Vendôme had now lost the initiative in the campaign. The French commander could no longer hold the line of the river without bringing on a major action, and so he fell back to Gavre, where pontoon bridges had been laid to allow his army to move behind the line of the Scheldt. Once beyond that wide and marshy obstacle, Vendôme could select a strong place from which to defy Marlborough with near impunity. The ground just beyond the river, rising in a series of low but pronounced ridges overlooking the town of Oudenarde, offered a number of promising opportunities for the French to stand and fight a pitched battle from a good position.

The Allied campaign, however, was now thoroughly alight, and Marlborough and his commanders were driving the army forward to overtake the French. By mid-morning on 11 July, William Cadogan stood on the hills at Eename, just downstream from Oudenarde, and watched the French army making its stately, unhurried way to their pontoon bridges at Gavre, a few miles away to the north-east. Messengers went galloping back along the road from Lessines to urge Marlborough and the main army onwards – if haste was made, the French could be brought to battle while they were crossing the river. In the meantime, Cadogan set his pioneers to work laying his own pontoon bridges over the Scheldt. Neither Vendôme or Burgundy had any notion of the close proximity of this advanced guard, as their own troops moved across the bridges over the river, much less that the main Allied army was actually bearing down on them and looking to fight a battle at the water's edge. Only at about 3.00 p.m. did Vendôme awake to the peril in which he stood. Two Swiss infantry brigades under command of the Marquis de Biron, who had been covering the left flank of the French army, presumably against any interference from the Allied garrison in Oudenarde, came under sudden attack from Cadogan's British and Dutch troops.

The French commander's immediate reaction to this attack was to throw the infantry of the right Wing of the army into an effort to eliminate Cadogan's bridgehead. The intention was sound but the execution was very poor. The troops were sent in without proper support or co-ordination and Marlborough's infantry, streaming down the hill to the pontoon bridges at Eename, got into place just in time to hold the French attacks. Meanwhile, the left Wing of the French army remained idle at the far end of the battlefield, as the Duke of Burgundy and his staff officers appeared not to realise the peril in which Vendôme now stood. As evening came on and the rain started, Marlborough sent Count Overkirk with his Dutch and Danish corps over the Boser Couter hill to the westwards of the fighting, outflanking Vendôme's troops in a crushing attack that encircled half the French army and left it struggling to survive in the gathering darkness. Only the onset of night saved Vendôme and his troops from complete destruction, as their the army fled northwards to take shelter in Ghent and Bruges.[10]

On the day that Vendôme's army received such a mauling beside the Scheldt, Marshal Berwick, by riding ahead with a small cavalry escort, reached Givet on the Meuse. His own army was still toiling along the roads from the Moselle valley, and it would be several days before he could deploy anything like his full strength. Even then, those fifty-six squadrons of cavalry and thirty-four infantry battalions, foot-weary from the long march, together with a few scattered garrison troops, would be virtually all that stood between the northern border of France and Marlborough's triumphant army. On 13 July, while at Sart La Bussiere on the Sambre river, the Marshal learned the details of the French defeat at Oudenarde from the governor of Mons. The gravity of the situation was obvious, and he took rapid action to try and limit the damage, as far as he was able. Hastening forward with an escort of twenty cavalry squadrons, Berwick reached Mons itself the next day and began to collect the stragglers and fugitives streaming in from the north, fleeing in despair from the recent disaster. In this way he was able in a fairly short time to gather together some 9,000 infantry in more or less formed units. Despite his popularity with the troops, there was a distinct limit to the Marshal's reassuring influence as the morale of these soldiers was fragile and they showed a tendency to panic at quite minor alarms. Berwick thought it best to put most of them in to reinforce the garrisons of Lille, Ypres and Tournai, which Vendôme had stripped bare to reinforce the field army earlier in the year. Little enough though this was, it went some way to restore the now-threadbare defence of the French border and the fortified obstacle belt there. Berwick recalled in his memors: 'It had always been found that the loss of one battle was followed by the loss of all Flanders for the want of garrisons.'[11]

The day after the battle, although he was suffering still with a headache, Marlborough held a council of war with his commanders in the Governor's palace in Oudenarde. A pursuit of the defeated French army was ordered and this was pressed northwards hard enough for their rearguard to have to turn and drive off the tormenting Allied cavalry, not far from Ghent. Simultaneously, Marlborough's attention switched to the south, towards the temporarily unoccupied

French lines of defence near Comines and Warneton. Late on 13 July, the Prussian Count Lottum was dispatched with a mixed corps of forty cavalry squadrons and thirty battalions of infantry to level and destroy the defences and so remove this obstacle on the road to France. Marlborough meanwhile found time to write with gentle reproof to the unsuccessful Allied commander of the citadel of Ghent:

> I have received your letter of the 11th instant with your [terms of] capitulation for your garrison, and wish you could have held out until Wednesday [the day of the battle]; it is probable then the enemy would not have pressed you anymore.[12]

In this respect the Duke was plainly wrong, as the French grip on northern Flanders, although undoubtedly weakened in battle, would take some time to prise loose, and Louis XIV's fresh instructions to his grandson ran: 'Your principal object now must be to keep Ghent well-garrisoned, and to sustain it.'

News soon came in to Berwick's makeshift headquarters that the Allied army was losing no time, and that a powerful force was already heading south towards the French border. With his own army steadily gathering at Valenciennes, Berwick moved to block the thrust with those troops that he had to hand but he was both too late and too weak in numbers still to seriously interrupt the Allied operation. Vendôme and Burgundy with their battered troops may have been forced back behind the Ghent-Bruges canal to the north, but once a dangerous opponent like Berwick had his forces in play, the freedom of action now enjoyed by Marlborough would be lessened. The most had to be made of the temporary advantage so daringly snatched at Oudenarde.

By 15 July 1708, Lottum's troops had reached the French lines and the work of demolition began at once, unimpeded by Berwick's tentative approach. Matthew Bishop, who laboured to help level the works wrote: 'Every man had a shovel. When we got to the top [of the obstacle] we began to throw it down as fast as possible to make way for the army.'[13] There was a brief skirmish with the few French troops in the area and some prisoners were taken by Lottum's soldiers. The same day Marlborough's main force reached Wervicq on the Lys river. Foremost in his mind was the lack of heavy guns with which to take on formal obstacles and fortifications 'For want of heavy cannon we are not able to do anything considerable … As long as the French are masters of Ghent we cannot make use of the Scheldt or the Lys.'[14] As so often, operations had to wait for the siege artillery to arrive and Marlborough's army was now in a very advanced position, well away from its depots and magazines. This was a concern with Berwick so close, even if Vendôme's troops were too battered to do much about it at that point. To the Duke's relief, on 16 July Prince Eugene's army was pouring through the streets of Brussels after its wearying march from the Moselle. Their arrival almost coincided with that of Berwick's main force, but of course the Marshal had been too late to avert the defeat at Oudenarde. The concentration of the Allied armies was accordingly far more potent than Berwick, now trying to co-ordinate some sort of campaign with the remnants of Vendôme's army. The Allies had won this round in the campaign handsomely, but it remained to be seen whether they could make the most of their success.

Eugene's army comprised forty-eight cavalry squadrons and eighteen infantry battalions, and more Imperial troops would join him in time. Any concerns Marlborough had, now tactically rather exposed with enemy forces to both the north and the south-east, were set at rest. With Eugene covering the rear of his army and the Allied lines of supply and communication now fairly secure, the Duke could press his campaign onward. A number of enticing possibilities presented themselves. Perhaps the most obvious of these, notwithstanding the success in spoiling the French lines at Comines and Warneton, was to pursue Vendôme northwards, break through the line of the Ghent-Bruges canal, and bring on another general action there. Given the sad state of morale in the French army at this point and the contrasting boundless confidence amongst the Allied troops, the outcome would seem to have been in little doubt. The practical difficulty of actually forcing the canal – almost certainly opposed by the French and without the advantage of surprise – made this an uninviting prospect. If it was going to be attempted, Berwick would surely manoeuvre against the flank of the Allied armies as they closed up towards Vendôme, and a substantial detachment, perhaps the whole of Eugene's corps, might be required to hold the Marshal off.

Vendôme was anxious to shield his army after the recent defeat and he was already strengthening the defences along the line of the canal. The option to attack him in place was understandably rejected by Marlborough, although Deputy Goslinga came up with a wholly unsuitable alternative to isolate Vendôme north of the canal and just starve him out. This time-consuming scheme would also entail the starvation of the civilian population of northern Flanders, and made it an impractical project which Marlborough politely but firmly set to one side. The Duke did however impose a blockade on the region to limit the movement of supplies, both military and civil. He also gave orders to the governor of Ostend that the sluice gates between Nieuport and Bruges should be opened to lower the water levels enough to deny as far as possible the use of the canal for the movement of munitions and supplies by the French along the coast.

The border with France was now open, devoid of decent garrisons, and both Vendôme and Berwick were out of position if they had to move rapidly to its defence. It was necessary to maintain the pace of the Allied campaign, and Marlborough sent Count Tilly, with a strong force of cavalry, raiding into northern France, fully bringing home to Louis XIV the realities of the weakness of his position after Oudenarde. Crops, forage, cattle, horses and mules were gathered in by Tilly's troopers, all valuable supplies for the Allied army. Farms were put to the torch and the populace harried and looted – even the suburbs of Arras were raided – while La Bassée and Le Quesnoy were occupied for a short time: 'One of the parties, consisting of five hundred horse and three hundred hussars, advanced as far as the gates of Arras, and having burnt the suburbs, returned this morning with little or no loss.'[15] The French King, ruefully aware that he could not protect his people, directed that huge contributions of money, demanded by Tilly from the magistrates of the towns along the French border, should be paid promptly to avert the full fury of the Allied cavalry.

Marlborough hoped that the ravaging of the border region would force Vendôme to come out from behind the canal, combine with Berwick, and give battle in the open. This he did not do, but instead clung to his defended position in the north. From there he obliquely exerted pressure on Marlborough's means of supply, particularly the useful waterways; as a result, his communications both with England and southern Holland were made more difficult. This tactical advantage gained by Vendôme, although a side-show overall, was significant for it slowed the pace of the Duke's operations, while permitting the French commander to rest his army in relative safety.

Alternatively, Marlborough could turn on Berwick and try to catch and destroy his smaller army. The Marshal had already garrisoned Mons, Tournai and Ypres, and could manoeuvre with their solid support if he was threatened – he could even fall back to the south-east towards Valenciennes, secure in the knowledge that his opponent would be embroiled in the fortress belt left behind. The Allied lines of supply would be uncomfortably stretched in the process. If the Duke then tried to move back against Vendôme, Berwick could move forward again to harry the rear of the Allied army as it did so. Louis XIV was striving to bolster the northern defences, pulling in troops and commanders from other theatres of war as fast as they could; Berwick was daily receiving reinforcements, and he was too astute and dangerous an opponent either to be easily caught or safely ignored.

Instead of going for either Vendôme or Berwick, Marlborough put forward to his commanders a daring plan for a thrust deep into northern France with Paris as the goal. Such a move would entail threading the Allied army through the deeply fortified belt along the border, leaving those garrisons intact and in place. As the advance on land progressed, an amphibious 'descent' on the French coast in the area of Abbeville would be made by troops carried by the Royal Navy. The ships would then ensure the provisioning of Marlborough's marching columns, whose lines of supply, vulnerable to the attention of the French garrisons left behind, would almost certainly be interrupted. Troops were available for the 'descent' as Lieutenant-General Erle had men already on board ships off the Isle of Wight, units which had been intended originally to reinforce the Allied army in Spain, but which could be deployed to Normandy instead.

Such an audacious move into the heart of France, so dramatic and potentially decisive in bringing the war to a close, unavoidably entailed enormous risks. The Allied army would advance and have to leave behind two French armies, sitting firmly on roads leading back to Holland. Despite the promised naval support – a concept not wholly tested or trusted at this time – it was a daunting prospect to have an army's communications and supply lines left exposed to the attentions of even one active enemy, let alone two (Vendôme must at some point throw off the lethargy into which he had subsided). Once the fortress belt was passed, the garrisons left behind were unlikely to sit still and do nothing, for the French commanders would draw them out to reinforce their armies once the immediate threat from Marlborough passed on. Unless the advance into France was so powerful and dramatic that pressure was exerted on Vendôme, Burgundy and Berwick to hurry to the rescue of Paris and Versailles, they could be counted on to create havoc in the Spanish Netherlands and might even march into southern Holland itself. Such an event would alarm the States-General, who would undoubtedly demand the prompt return of their own troops to defend their border. If the plan had just one major flaw (leaving to one side the unproven capabilities of the Royal Navy to support such an operation at all), this was it: the danger of leaving Holland exposed. Marlborough, with his eye set firmly on the horizon of a war-winning campaign around Paris, was for once not alert enough to the concerns of his allies.

All this the Allied generals discussed in council of war. Alone among them, Marlborough advocated the advance on Paris, passionately explaining the great prize to be had: a massive campaign rampaging across the open country of northern France, where either Paris would fall or the French army would have to stand and fight to save the city. The Duke's veteran officers were unconvinced and wary; their training and experience gave them no confidence in deep thrusts into enemy territory, especially when powerful forces remained in their rear and a major fortress belt, intact in most respects, spread across their communications. Re-supply by sea sounded well enough, but few were convinced that the Royal Navy had the will or the means to ensure the sustenance of a huge army throughout protracted operations, in all weathers and at all hazards. This was all too daring; there seemed to be too many questions that could not be answered with certainty. So much had been gained at Ramillies and Oudenarde it could not now put all be put at such risk, no matter how glittering the potential prize. Eugene, the most daring of Marlborough's colleagues, was against the plan, being unwilling to move forward while the French obstacle belt remained intact. He felt that Lille, the most important city in northern France, and a major fortress in its own right, should be in Allied hands before a further advance was undertaken; and Lille would provide a good base for the projected advance on Paris, whenever that might come.

Disappointed, Marlborough accepted the opinion of his generals with his customary good grace and turned his attention to Lille. On 26 July 1708, he wrote in resigned tones to Lord Halifax: 'Your notion of entering France agrees very well with my own inclination, and were our army all English, it would be feasible, but we have a great many among us who are more afraid of wanting provisions than of the enemy.'[16] This was certainly a little unfair: his generals did not lack energy or bravery, as their records demonstrate. The Duke had developed a kind of blind spot to the perils of the projected advance, and it is difficult not to sympathise with the colleagues who did not share his enthusiasm. Their caution was understandable and valid, and it could be argued that the best way to win the war was not an expensive and hazardous campaign deep in northern France, but just what Marlborough had yearned for so many years – the destruction in open battle of Louis XIV's field armies, wherever they might be found. If the most pressing need was to get the French commanders to stand and fight, the impending loss of the second city of France, Lille, would surely bring on such a battle, and that was the course favoured by Eugene. Marlborough went on in his letter: 'If we can get up our battering train, Lille would be of infinite use in our projects.'

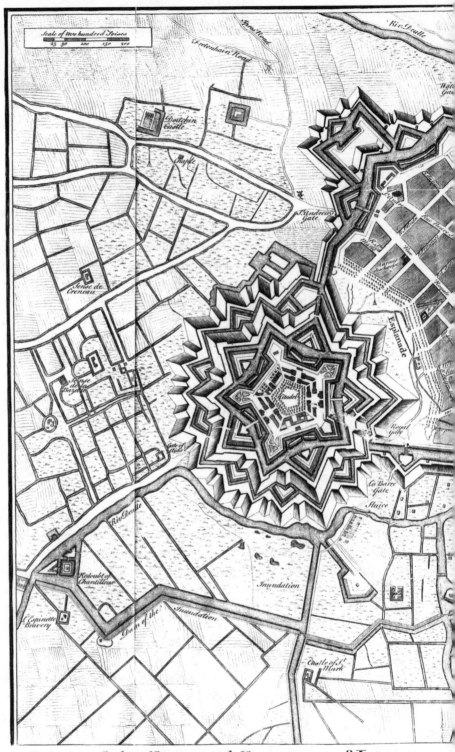

Scale of two hundred Toises
25 50   100   150   200

Riv:Deule

Ypres Road

Fretenhain Road

Deutchin Castle

Chapple

St Andrews Gate

Water Gate

Rue Dengilestu

Carnas dechamps

Sense de Creneau

Esplanade

Sense de la Bazelle

Citadel

Gate of Fishes

Royal Gate

la Barre Gate

Sluice

Riv:Deule

Redoubt of Chantilleur

Inundation

L'Espinette Brewery

Dam of the   Inundation

Castle of St Mark

PLAN of the CITY and CITADEL of LISLE

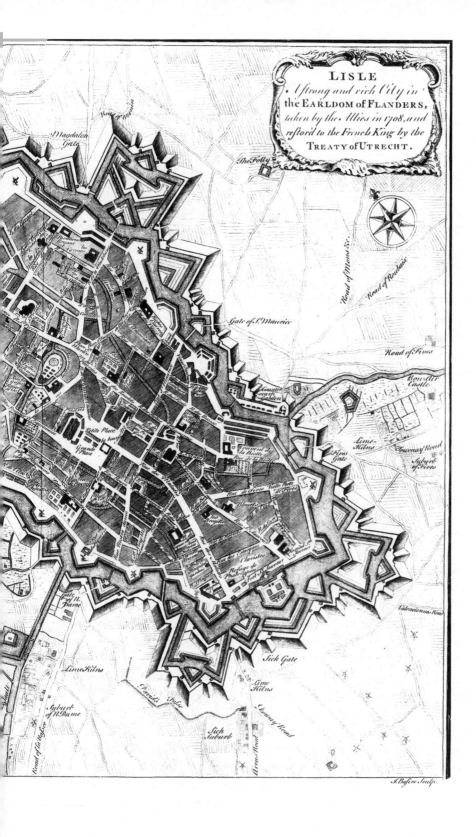

LISLE A strong and rich City in the EARLDOM of FLANDERS, taken by the Allies in 1708, and restor'd to the French King by the TREATY of UTRECHT.

Magdalen Gate

The Folly

Gate of St Maurice

Road of Mons &c.

Road of Roubaix

Road of Fives

Bon-Air Castle

Austin Convent Garden

Petite Place

Grande Place

Convent de la Riotte

Lime-Kilns

Tournay Road

Fives Gate

Suburb of Fives

Rue de Fives

Velle Porte de Fives

Bleuets

les Brigitts

Rue des Cinques

Clarisses

Refuge de Phalempins

Fort St Sauveur

Valenciennes Road

Gate St Dame

Sick Gate

Lime Kilns

Lime Kilns

Barach Police

Suburb of NºDame

Sick Suburb

Road of Carbagere

Arren Road

Tournay Road

A. Basire Sculp.

Given the size and strength of the fortifications of Lille, the master-piece of Marshal Vauban on which he had exerted the utmost of his skill, such a campaign was bound to be complex and expensive. One Allied army would have to lay siege to the town and citadel, while the other held off the French forces which would come to its aid. A major operation to maintain and supply the besieging troops and the cover-ing army inside France would also be necessary. This would be a vast and testing campaign, and the French were to be kept in ignorance of Allied intentions as long as possible. Helping in this task was the simple fact that it seemed quite incredible that Marlborough should so rashly assault a major first-rate fortress, well in advance of his own depots and magazines, rather than one of several lesser potential victims (Ypres, Mons or Tournai), while powerful enemy field armies operated against him. When combined, the French would outnum-ber the Allies by about 110,000 troops to 100,000, and could probably match any subsequent increase in Allied strength by drawing troops from elsewhere. Such were the odds against success that Vendôme incorrectly predicted: 'So wise a commander as Prince Eugene would not venture upon such an enterprise.'[17]

This was not complacency on the part of the French general, for there were many risks with such an ambitious siege operation. Once French reinforcements gathered in response to the defeat at Oudenarde, Berwick would be able to move against the southern flank of the Allied armies, while Vendôme simultaneously operated against their flank in the north. Well handled, the French might well cut the Allies off entirely from their bases and supplies. However, these things are not simple to arrange. Vendôme and Berwick were not on the best of terms, and Burgundy was virtually irrelevant, while Marlborough and Eugene, such close friends, could be counted on to co-operate in complete harmony to foil the French.

The Allied commanders faced several immediate and daunting difficulties, quite apart from the French armies and what their com-manders might try and do. Marlborough's army lay at Menin, while Eugene kept his troops near to Brussels to cover the rear of the Allied deployment. It was decided that Eugene should move to supervise the siege operations against Lille, while the Duke commanded the covering army and kept the French at bay. Before any of this could begin, the practical preparations for the siege had to be completed. These entailed the bringing forward of huge amounts of stores, ord-nance and munitions from depots deep in the Spanish Netherlands, Holland, and even across the Channel from England. Supplies of this nature and quantity were not carried by a field army on a day-to-day basis and the most obvious lack, as usual, was that of the heavy siege artillery. Largely denied the use of the waterways of northern Flanders (validating in part Vendôme's determination to sit tight behind the Ghent-Bruges canal), the Allies had to rely on the rough roads of the region. Deep in mud when it was raining and swirling with dust when dry, their use to bring forward the supplies and guns was always laborious and required great effort and protection against attack. Marlborough wrote on 23 July 1708:

> We are at present at a stand for want of our heavy artillery, which we are using all possible diligence to bring up; but as we shall have occasion for about sixteen thousand horses for this service you may believe we labour under some difficulties, being obliged to send as far as Maastricht for some of them, as well as for some of our artillery. In the mean time we are doing all we can to annoy the enemy.[18]

The Duke added 'This morning we sent a detachment of sixteen hundred men to get possession of the town of Armentières.'

Berwick gamely tried to prevent these raids, but Allied foraging parties were now scouring the border region and even sweeping into France itself to gather draught animals and wagons to add to those being gathered in throughout the Spanish Netherlands. The Allied army also contributed to the effort and quartermasters' wagons and officers' equipages were taken, while any spare horses and mules were pressed into service. William Cadogan picked the province of Brabant clean. Every cart, tumbrel, coach and wagon was gathered in for use in the huge and complex operation, as were the thousands of horses, mules and oxen that were required to bring forward the guns and mortars of the siege train, together with sufficient powder and shot for sustained battery firing. Neither Berwick or Vendôme had the ability to prevent the operation taking place right in front of them, and that was a good measure of the ascendancy that the Allied commanders had established at this time.

Before the decision to attack Lille was even taken, it had been necessary to bring forward the immediate supplies and baggage of the army, without which the soldiers were campaigning with just what they carried on their backs. This first convoy, dragged by 8,000 horses and mules, left Brussels on 22 July and negotiated the seventy miles of road without hindrance, arriving at Menin three days later. The covering force of cavalry was commanded by the Earl of Albemarle. Marlborough brought a detachment of his army to Pottes on the Scheldt to cover the convoy from the north, while Eugene manoeuvred to the south of the route taken, ready to foil Berwick if he prowled out of Mons towards the long column of wagons. In any case, it seemed that the Marshal was taken unawares by the Allied operation and no serious effort was made to interrupt the convoy's progress. This neglect was in part due to Louis XIV's being concerned for the security of the fortress belt and having instructed Berwick not to move too far north for the time being. Vendôme was still lethargic, and despite the two French commanders now having over 100,000 troops available between them, the valuable convoy went through unchallenged. By 25 July, the baggage was safely in the Allied camp and the army could proceed with the campaign, while the French had missed their first chance to stop their opponents in their tracks.

Louis XIV sent Marshal Boufflers to take command of the garrison in Lille. On 28 July, he arrived with a small cavalry escort, their saddlebags bulged with gold coins with which to settle the arrears of pay of the troops there. Marlborough wrote to the Secretary of State at War, Henry Boyle, on 30 July: 'M. Boufflers arrived two days ago at his government of Lille, and is putting the place in the best posture of defence he can.'[19] The veteran Marshal also brought along in his small party the Marquis de Surville, a bruising infantry commander, and a notable exponent of aggressive artillery tactics, the Marquis de la Frequeliére, who had worked the French guns so well at Blenheim. Both officers had been waiting for some weeks at Versailles without a command, and Boufflers just took them to add their skills to the forthcoming defence of the city. His arrival in Lille was greeted with rapturous applause from soldiers and citizens alike, for the Marshal was known to be a close confidante of the King, and his appointment was a mark of the high regard in which Lille was held at Versailles. Work immediately began to improve and strengthen the already formidable defences, clearing fields of fire around the city by demolishing cottages and felling groves of trees, and planting mines on the likely approaches that the Allies would take. The more substantial buildings on the outskirts of Lille were fortified and turned into strong-points, dense hedges of abbatis were laid around them; each one became a minor block-house ready to impede and delay the attacking army and force costly and time-consuming battles for possession.

For the time being, all Marlborough's attention was on the passage of the next great convoy, bringing the necessary armaments and materiel for the siege of Lille. Despite the problems in finding enough draught animals available for the task, by 2 August 1708, the vast assembly of the battering train and its associated baggage was ready in Brussels ready to move. The Duke wrote that same day to Henry Boyle:

> Our greatest difficulty of bringing our heavy train of artillery to Brussels is almost over, the greatest part being safely arrived, and I hope we have got a sufficient number of horses and wagons together to bring it forward. No doubt the enemy will do their utmost to obstruct us. The wagons are now loading, and the whole will be ready to come away in two or three days ... Count Tilly, having recalled all the detachments he sent into Picardy, where they have burnt and ravaged a good way into the country, began his march back today.[20]

The huge convoy, 3,000 wagons loaded with munitions and materiel of every kind, together with 154 guns and mortars, was tugged along by the 16,000 horses, mules and oxen. They took to the road, under the supervision of William Cadogan, and Albemarle again led the covering force as the ponderous 15-mile-long column set off. The importance of the success of this operation could not be greater, should the French interrupt its progress, or even seriously damage or destroy the convoy, Marlborough's plans would be in ruins. A marvellous prize, affecting the campaign for the remainder of the year, was dangled in front of the French commanders. If the Allies lost this convoy, it was unlikely that they could mount another in good time to proceed with the siege of Lille.

Marlborough was, as always, concerned for the security of the siege train in particular. Without this, the Allied campaign was at a standstill, unable to even think of attempting the fortifications of Lille; the hard-won gains of Oudenarde would be lost. On 3 August, as preparations for the convoy progressed, he wrote to Cadogan: 'For God's sake, be sure you do not risk the cannon ... Let me hear from you as often as you can.'[21] The following day, Eugene, who had been conferring with the Duke at his headquarters at Werwicq, returned to his own army near Ath. Marlborough sent him a powerful corps comprising twenty-five squadrons of cavalry and twenty-five infantry battalions, under the command of Count Lottum. With this additonal force, Eugene could deploy about 50,000 troops to protect the convoy and siege train, and could probably face down any opponent who tried to interfere with the operation.

The second great convoy was split into two parts to aid tactical control on the march. Slowly, on 6 August, the wagons, carts and guns lumbered southwards from Brussels. The close covering force of infantry, commanded by the Prince of Hesse-Cassell, threw an iron cloak around the huge columns, while a rearguard of six squadrons of Hessian cavalry watched the road from Brussels. By the early hours of 7 August, the leading wagons reached Soignies, and the following day they swung westwards to Enghien and Ath, coming under the protection of Eugene's waiting army. Meanwhile, Marlborough sent a strong detachment of thirty cavalry squadrons, under the Duke of Württemberg, towards Oudenarde to watch for any movement by Vendôme towards Brussels. The garrison there was also reinforced to guard against any French attempt to surprise the city. This was just as well, for the French commander pushed forward a powerful detachment 12,000 strong across the Ghent-Bruges canal, looking for an opening as they probed towards Ninove. Failing in this, and finding that they brushed against Württemberg's alert scouts, the French force drew off and avoided serious contact.

By 8 August, the convoy was crossing the Dender at Ath and two days later the pontoon bridges that had been thrown across the Scheldt at Pottes were reached. On 12 August, the wagons were trundling into Menin with the loss of not a single vehicle, having met no opposition on the road. Marlborough wrote to Lord Townsend the next day: 'Our heavy cannon being come up safe to Menin, the Prince of Savoy has this day invested Lille with his army. The French threaten hard to oblige us to raise the siege.'[22] The lack of action against the vital Allied convoy is less strange than it seems. The French commanders still found it difficult to co-ordinate a joint campaign and Berwick seemed to think that the Allies might turn aside to attack Mons. Accordingly, the Marshal marched and counter-marched to protect that town, but came no closer to the convoy route than Mortagne and he thereby lost the chance to strike at the convoy as it ground its slow way past. Vendôme meanwhile had been deterred from advancing southwards by Württemberg's presence near to Oudenarde and Ninove. Such a chance is rarely offered twice, and a French observer wrote: 'Posterity will hardly believe this fact, though it is an indisputable truth. Never was a daring enterprise so conducted with more skill or greater circumspection.'[23] Neither Vendôme nor Berwick were lacking in tactical skill and this failure to act shows very well the disarray and doubt amongst the French.

On 10 August, while the vital convoy slowly drew near, John Friso, the Prince of Orange-Nassau, and Lieutenant-General Cornelius Wood combined their forces to form the besieging army near to the village of Marquette. They began the approach to Lille from the north; Boufflers immediately set ablaze the suburbs of the city on that side to hamper the Allied deployment. Despite this, the great siege had now begun. On the following day Berwick, having realised his error in moving to cover Mons at the expense of the chance to scatter Marlborough's convoys, diverted a brigade of infantry into Lille to reinforce the garrison . Boufflers could now deploy twenty battalions of infantry in defence, in addition to seven dismounted squadrons of dragoons and sixty heavy guns – he also had the 2,000-strong locally recruited militia and in all could use a garrison of about 15,000 men.

The first attack on Lille went in from the north on 11 August 1708, when an outer-work at the Marquette Abbey was stormed by Dutch and British troops. The immense hornworks at the St Mark and St Magdalene gates, so prominent in all the plans of the city, were the immediate objectives of Eugene's opening assault. This approach was plainly the most obvious option open to him, despite the seeming lack of subtlety and apparently neglectful signalling of intentions to Boufflers. However, the main road from Menin also came from that direction, and along that way must pass all the ordnance and supplies for the siege operations. This was the governing consideration in Eugene's decision. The waters of the Deule close at hand could best be controlled from the north also, allowing the Allies to lower the water defences of Lille to a certain extent. In addition, the high ground of the nearby Magdalene feature offered a valuable vantage point for the besiegers and their breaching batteries. If Eugene could break into the city at this point then the siege might prove to be a surprisingly short affair despite the strength of the hornworks.

Soon after the attacks began on the outskirts, the citizens of Lille asked Eugene, with the permission of Boufflers, to spare the city and its inhabitants the rigours of a bombardment. The Prince replied firmly: 'They might be assured of his protection, provided that he should be satisfied that they had endeavoured to deserve it.'[24] This was in fact a fairly impossible demand, as the town-recruited militia quite legitimately formed part of the garrison, and Eugene would have been well aware of this. Eugene's officers, while escorting a number of civilians who had obtained passes to leave the place, took advantage of the chance to scout the defences and the preparations to receive the Allied attacks, particularly at the St Magdalene and St Mark gates. Some French officers, noticing this, protested at the supposed breach of etiquette in the ceasefire, but Eugene shrugged their comments off – such opportunities were really just a part of the fortunes of war and were not to be missed.

The day after the storm of the Marquette Abbey, Cornelius Wood swept round Lille with thirty-four squadrons of cavalry, neatly cutting off all means of supply and communication for the garrison. His detachment took up position between Rollegem and Helchin, where Marlborough joined him the same day; simultaneously, Eugene's troops – the investing army proper – closed up to the defences of the city and one of the greatest sieges in military history began. On 13 August, Marlborough wrote to his friend the Lord Treasurer Sidney Godolphin: 'Our cannon being arrived in safety we are divided in two armies, that of Prince Eugene is to invest Lille this day. I am to observe as well as I can the motions of the Duke of Vendôme's army.'[25] Eugene deployed fifty infantry battalions into the siege lines. Amongst the assault brigades (mostly Dutch and Imperial Germans) were a number of British regiments: those of Derby, De Lalo, Sabine, Tatton and the Royal Irish. Sergeant Littler of Derby's had already distinguished himself during the storm of the abbey by swimming the Marquette stream under a hail of French musketry to let down a foot-bridge. He had thus earned himself a commission for his notable bravery.

The Allied heavy guns, with their close escort of 5,000 infantry, trundled into camp on 17 August. In the meantime work had begun on constructing the huge lines of contravallation and circumvallation, nine feet high and nine miles all around, each comprising a parapet and a ditch with fire-step. Despite having to work in oppressively hot weather, the labourers and pioneers completed these by 21 August. All the mass of material to build the firing platforms and shelters for the siege guns had been hauled along from Brussels under the noses of Vendôme and Berwick, and now had to be lugged into place in full view of the garrison. As was to be expected, the French gunners did their best to impede these preparations with a vicious counter-bombardment. In the process, the Prince of Orange was splashed from head to toe with the blood of his unfortunate valet one morning, as a round-shot flew through his tent while he was dressing. Prudently, Orange move his quarters to a less exposed spot without delay.

The trenches were opened during the night of 22 August; 4,000 workmen labouring at the task, covered by sixteen infantry battalions and nine cavalry squadrons. Two days later a fortified chapel and water-mill near the St Magdalene gate was captured in a very neat surprise attack by Dutch troops, although it took sharp hand-to-hand fighting with the French before the place was secure. Boufflers's response was swift, and a sortie by 400 French volunteers on 26 August managed to spoil some of the newly constructed Dutch trenches and retook the chapel, which was then burned to the ground to prevent its further occupation. The following day, at 7.00 a.m., the Allied bombardment of the city defences began in earnest, with Prince Eugene firing the first shot. Although one hundred and twenty heavy guns, twenty howitzers and forty large siege-mortars were in place, it was soon found that they were not very well sited: the pieces had been placed too far back for some reason and were unable to bring effective fire to bear on the fortifications. The expenditure of ammunition and powder in this futile cannonade was enormous, raising immediate concerns at the continuing supply of the army. Despite this, Eugene's engineer officers, Colonel Du Mey and Colonel Des Rogues, were initially very confident that their efforts would soon be successful. Marlborough wrote to Sidney Godolphin on 27 August:

> Our engineers promise that we shall have the town in ten days, after which we must attack the citadel ... I think they [the French] will not venture a battle though it is said they have positive orders to succour the place ... I have this minute advice that M. de Vendôme has begun his march ... as I am now posted it is impossible for him to get between me and the siege.[26]

The previous day, to coincide with the French sortie against the ruined chapel at St Madgalene gate, Berwick had marched out of Mons with his army, while Vendôme and Burgundy came south across the Ghent-Bruges canal with almost their whole strength. Instructions had come from Versailles for the King's generals to do something and save Lille – nothing was to be spared in defence of the place.

The French commanders combined their two armies for the first time on 29 August at Grammont near to the Dender, moving forward to Tournai on 1 September. Able to now deploy a theoretically very imposing force, with some 110,000 troops between them (against only 70,000 men available to Marlborough with the Allied covering army) they advanced past Orchies on 3 September, then came westwards along the road from Douai before turning north towards Lille between the rivers Deule and Marque. The first real contact between the opposing armies came the next day – Marlborough had moved out with his covering army to counter the French approach, but had not yet deployed his full strength. A chance might have offered to attack the Duke before he could really establish his blocking force, but Vendôme decided the day was too far advanced to start a major action and deferred the need for a decision until next day.

As the French came forward Marlborough manoeuvred to meet them, shielding his lack of numbers by anchoring the flanks of his army on the two rivers; the marshes of the Deule near to Noyelles covered his right, while those of the Marque at Peronne protected his left. No sooner was the Duke in position than the combined French army approached as if to give battle. Their march was impeded by the densely cultivated ground between the two rivers, and the gardens and orchards prevented rapid deployment so that delay and confusion resulted. Vendôme now pressed for an immediate attack despite the difficult going, but Burgundy and Berwick were not in favour and their army came to a halt. The matter once again had to be referred to Versailles for a decision and Marlborough used the resulting delay to massively fortify his position. These preparations included a great defensive ditch, twelve feet wide and six feet deep, which was dug across the front of the army; and Ennetières village just in advance of his main line was occupied with infantry and guns, and prepared as a strongpoint. So stout were these preparations that the Duke felt able to send back to the siege trenches before Lille a number of troops that he had called forward to support him in confronting the French army. An added advantage was that this concentration of the forces to the south of Lille left the vital road to Brussels wide open to the scores of Allied wagons that, unmolested, daily rolled southwards with their vital munitions and supplies. Marlborough could afford to bide his time and see what his opponents would attempt next. He had no real reason to fear an attack where he stood and if his opponents manoe uvred for position instead, he could march on internal lines to check them again; meanwhile his hungry army was being daily resupplied without much hindrance.

Detailed reconnaissance of the Allied position on 5 and 6 September brought no comfort to the French commanders. The chances for a successful assault on Marlborough's strong position were poor, and Vendôme's repeated calls for action seemed unconvincing. He could afford to appear aggressive, knowing that this would be well received in Versailles, but was fairly certain that his plans would not be approved by Burgundy. Marshal Berwick wrote to Michel de Chamillart:

It would not be possible to attack an enemy at least as strong as we [this was not so], well posted, entrenched, whose flanks are covered and who cannot be dislodged … It is sad to see Lille taken, but it would be even more sad to lose the only army which now remains to us, or which can stop the enemy after the fall of Lille.[27]

The French were firmly checked, while the siege operations against Lille ground on. Louis XIV now expressed his surprise that clear instructions sent to his commanders in the field to get on and do something had not brought forth a prompt and active response – other than the sending of yet more letters to Versailles to explain why nothing could be attempted, and pleading for his advice. The King urged his grandson to make the attack. This was now his explicit order, even if it led to a failure: 'Less dishonouring, however, both for his person and for the army, than to become spectators of the capture of Lille.'[28] Berwick had found it impossible to work with Vendôme, and resigned his command. He did however continue to accompany the army in the capacity of adviser to Burgundy.

The French commanders were plainly in something of a bind. Marlborough's covering force lay between them and Lille with flanks nicely secured on small, but impossibly marshy streams. To attempt to force this position was fraught with uncertainty, particularly when the morale of their army was still rather fragile. If, on the other hand, they attempted to move around either of Marlborough's flanks in order to edge him out position or get between the Allied covering army and Eugene's troops, the Duke could simply shift sideways and take up a new position. Marlborough might of course throw caution to the winds and move out to attack the French, but such a course, with the known imbalance in troop numbers, would be very rash and was not really to be expected.

Meanwhile, the Allied sappers and miners were burrowing and digging their perilous way forward at a steady pace towards the defences of the city. In the circumstances, and despite the best efforts of the gunners in the garrison to slow the work, the trenches were pushed forward quite well; the ever-lengthening parallels snaking around the fortifications. The battering artillery was also at work and, after a hesitant start, a breach was begun on the northern side of the defences. An attempt on the counterscarp of Lille was delayed for some days, but late on Friday 7 September the storming party was ready – a huge body of troops reportedly some 15,000 strong. The 'forlorn hope' of volunteers, raised as usual by means of offering extra pay and the prospect of accelerated promotion, led the assault on the glacis of the salient angles of the counterscarp, on either side of the Deule, at the gates of St Andrew and St Magdalene.

The firing of three signal guns in rapid succession started the assault, but as the troops rushed towards the tumbled earth and stones of the breach they were received with a heavy French musketry fire. Batteries on either flank poured canister-shot into their massed ranks, while four *fougasse* defensive mines were blown in their faces by the defenders. Hundreds of men were shot down in the opening moments and the attack shuddered to a ghastly halt with the storming parties milling about in the open ground. The attempt was an expensive failure: over 3,000 casualties were suffered in exchange for trifling French losses, and only the slightest foothold gained at two points in the defences. Marlborough's report on the attack went:

> We had made a lodgement on the counterscarp, but it was not with so much success as I expected, having been deferred until it was quite dark, by which means our people were in some confusion, and the workmen not finding their ground readily, our men were for some time exposed to the enemy's fire before they could be covered.[29]

Many of the pioneers who were intended to give some protection to the storming parties by laying fascines at intervals on the glacis had hung back and in some cases, taken advantage of the darkness to make off to a safer spot. Boufflers had also flouted the general convention, which maintained that a covered-way could not be held for long once an attacking force had made a serious lodgement. In consultation with his artillery commander the Marquis de la Frequeliere, he had sited his guns well forward to hold the defences at all costs, and it was noticed the following day that the grass on the glacis and on either side of the saps and third parallel was entirely covered with bodies, mangled and torn by musketry and canister.

The morning after this dismal episode, the garrison put in a sharp counter-attack that caused a lot of alarm, dispersed two Allied battalions, and almost captured the Duke of Argyll before it was beaten off. Marlborough also learned that a force of thirty squadrons of French cavalry had been detached from their main army to sweep back to the north, hoping to catch the Allied commanders unawares and intercept the latest supply convoy trundling its way southwards from Brussels. The Duke sent orders for the Earl of Albemarle to take a similar-sized force of cavalry to screen the convoy and add weight to its escort of eight infantry battalions commanded by Major-General Pascal. Albemarle's horsemen were moving on a shorter route and accordingly made better time, so that the French raid came to nothing. By 11 September, the convoy had come through to the Allied camp in safety.

The French commanders, aware that a great attempt had been made to storm Lille and had failed entirely, carried out a fresh reconnaissance of Marlborough's position. The Minister of War accompanied them, having just arrived from Versailles with instructions to see that an attack was made. There was soon no doubt at all that an assault on the Duke's heavily fortified line would be very expensive and have faint chance of success. The French artillery did, however, subject the Allies near to the village of Ennetières to a heavy cannonade, as if hoping to provoke a rash response. The Allied soldiers gratefully collected the French roundshot wasted in this way and sent them to Eugene's gunners for use against the city. For once, Marlborough seemed disinclined to venture out to give battle in the open, but on 14 September he did confer with his generals on the likely prospects for mounting a raid on the French army. He summoned Eugene again from the trenches to give support, but with the numerical disparity between the two forces, any attack would plainly be very risky and the project was not taken forward. Berwick afterwards remembered that there was still such a lack of accord between Vendôme and Burgundy that such an attack on their army would very likely have been successful.

Although it seemed that the French campaign was drifting, it was also apparent that the Allied siege operations were beginning to stall. Marlborough had not been able to entice an attack on the covering army in its strong position between the Deule and the Marque, nor had he been able to drive off, or inflict any real damage on, the French field army. He had certainly maintained the resupply of his troops, but in the meantime the assault by Eugene's troops on the northern defences of Lille had been a bloody, ghastly failure. The French army now fell back towards Tournai. The movement began on Saturday 15 September, while their commanders decided on other ways to tackle the Allied operations against Lille rather than forcing an outright battle on Marlborough and Eugene. The potentially vulnerable extended lines of supply and communication reaching back to Brussels and Antwerp were an enticing prospect. To this target, Vendôme now turned his attention. This switch in effort by the French came as no great surprise to Marlborough. In many ways it would prove to be a greater concern to him than having to fight an outright battle, albeit with inferior numbers, from a comfortingly strong defensive position. He expressed this anxiety when he wrote wearily to his wife on 17 September:

M. de Vendôme having gathered much more strength than we could imagine, and being encamped so near that in one hour's time we might be engaged, obliges us to be so diligent that we have every little rest ... The siege goes on very slowly, that I am in perpetual fear that it may continue so long, and consequently consume so much stores, that we may at last not have where-withal to finish, which would be very cruel. These are my fears ... but I am in the galley, and must row as long as the war lasts ... Since I had finished this letter, I have notice that the French are passing the Scheldt.[30]

A special corps of 5,000 British troops was sent to add weight to the siege operations, and a renewed Allied assault on Lille to try and force the issue went in the same day that the letter was written. This attempt had rather more success that the first dreadful failure, although resistance was still strong, and the besiegers did manage to move their big guns to better positions in the third parallel for the breaching work. To the north, Comte de la Motte came across the Ghent-Bruges canal to threaten Brussels, but he drew off when Major-General Murray approached with four infantry battalions and six squadrons of Imperial cavalry. Vendôme in the meantime was establishing his army at the crossing points along the Sheldt, and screening the Allied garrison in Oudenarde.

On 20 September an attack was mounted against the St Mark and St Magdalene gates which cost nearly 2,000 casualties. Eugene rather rashly led the storming parties towards the insufficiently widened breach and was wounded in the forehead by a French musket-ball. The stiffened brim of the Prince's hat took most of the force of the blow, but he was badly concussed and had to be helped off the field. Taken to his quarters, Eugene was visited there the next morning by Marlborough, anxious to see how his friend did. The Duke was alarmed to find him in the act of dressing, ready to go back into the trenches. Marlborough persuaded the Prince to go back to his bed to recover properly, promising that he would direct the siege operations personally until he was quite well again. Eugene's wound, alarming though it undoubtedly was, had no serious lasting effect, but the additional burden thrown onto Marlborough was considerable. At a moment when the operations in the trenches were stalled by the ferocious resistance of Boufflers's garrison, enemy armies were prowling along his lines of supply and looking for any weak spot in the Duke's arrangements.

The Duke soon found for himself how bad things had become in the management of the operations in the trenches. He wrote to Sidney Godolphin that same evening:

It is impossible for me to express the uneasiness I suffer for the ill-conduct of our engineers at the siege, where I think every-thing goes very wrong. It would be a cruel thing, if after all we have obliged the enemy to quit all thoughts of relieving the place by force, which they have done, by re-passing the Scheldt, we should fail of taking it by the ignorance of our engineers, and the want of stores, for we have already fired very near as much as was demanded for the taking of the town and citadel; and as yet we are not entire masters of the counterscarp.[31]

The strain was considerable, but the silver lining was that with Marlborough involved in the day to day siege operations, he was able to put a stop to what were developing into a series of prema-ture, ill-prepared and dreadfully expensive assaults. The Duke also had a chance to inspect the engineers' stores and the stockpiles of munitions available to the batteries. He was immediately concerned to find that the stock of powder in particular was far lower than he had thought and much of that was damp or bad. Inefficiency or corruption was evident, although it also seems most likely that the engineers Colonel Des Rogues and Colonel Du Mey were at first too optmistic, then overworked and simply overwhelmed with the scale of the operations which they had to supervise. If no remedy was found, it seemed certain that the breaching bombardment must soon cease and that effectively meant the end of the siege.

Despite the heavy demands on his time and attention, the Duke supervised a raid on the defences which, though modest in scale compared with previous efforts, produced a neat success. On 23 September an attack was successfully launched against the tenaillon on the eastern side, and several valiant French attempts to retake the position failed completely. Marlborough wrote to a friend that evening that, despite this day's satisfactory work, 'It is now a month since we began to fire before Lille. We should have been masters both of the town and citadel by this time, but I am sorry to tell you it goes still on very slowly.[32] The success of the whole Allied operation was in doubt.

NOTES

1. W.S. Churchill, *Marlborough, His Life and Times*, Vol II, 1947, p. 67. In their post-Ramillies euphoria, the Dutch demanded that a strong line of fortresses be established as their new 'Barrier' along

the French frontier. These were to be held by Dutch troops with Dutch governors but paid for by Spanish revenues. The towns that they had in mind fell into three supposedly mutually supporting groups: (a) Namur, Luxembourg, Thionville, Charleroi and Mons, (b) Mauberge, Valenciennes, Tournai, Lille, Menin, Ypres, Furnes and Conde, and (c) Nieuport, Ostend and Dendermonde. Just how far Marlborough's efforts delivered these places into Allied hands will be seen.

2. G. Murray, *Letters and Dispatches of the Duke of Marlborough*, Vol III, 1845, p. 379.

3. Churchill, *Marlborough*, p. 239.

4. Murray, *Letters and Dispatches*, p. 513.

5. R. Kane, *Campaigns of King William and Queen Anne*, 1745, p. 71.

6. Murray, *Letters and Dispatches*, p. 567.

7. *Ibid.*, Vol IV, p. 90.

8. George, Elector of Hanover, (George I of Great Britain from 1714 onwards) was an active and energetic soldier and had undoubted ability. Although this ability might not have been of the same high order as that of Eugene and Marlborough, he was undeniably a 'safe pair of hands' and someone of significant importance. He was a staunch friend of the Grand Alliance, the provider of large numbers of excellent troops for the Allied armies, and the heir apparent to the British throne. The decision to exclude him from the plan to march north from the Moselle was an undoubted snub, as if he could not be trusted with the information, and gave the Elector offence that was not quickly forgotten or forgiven.

9. Murray, *Letters and Dispatches*, p. 95.

10. The French army commanders Vendôme and Burgundy allowed their troops to drift into exactly the kind of tumbling infantry battle in close country that they, with their advantage in cavalry, really should have avoided. In fact, Louis XIV had particularly warned them of the danger of this in one of his frequent letters of advice to his generals. If the two men had managed a good

working relationship, of course, instead of heartily disliking each other, things might have turned out better for France. As it was, the French infantry attacks at Oudenarde, for all the energy and bravery of the soldiers, were repeatedly driven back and half of their army did not manage to engage the Allies at all. Marlborough and Eugene by contrast worked together in confident harmony and, despite being heavily outnumbered many times that July afternoon, achieved a remarkable victory against all the odds.

11. C. Petrie, *The Marshal Duke of Berwick*, 1954, p. 229.

12. Murray, *Letters and Dispatches*, p. 105.

13. Churchill, *Marlborough*, p. 393.

14. Murray, *Letters and Dispatches*, pp. 115–116.

15. *Ibid.*, p. 120.

16. F. Taylor, *The Wars of Marlborough*, 1921, p. 160.

17. Churchill, *Marlborough*, p. 425.

18. Murray, *Letters and Dispatches*, p. 126.

19. *Ibid.*, p. 136.

20. *Ibid.*, p. 143.

21. *Ibid.*, p. 144.

22. *Ibid.*, p. 164.

23. W. Coxe, *Life of John, Duke of Marlborough*, Vol II, 1848, p. 301.

24. Churchill, *Marlborough*, p. 428.

25. *Ibid.*, p. 425.

26. Coxe, *Life of John*, p. 305.

27. Churchill, *Marlborough*, p. 435.

28. *Ibid.*, p. 436.

29. Murray, *Letters and Dispatches*, p. 217.

30. Coxe, *Life of John*, p. 310.

31. *Ibid.*, pp. 311–312.

32. Murray, *Letters and Despatches*, p. 234.

VII

The Battles for Supply: Wynendael and the Fall of Lille, Autumn 1708

By mid-September 1708, the French were well aware of just how precarious the supply situation of the Allied army before Lille must be, given the massive daily expenditure in powder and shot in the bombardment of the city defences. Marlborough was concerned at the continued ability to feed the big siege guns, given the sustained programme of battery firing. The move of the French army to the south of Lille in August had for a time eased the pressure on the Duke's lines of supply, but Vendôme had now drawn off and prepared to move into position to threaten Brussels, Menin or Oudenarde as the opportunity arose. The line he chose to occupy, very sensibly, was that of the Scheldt river, where his troops quickly took post at all the major crossing places (except Oudenarde, which remained firmly in Allied hands). In this way, the French enjoyed the protection of the wide water obstacle against any sudden attack, while neatly severing Marlborough's communications with Holland. In effect, they established a blockade of the Allied army to their south and Marlborough's troops, if they could not be defeated in battle, might well be starved out instead.

Marlborough and Eugene were now in a very exposed position, deep in the French fortress belt with no easy way of obtaining the resupply of material, munitions, fodder and food necessary to sustain their campaign. Vendôme was playing his cards rather well after a poor start and was putting pressure on the Allies undoubted weak spot. Just the sea route across the English Channel remained open as a means by which the Duke could get supplies. Ostend was still in Allied hands, but Bruges and Nieuport on either flank were firmly held by the French. If the Allied army could be provisioned along the road from the coast, Marlborough's campaign could continue and all would yet be well; otherwise, he must dislodge Vendôme's army from the line of the Scheldt. Such an operation would entail the drawing off of his army from Lille, and so the siege of the city would be lifted. Boufflers would take immediate advantage of this to supply and reinforce the garrison and the probability was that the siege would not successfully be reimposed that year, if ever.

The strategic opportunity that was now presented to Vendôme was dazzling both in scope and potential effect. His opponent, fielding the smaller army, must press forward vigorously with the siege operations against Lille, otherwise his plan would fail. At the same time, the very existence and security of the Allied army was in doubt. If Marlborough could not feed his troops and supply his guns, not just that day but every day and as far ahead as could be seen, then his campaign would collapse in confusion, retreat and potential ruin. Yet it was difficult to see that Marlborough could both maintain the siege at full pitch and at the same time drive the French field army away from the Scheldt. The battle for supply was crucial to the success of the campaign and all rested on the road southwards from Ostend; Marlborough must get his wagons safely through on that precarious path, or his men and his guns would go hungry.

At times, it seemed that the besiegers really would starve in their trenches before the Lille garrison had to submit. In mid-September Marlborough brought Lieutenant-General Erle with his troops, who had been intended for the abortive 'descent' on the French coast, to Ostend to strengthen the garrison and guard the road leading southwards to the main army. The Duke had no other choice but to to win the battle of supply or lose the campaign. Oudenburg was garrisoned, as was Leffinghe, and the flooded meadows between Ostend and Nieuport were drained. In addition, bridges over the Nieuport-Bruges canal were strengthened ready for use. Some 700 wagons were gathered at Ostend for a great resupply operation, most particularly to replenish the depleted stocks of powder and shot for the siege guns in continuous action before the walls of the city.

Towards the last week of September, matters had become urgent in the Allied camp; ammunition stocks were getting to be low, and the convoy laden with supplies from Ostend was eagerly awaited. Erle was to command the covering force for the vital munitions, but had only twelve infantry battalions (about 6,000 men) and a single squadron of cavalry with which to undertake the task. So Marlborough deployed Major-General John Richmond Webb to Thorout with twelve more battalions, and a strong force of cavalry under William Cadogan was sent to Roulers to be ready to move to his support. Late on 27 September, the convoy began to move southwards from

Ostend and the following day Comte de la Motte, the French commander in Ghent and Bruges, moved out to intercept the wagons. He had a vastly more powerful force of thirty-five battalions and sixty-two squadrons and may well have hoped for an easy success over the Allied escort. Whether or not this was so, for de la Motte to destroy or seriously impede the convoy would deal a terrible blow to Marlborough's campaign.

The initial action came in Oudenburg the next day when de la Motte's advanced guard clashed in the market-square with a Scots battalion in Dutch service, which had been sent there to guard the flank of the approaching convoy. After a brief but fierce engagement, a fresh brigade of infantry under Brigadier-General Landsberg was sent in to help the Scots, and the French drew off, looking for a fresh opening further along the road: 'They came in at one end of the village just as a detachment of twelve companies of grenadiers of our troops came in at the other ... Our people obliged the enemy to retire with the loss of about two hundred men.'[1] Count Lottum, commanding a detachment of Cadogan's cavalry, had pressed on from Roulers and detected the main French force approaching from the north, near to the hamlet of Ichtegem, just a few miles from Wynendael. Lottum promptly alerted Webb to de la Motte's advance. By taking this route, the French would neatly intercept the convoy on the road to Menin, but Webb quickly gathered his infantry and took up a good position between woods, close to Wynendael Chateau. Lottum used his few squadrons to cover this deployment, and his troopers soon brushed with the French, slowing the pace of their approach as they groped forward to establish the strength of the opposition ahead of them.

Webb now ordered Lottum's squadrons out of the way, pulling them back behind the infantry to cover the wagons trundling along the road leading south. Taking advantage of the wooded terrain, Webb deployed a Prussian and a Hanoverian battalion into the copses nearest to the road from Bruges while the rest of his infantry drew up between the trees themselves. The avenue of approach was very restricted and offered de la Motte no room to manoeuvre, but the Comte got a battery into place and opened fire on the Allied infantry. These troops were ordered to lie down for shelter from the artillery: 'Webb ordered his men to lie flat on the ground, by which the cannon did little, or no hurt'.[2] In any case, the advance of the French infantry soon masked the battery, forcing the gunners to stop firing for fear of hitting their own comrades.

At about 5.00 p.m. on 28 September, de la Motte sent his infantry in to the attack on Webb's small army. The French troops came on in four lines in perfect order, but due to the limited frontage available their flanks almost literally brushed the woods on either side, and these copses were thick with Allied soldiers. Suddenly, the French were struck by intense musketry from their front and both flanks; those on the outside instinctively crowded inwards away from the fire, and the centre companies were thrown into disarray. The advance ground to an abrupt halt in ghastly confusion, and it took some time for the attacking infantry to recover their order in the gathering twilight.

The French officers led their soldiers forward into the attack once again, but the dead and wounded choked the ground, tripping them and throwing their ranks into disarray once more. Squadrons of French cavalry forming the second echelon were ordered forward to force a way through, but the thunderous noise of the musketry volleys maddened the horses, adding to the mayhem in the smoke-filled avenue between the trees. Reforming their ravaged ranks, the French soldiers came on a third time, and with great determination some even broke through two battalions of Allied infantry in a vicious bayonet-point struggle. Webb had just hurried in to support his last reserve – three battalions of infantry who had been the close escort for the convoy. If they gave way then the wagons and Marlborough's campaign would be lost. These fresh troops were equal to the task and coolly poured murderous volleys into the French ranks, whose leading companies were annihilated in the storm of fire. Marlborough wrote afterwards that about 1,000 dead French soldiers were counted lying all tumbled together in the congested gap between the woods. Utterly exhausted, de la Motte's soldiers fell back from contact with Webb's line of battle.

So intent was de la Motte in forcing his way through the line of Allied infantry that he lost the chance to use his own cavalry to strike at the convoy which, only thinly protected by Lottum, was making off in ponderous fashion towards Cadogan's approaching cavalry. The opportunity slipped away from the French commander, who had been able to see the wagons passing behind the Allied infantry, and the convoy reached safety. Cadogan offered to put in a counter-attack on the battered French units, but Webb rightly felt that he had insufficient strength to achieve very much in the growing darkness. He withdrew his infantry as night came on, and de la Motte's troops did not try to pursue them. The action had been brief but very fierce indeed: over 3,000 French had fallen, killed or wounded; and Webb's losses, at nearly 1,000, were not by any measure slight (as a percentage of the troops engaged, they were actually a greater loss than that suffered by de la Motte). The French commander had not scouted the position between the woods properly, and in the withering crossfire of Allied musketry his troops had paid a terrible price for his impatience to get at the convoy. The real success of the day came in the successful passage of the wagons, free from harm. Not all the Allied troops performed as well as they might have done, however, for a subsequent court-martial heard: 'Ensign Colville [Cameronians] stated that he had heard say that during the action Sinclair had bowed himself towards the ground for a considerable time together.'[3]

An unfortunate disagreement resulted from the success at Wynendael. Marlborough's despatch to London appeared to credit his close friend William Cadogan with the success, on terms at least equally glowing as those to Webb, whose victory it truly was. The Duke wrote to Godolphin: 'Webb and Cadogan have on this occasion, as they always will do, behaved themselves extremely well. The success of this vigorous action is, in great measure, owing to them.'[4] Marlborough soon amended his account to give added and proper recognition to Webb for his fine achievement, but great offence had been taken at the supposed insult, and the two men were never really on good terms again. Richard Kane's laconic comment on the whole affair was: 'Webb gained great honour by the gallant action, though a great deal was owing to Lamotte's ill-conduct; and Webb spoiled it, by boasting too much of it.'[5]

The Duke of Vendôme was understandably exasperated at the failure at Wynendael to intercept the important Allied convoy, the destruction of which would have ruined the whole campaign against Lille. The resupply operation had provided the Allied army with a quarter of a million pounds of gunpowder – enough to sustain two week's bombardment at the present rate of firing. On the same day that the battle was fought, the Chevalier de Luxembourg managed to get a resupply of gunpowder into Lille. He used the desperate expedient of having 600 dragoons bluff their way through the Allied lines (using in their hats the green bough field symbol of their opponents and giving the answers to challenges in German) with bags of the powder strapped across the saddle-bows. They came along the main road from Douai, and in the resulting confusion and exchange of shots some of the bags caught fire, the resulting explosions destroying riders and mounts. A surprising number of the dragoons got through the chaos all the same, with enough powder to sustain Boufflers's batteries for several weeks. The Marquis de Béthune, who led the dragoons, was taken prisoner along with sixty of his men. The Duc de St Simon wrote of the exploit: 'It enabled the garrison to sustain with vigour the fresh attacks that were directed at them ... but all was in vain.'[6]

The tenaillon on which Marlborough's troops had gained a foot-hold on 23 September was finally secured after ten days' fighting; the final attack was made in broad daylight and succeeded, unlike many of the efforts mounted at night. On 5 October, in an effort to take the initiative and prevent any more such resupply oper-ations from Ostend, the French army commander reinforced the troops in place between Nieuport and Plaes-Endal. 'He has cut all the dykes', Marlborough wrote, 'so that the whole country is under water.'[7] Vendôme then advanced upon Ostend, but on learning that Marlborough had moved reinforcements to Rosselaer and was there in person with about 45,000 troops, he turned back, taking up a posi-tion at Oudenburg. Hampered from finding a good place to position his army by the rapidly spreading floodwaters in the area, a major part of which was the result of hard work by his own engineers, Vendôme then fell back once more behind the Ghent-Bruges canal on 9 October.

By 12 October, a significant part of the main counterscarp of Lille was in Allied hands, and preparations were being made to drain the water-filled ditch. A substantial quantity of munitions and provisions in Ostend was again ready to be taken along to the hungry Allied army. William Cadogan was sent by Marlborough with eight infantry battalions and nine squadrons of cavalry and dragoons to escort the fresh convoy past the French posts on either side of the precarious route. Brigadier-General Grumbkow was detached with a large bri-gade of five Prussian battalions to meet Cadogan on the road. The supplies had first to be ferried in barges across the flooded terrain to the drier ground to the south of Leffinghem. There the wagons, fitted with outsize wheels to keep their cargo dry, would be able to operate almost normally. Marlborough had the whole Allied covering army standing by at one hour's notice to march in case word was received that Vendôme was coming out from behind the canal to threaten the resupply operation once more. On 15 October, Baron Fagel was sent northwards with another twenty infantry battalions and twenty mounted squadrons to support Cadogan,.

The tactics now used by the French were, however, something of a surprise. Six armed galleys, packed with cannon and musketeers, sailed out from Nieuport along the Bruges canal under the command of the Marquis de Langeon. They attacked the Allied-held post at Leffinghem, the loss of which would neatly interrupt the route by which the supplies were being taken. The French attempt was spirited and had a certain novelty about it, but after a promising start it failed, and the galleys were driven off. On 19 October, Cadogan was able to get a large quantity of gunpowder and other stores safely through to the hungry besieging army. Marlborough wrote to London:

> Their galleys and armed boats roamed over the very places where we had posted our men, whereby they have destroyed a great tract of land for many years and prevented our drawing any thing from there, however we have got over nearly seventeen hundred barrels of powder.[8]

A few days earlier Marlborough had been forced to reduce his troops' rations by one third to conserve stocks, the soldiers being given a cash payment instead. There was little food to buy in the sutler's tents by this time, so this was compensation for hardship rather than anything else, although Marlborough did arrange an extra salt ration to be given out. This reduction was necessary despite the Duke's foraging parties ranging into France once again as far as La Bassée and Armentières in their search for supplies. On 19 October, Veldt-Marshal Overkirk, the stalwart 67-year-old Dutch veteran, died of strain at Rosselaer, removing from Marlborough's side one of his most reliable colleagues. The highly capable Arnold Joost van Keppel, Earl Albemarle, took his place for the time being.

French efforts to interrupt the supply of the army continued but were mostly unsuccessful. At Lille, the defences were crumbling under the remorseless weight of Allied battery fire forward of the third parallel. 'They have mounted nearly fifty pieces of cannon', Marlborough wrote with satisfaction (although he understated the actual number), 'besides a battery of mortars upon the counterscarp.'[9] A thirty-yard-wide breach had been made in the main fortifications, and at 4.00 p.m. on 22 October the Marshal offered to capitulate the city. The defence had endured for a very creditable sixty days, but the ruined St Magdalene gate, scene of much bitter fighting in the previous weeks, was handed over to Allied troops the next day as a symbol of submission. 'The place had become untenable', St Simon remembered, 'the provisions were all eaten up; there was nothing for it but to submit.'[10] On 25 October, the French commander withdrew his surviving troops, some 6,000 strong, into the citadel, from where he would fight on. The locally recruited citizen militia were released from service and permitted to go home; Boufflers realised he would have mouths enough to feed in the citadel without their help. Prince Eugene signed the articles of capitulation without reading the terms in detail, declaring, as a compliment to the fine performance of the defenders, that there was nothing that the Marshal, as a man of honour, could request of him that would not immediately be granted. The Duke wrote on 1 November that he could report:

> No news from the siege where our batteries were to begin to fire this morning against the citadel. Our people took the advantage of the cessation to carry on the approaches with very good success, and without any loss.[11]

That same week, the French had made a number of probing attacks on the small garrison in Leffinghem, all of which were stoutly resisted. However, on 28 October, after a relieving Allied force had got to the place, the French tried again, and this time they had been successful. The garrison, all of whom were killed or taken prisoner, were said to have celebrated the fall of Lille more than was wise and been too drunk to fight properly. However this might have been, the road south from Ostend was once again under pressure, and Marlborough resumed his raids into Artois to gather what supplies were to be obtained from that ravaged region instead.

The citadel soon proved to be just as formidable as the main fortress. John Millner wrote that the besiegers:

> By sapping and otherwise, expeditiously encroached and approached to the farthest extent that possibly they could, until at last they erected their batteries on the glacis, with the muzzles of their cannon quite over the very top of the pallisadoes.'[12]

Millner also recalled that the French sent in frequent small sorties to disrupt the siege operations, and these were driven off in fierce, close-quarter fighting, with many casualties on both sides.

Vendôme still held the line of the Scheldt, but the Ostend resupply convoys had been Marlborough's effective answer to the blockade of the Allied army. The muddy track that led from the coast had enabled Marlborough to feed his army and his guns; however, the French army commander now attempted to lift the siege of Lille citadel by having the Elector of Bavaria march on Brussels. The Elector had newly arrived in the Spanish Netherlands from his duties on the Rhine, and liked to believe that the citzens retained fond memories of him when he was the Governor-General. On 21 November, he advanced from Hal with eighteen cavalry squadrons and fourteen infantry battalion (about 15,000 troops), and the following day they were before the gates of Brussels. The city was now only lightly garrisoned as Allied troops had been drawn away to the siege operations. Still, the governor of the city, Colonel (subsequently Major-General) Pasqual, was a tough character. He refused an imperious summons to submit or face a storm, regretting that he had not the honour of being acquainted with the Elector, but he was quite satisfied with his small garrison and the position they held. Pasqual coolly added that he would defend the city against any attack as his duty required him to do – that was that. The Elector had to begin an artillery bombardment on the Namur gate in an attempt to intimidate Pasqual into surrender. This, however, was slow work as only a small siege train was present. The rather scratch garrison, consisting of four under-strength infantry battalions including sick men who were drafted into the trenches, put up a good fight. Pasqual was evidently very resourceful, and understood his men well. He ordered that each soldier who helped defend the rather outdated fortifications of Brussels should receive an extra ration of fresh meat, beer and brandy for each day that they manned their posts. Some severe fighting took place, but all the Elector's efforts to break into the city were driven back.

Marlborough could manage with the line of the Scheldt in the hands of the French, but the loss of Brussels would alarm the Dutch and became a serious embarrassment. On 26 November, the Duke's army, reinforced with as many troops as Eugene could spare from the siege, moved rapidly forward from Courtrai. The line of the Scheldt was forced at two points: Kerkhoff and Gavre. The troops crossed the wide river on pontoon bridges, taking the French by such surprise that little resistance was met, and they 'Made off in great haste and hurry, disorder and confusions.'[13] A crossing was also made at Oudenarde, and a strong Allied advanced guard, formed of English Foot Guards with cavalry support, was pushed to Alost to the west of Brussels. The Elector had no choice but to draw off from his attempt to take the city, abandoning twelve heavy guns and four mortars, stores and even his wounded in the haste. 'About the break of day, a great deal of deserters from the French were at our port [gate], and gave us an account of their flying ... the governor of the city ordered to every gunner ten pistoles of Smart Money.'[14] With the city secure and the line of the Scheldt now safely in his hands, Marlborough's lines of supply into Holland were once again open, at a cost of 413 killed and wounded in the Brussels garrison. Vendôme and the Elector fell back grudgingly to the south, leaving the troops north of the Ghent-Bruges canal under the command of Comte de la Motte who more or less had to fend for himself. In the trenches meanwhile, the siege operations against the citadel of Lille ground on under Eugene's direction; the cost was still heavy, but it was now just a matter of time.

The Duke of Berwick, who had now returned to command the French army in Alsace, wrote: 'I received a private letter from the Duke of Marlborough signifying that the present occasion was a very favourable one, to set on foot a negotiation for peace.'[15] The timing had a certain promise, as can easily be seen: with the French suffering such setbacks in the Low Countries, they might be amenable to a fair offer of peace terms. In the same way, the Allies, having gained so much since the start of the year, might be able on the back of that success to drive a satisfyingly hard bargain. However, Berwick went on to scoff: 'De Chamillart has taken it into his head that this proposal of the Duke of Marlborough proceeded only from the bad situation the Allied army was in.' This was not the first occasion the French Minister of War had misread the signals in the conduct of the operations.

The laborious work of setting up the batteries at the closest possible point to the citadel of Lille was complete by 6 December, the onset of cold weather having hardened the ground and made the movement of the pieces easier. Twenty-six 24-pounder guns, twelve large mortars and twelve howitzers were in place, and Eugene issued a formal summons to Boufflers to capitulate. Three days later at 9.00 p.m. in the evening the Marshal signed the articles of capitulation. A distinguished veteran of many wars, Boufflers had fought a skilful and vigorous campaign, tying down the Allied armies and occupying the attentions of Marlborough and Eugene for over four precious months. This valour, both in defence of the city and the citadel, was recognised by the Duke; the Marshal and his surviving troops, without giving their parole, were permitted to march away to Douai on 11 December 1708 with all the honours of war, their regimental colours and arms intact, and with drums beating bravely. John Deane of the 1st English Foot Guards recalled:

> Marshal de Boufflers was admitted to march out at the head of his troops with flying colours, six pieces of cannon and ten covered wagons, and to be safe conducted to Douai, which was accordingly done. The number of what marched out in all, both sick, well and wounded, was computed to be about 6,000.[16]

Louis XIV was aware of the impending submission, and Boufflers had consulted him on the terms to be sought for the garrison. The King wrote from Versailles two days later, with warm praise for the Marshal, acknowledging the fine effort made to defend Lille and the citadel:

I cannot sufficiently praise your vigour, and the pertinacity of the troops under your command. To the very end they have backed up your courage and zeal. I have given the senior officers special proof of my satisfaction with the manner in which they have defended the town. You are to assure them, and the whole of the garrison, that I have every reason to be satisfied with them. You are to report to me as soon as you have made the necessary arrangements for the troops. I hope these will not detain you, and that I shall have the satisfaction of telling you myself that the latest proof you have given of your devotion to my service strengthens the sentiments of respect and friendship which I have for you, and of which you shall receive proof on every occasion which presents itself.[17]

The overall cost of the huge operation is well illustrated by John Millner when he calculates that overall, including the casualties at Wynendael in late September, it had cost the Allied army some 16,000 men to gain Lille:

It was said that Monsieur Boufflers said, that if the Allies must needs take Lille, before that they left it, that they must gain it inch by inch; and indeed we may safely say that he in a manner was as good as his word; and no wonder, the great hindrance of the want of ammunition was a great baulk to the besiegers vigorous proceeding, all our passes most of time thereof being obstructed by their huge army dispersed up and down between us and our garrisons [bases] … Nevertheless, the valour, vigilance, activity, consummate skill, and unanimity of the Duke and Prince Eugene, with our other generals, together with the resolution, courage, and indefatigable labour of the troops, in their good conduct and care, did at last overcome all difficulties.[18]

The actual loss suffered by the Allied army was given as 11,947 in the siege of the city, with another 1,044 casualties in the attack on the citadel. This takes no account of the casualties in the various covering force operations, foraging raids into France, the actions at Wynendael and Brussels or the land-sea actions around Plas-Endael, Leffinghem and Ostend to bring forward the supply wagons; so Millner may not be far off the mark with his estimate.

Despite the elaborate courtesies of the surrender ceremony, nothing could disguise the gravity and significance of the series of defeats for France at this time. Lille was the second largest and most populous city in France, and its loss was felt keenly by Louis XIV. Of Boufflers's original garrison of over 15,000 men, some 7,000 had been killed or wounded, or become invalid through sickness. An enemy army, commanded by an Englishman who had once been in the King's own service, was now camped in his realm, levying contributions and supplies at will across a wide area of Artois and Picardy. Huge sums of money were still being authorised to be paid to save the towns along France's northern border from being sacked and burned at Marlborough's pleasure. 'Without an infinite number of extraordinary events. It was impossible for us to have lost Lille.'[19] To the observer, this had undeniably been a dire campaign for France.

However, the fortification of Lille, constructed at massive expense under the direction of Marshal Vauban, had undoubtedly served its intended purpose. The Allied army, victorious after Oudenarde in July, had devoted more than four grinding months and spent the lives of thousands of its veterans to take the place. Despite the very natural regret felt in Versailles at the loss of the city, time had been traded for space, and the French army, so prostrate after the grossly misman-aged battle beside the Scheldt river, had been allowed enough space in which to catch its breath and, to a degree, recover. Quite literally, it had survived to fight another day. This, in the grim autumn months of 1708, was as much of an achievement as Louis XIV could wish for, even if cherished Lille had been the price that had to be paid. One of the main purposes of a fortress in warfare, to impose delay upon an opponent, has rarely been shown to better effect.

By 11 December, as the weather deteriorated, Marlborough began moving his army northwards to threaten Ghent. The investment of the city began two days later and was completed by 18 December, when Eugene closed up with a strong detachment from Lille. Although Vendôme at least half-expected it, the French commander in Ghent, the Comte de la Motte, was caught off-guard by this march, and the crossing places over the Ghent-Bruge canal were poorly guarded. Louis XIV, however, had convinced himself that after the exertions of the siege of Lille, Marlborough and Eugene would send their troops off to winter quarters without attempting anything more. This would have certainly been the normal course to take so late in the season; the French garrisons to the north of the canal had already begun to disperse to winter quarters themselves and had to be hastily reas-sembled to meet the new Allied advance. They were too slow to stop Marlborough's investment of Ghent. As soon as the French King learned of the new Allied move, he sent Marshal Boufflers to Douai to gather together a force with which to interfere with Marlborough's plans, but by then it was too late.

A deputation of prominent citizens from Ghent came to the Duke with a plea that they should be spared a bombardment: 'That the town might not be destroyed by the bombs and fire-balls.' The Duke was unbending, and he wrote on 17 December to London: 'Since they had brought this misfortune upon themselves [by their prompt defection in July] they must either assist us against the garrison or expect we should use all manner of extremity to reduce them to their duty.' The citizens replied: 'They were over-awed by a numerous garrison of thirty battalions and nineteen squadrons so that all they could do was not to assist the garrison.' The Duke then suggested that they 'Declare to the Spanish and Walloon troops which make part of the garrison that if they would immediately quit the French interest and come over to us, they would [all] be favourably received.'[20]

Count Lottum was tasked with the siege of the place while Eugene's troops, relieved from their arduous duties around Lille, provided the covering force between the Scheldt and the Dender. The French garrison in Ghent was nearly 18,000 strong, well posted and amply supplied with artillery and provisions. Nonetheless, frost hardened the ground, movement became easy and Lottum pressed the operations forward vigorously. The trenches were opened on Christmas Eve, and the main batteries were quickly established now that he could move his guns freely. At least one sally by the French garrison drove North and Grey's Regiment back some way before they recovered their order, but an outwork known as Fort Rouge was evacuated by the French, conveniently opening up a direct line of supply northwards to Holland.

De la Motte received rather pointed exhortations from the Michel de Chamillart that he should trust to the strength of his defences and stand firm, at the risk of his own reputation if he gave way too quickly:

> The preservation of Ghent is of so great importance, that you can never take too many precautions ... You have good officers, capable of seconding you ... it is for your interest, in the present occasion, to merit, by your conduct, the rewards of his Majesty to which you have been so long aspiring ... Dispute the ground inch by inch, as Marshal Boufflers has done at Lille.'[21]

A copy of de Chamillart's letter actually fell into Marlborough's hands, and he wrote to a friend with a word of caution lest the

French should find it out: 'The enclosed is a copy of a letter written by M. Chamillart to the Comte de la Motte. It should not be seen by many, for fear the French should hear of my having a copy.'[22] The Allied bombardment began in earnest at 10.00 a.m. on 29 December with heavy mortars adding to the onslaught. Within two hours, a deputation was sent by de la Motte to negotiate terms. It was agreed that the garrison would give up both town and citadel within three days and withdraw with 'all the usual marks of honour' if the Allies had not been forced to abandon their operations by then. There was plainly going to be no French attempt at a relief operation, and so de la Motte was permitted to march away with his troops on 2 January 1709. Marlborough wrote the next day:

> The garrison was so numerous that they were from ten in the morning until near seven at night before they had all passed the gate. This morning I visited the works, which I find in as good a condition, that they might have given me much trouble.[23]

Marlborough had been willing to grant the Comte good terms promptly and bring operations to a close as the recent spell of fine weather was over; his soldiers in the trenches were exposed to the increasingly bitter cold and needed shelter. Bruges followed suit shortly afterwards when the Marquis de Grimaldi evacuated the place, as did the lesser French garrisons in Leffinghem and Plas-Endael. The citizens of the region, bending this way and that with the varying fortunes of the war, received Marlborough with all pomp and ceremony. They expressed themselves very glad to be, once again, subjects of Archduke Charles and free from French oppression.

It had been an astonishing, epic campaign. Marlborough and Eugene, with boundless confidence in their own abilities and those of the men they commanded, had defeated a numerically stronger French army on the banks of the Scheldt in July, and then stepped deep into northern France to seize one of Louis XIV's most cherished city and fortress. A complex and demanding siege operation lasting many months had been required for this, but all the efforts of skilled and brave French commanders to save Lille had failed. When that fell, and even with the onset of the bitterest cold weather in living memory, the Allied commanders had not paused. They struck northwards to regain Ghent and Bruges and force the withdrawal of the powerful French garrisons, once more freeing the valuable waterways in the region for the use of Allied supply convoys in the next campaign.

Marlborough could now send his shivering soldiers off to their winter quarters. It was not a moment too soon as they suffered in the severe weather, which really set in with increasing effect from 5 January onwards. The Duke wrote from Brussels two days later: 'I was afraid we should have had a very wet season here, it having rained two days together, but since yesterday morning it has frozen very hard, which comes very opportunely for the march of the troops to their winter quarters.'[24] The 'Great Frost' as it became known would soon cause terrible hardship: as the soldiers shivered in the billets, sentries were found frozen to death at their posts and even, as one veteran recalled, died of cold while on the march. In France, where the population had been weakened by years of war, starvation gripped many areas, livestock and mature vines died of the cold, and there was unrest in some towns. The currency was devalued, and noble families were encouraged to donate their silver plate to the Mint – rather reluctantly, many did so. French plenipotentiaries were in discussion with the Allies and attempting to find terms for an acceptable peace; they were ordered by Versailles to redouble their efforts.

NOTES

1. G. Murray, *Letters and Dispatches of the Duke of Marlborough*, Vol IV, 1845, p. 243.

2. R. Kane, *Campaigns of King William and Queen Anne*, 1745, p. 79.

3. C.T. Atkinson, *Wynendael*, JSAHR, 1956, p. 125.

4. W.S. Churchill, *Marlborough, His Life and Times*, Vol II, 1947, p. 450.

5. Kane, *Campaigns* p. 79.

6. B. St John, *Memoirs of the Duc de St Simon*, Vol II, 1879, p. 41.

7. W. Coxe, *Memoirs of John, Duke of Marlborough*, Vol II, 1848, p. 303.

8. Churchill, *Marlborough* p. 453.

9. Murray, *Letters and Dispatches*, p. 269.

10. St John, *Memoirs*, p. 41.

11. Murray, *Letters and Dispatches*, p. 287.

12. J.A. Millner, *A Compendious Journal, 1702–1711*, 1736, p. 242.

13. *Ibid.*, p. 244.

14. D. McBane, *The Expert Swordsman's Companion*, 1728, pp. 137–138.

15. C. Petrie, *The Marshal Duke of Berwick*, 1953, pp. 232–233.

16. D.G. Chandler, (ed.), *Journal of John Deane*, 1984, p. 74.

17. Petrie, *The Marshal Duke*, p. 232.

18. Millner, *A Compendious Journal*, pp. 250–251.

19. Petrie, The *Marshal Duke*, p. 230.

20. Murray, *Letters and Dispatches*, p. 362. See also T. Lediard, *Life of John, Duke of Marlborough*, Vol II, 1736, p. 404.

21. Lediard, *Life of John*, p. 405.

22. Coxe, *Memoirs of John*, p. 343.

23. Murray, *Letters and Dispatches*, p. 389.

24. *Ibid.*, pp. 395–396.

VIII

The Daily Springing of New Mines: Tournai and Mons, 1709

The French defeat at Oudenarde in July 1708, the fall of Lille and the recapture by the Allies of Ghent and Bruges were closely followed by the ravages of the famous Great Frost in the winter of 1708–09. With famine in much of France – even bread riots in some towns – and his Treasury in a sorry state, Louis XIV urgently sought peace. His Minister of Foreign Affairs, the Marquis de Torcy, was in negotiation with the representatives of the Grand Alliance, with clear instructions to arrange a settlement. Matters appeared to progress well for a time, but the French, for all the plight of their country, drove a hard bargain, and the Allies were prone to divisions between themselves. The Dutch States-General felt assured that the war was now won, and became more insistent in their demands for a renewed and enlarged Barrier against future French aggression. This would unavoidably have to be carved out of the territory of the Spanish Netherlands, and Marlborough wrote to the Secretary of State, Henry Boyle, in London on 19 April 1709:

> Yesterday in the afternoon, I had a long conference with the Deputies of the States on the subject matter of their barrier in the Low Countries. They opened it by acquainting me they now expected several places more than had been formerly mentioned … I hoped at the same time they would not insist on any place but what might be absolutely necessary for their own security.[1]

Marlborough had to point out to the Dutch that the agreement had yet to be reached as to which towns were to constitute any new Barrier. Also, it was uncertain where the money was to come from to pay for the garrisons. The revenues of the Spanish Netherlands, properly part of the domain of Archduke Charles, would, after the ravages of years of war, probably prove inadequate for such a purpose. However, the Dutch also were in something of a financial plight: their expenses in the war had been ruinous, and their demands reflected this sorry fact.

There were also differences of opinion within the Grand Alliance over the likelihood of continued success in the war. Marlborough's account of a conversation he held with Hiensius, the Grand Pensionary of Holland, in April illustrates the point very well. The Duke talked of 'the misery and low ebb the French were reduced to, which was confirmed from all parts, so as to render it almost impossible for them to continue the war.'[2] Hiensius, on the other hand, was not convinced that the Allied powers were in quite such a strong position, and replied that:

> he was sorry to tell me, in confidence, he was persuaded the States [General of Holland] were under worse circumstances, though their people had been encouraged to go on hitherto by the hopes of a speedy peace, and that he dreaded the consequences if these negotiations should prove abortive.

It would soon be seen that both men were wide of the mark – France was not so reduced in power or spirits as Marlborough hoped, and the resilience of the Dutch proved greater than the Pensionary feared.

The negotiations went on and things seemed to progress for a while, with Marlborough writing in May: 'M. de Torcy has offered so much, that I have no doubt it will end in a good peace.'[3] Torcy, not for the first time, was trying to drive a wedge between the Allies and so offered the States-General a separate peace if they would withdraw from the war, but Hiensius would have none of it. The French then tried the same thing with both Britain and Austria, but the Alliance remained firm, at least for the time being. Louis XIV felt obliged to agree to almost all the terms presented to him by the Grand Alliance. Some of these were very humiliating indeed, but he could not agree to the final clause (Number 37) in the treaty he was asked to sign. This clause required the King to send his own troops to depose his grandson if Philip V refused to vacate the throne in Madrid within a strict timescale. Everything seemed settled however when Marlborough wrote on 31 May to Sir Philip Meadows: 'We have, at last, I hope, brought our affairs to a happy issue, and that the Allies will soon reap the fruits of this bloody and expensive war.'[4]

The Alliance obstinately insisted on Clause 37, and Louis XIV was equally adamant. Torcy was recalled to Versailles early in June; the peace terms were rejected by France on that one point. Marlborough was as surprised as anyone at the failure of the talks. In a letter from the Hague dated 7 June he wrote: 'Our negotiations here are at an end, by the French King's refusing to agree to our preliminary treaty … I am hastening to the army.'[5] Although the Duke had sounded rather complacent in his expectations of success in his letters during May, he had nonetheless taken care to keep his troops at a few hours notice to march, had it proved necessary.

The successful conclusion of the negotiations had been widely anticipated on both sides, and the French also looked forward to peace. Louis XIV felt obliged to explain his refusal of the terms offered to his provincial governors. This was a concession by the unbending king that was remarkable in its rarity, but their tax-gathering efforts, amongst an increasingly desperate population, had now to be renewed:

> As the hope of an early peace was so widely entertained in my kingdom, I feel that I owe it to the loyalty which my people displayed towards me throughout my reign to tell them what still prevents them from enjoying the repose which I was trying to secure for them … I pass in silence over the suggestions made to me that I should join my forces to those of the league [the Grand Alliance] and oblige the King my grandson, to abdicate if would not voluntarily consent to live in future without a kingdom, and be reduced to the condition of a private individual.[6]

There it was, and the French people by and large agreed with their King – that what was demanded of him by the Allies could not with honour be performed. Louis XIV could not be expected to force his grandson off his throne – even Marlborough recognised this in private – and so the war went on.

The entirely unexpected failure of the peace negotiations meant that the rival armies took to the field later in the year than would normally have been the case. The spring had already passed, notable for its unseasonably miserable weather, and preparations had been made to disband many of the troops in the Allied army to save money. The inevitable result of this unexpected news was some confusion and delay, and the campaign season would now be quite short. Marlborough would have no chance to revive his grand plan for a deep thrust into northern France until the following year – if his colleagues could be brought to agree of course. So the Duke turned his energy to eliminating the remaining major fortresses still held by the French along the border with the Spanish Netherlands. By the middle of the month, scouts reported that French dragoons were sweeping the region clear of the little forage that was available, and what they could not carry off they burned: 'We have a dismal account of the scarcity of forage on the ground, besides that the French troops forage and destroy the little there is before them, to distress us the more when we approach them.'[7]

The Duke of Vendôme had been removed from command of the army early in the new year, once the extent of his mismanagement at Oudenarde became known at Versailles. He was replaced by the flamboyant Claude-Louis-Hector, Marshal Villars.[8] The new commander insisted that the Duke of Burgundy should not accompany the army and get in the way. He was on the alert for Marlborough's opening moves, but his 90,000 troops had not recovered their morale and strength after the awful events of the previous autumn, so that the Marshal had to stay within his lines of defence, watching for the moment that his opponent made a mistake. In this he really had little choice, given the state of the French army, and the Marshal wrote to Louis XIV that the soldiers at this time were in a deplorable condition, with officers selling their coats to get bread for their men. Villars soon put a stop to this: he openly commandeered food supplies to feed the army, bullied contractors to provide stores and demanded regular drafts of money for his regimental paymasters to disburse.

The weather in the early summer of 1709 was poor, and preparations for the new campaign were made particularly difficult by the miserable, sodden, state of the fields, which made forage virtually unobtainable. The Duke of Marlborough carefully considered making a frontal attack on the French defensive lines, which stretched for 40 miles from St Venant on the Lys river, through La Bassée to Douai. He hoped by doing so to force a major engagement on Villars at an early stage with the 100,000 troops he had under command. William Cadogan and Daniel Dopff, having carried out a careful reconnaissance of the lines, advised against such a course, which must result in heavy losses for an uncertain result. 'If it had been reasonable, this letter would have brought you news of a battle', Marlborough wrote to his wife on 27 June, 'but Prince Eugene, myself and all the generals did not think it advisable.'[9] So Marlborough turned his attentions instead to the rival merits of the fortresses of Ypres and Tournai. He favoured the former, for that would take the Allied army close to the Channel ports, put Dunkirk and Calais under threat and hold out the chance of a revival of the plan to advance deep into northern France with the support of the Royal Navy. Prince Eugene and the Dutch generals urged that Tournai, relatively exposed between Allied-held fortresses of Lille and Ath, would be a greater prize, opening up the road for a subsequent advance on Mons with Mauberge and Le Quesnoy beyond. This also had the attraction of covering Brussels, Limburg and Brabant, while threatening to turn the French right flank with the suggestion of an advance against Namur on the Meuse. Field deputy Sicco van Goslinga wrote: 'The Duke voted for the siege of Ypres, the prince for that of Tournai. Our people, as well as Count Tilly, ranged themselves with the prince.'[10]

On 24 June 1709, the decision was taken to attack Tournai. The Allied army at first gathered with the appearance of being about to hurl itself at the French lines near La Bassée. The siege train moved by water towards Menin, as if Ypres was the intended victim (which would have been the case had Marlborough got his way). On 25 June, a new, more powerful probe was made on the French lines, strengthening the impression that an attack would be made. The French commander watched all this, uncertain just where the blow would fall, and five days later Marlborough's informant at the French court wrote: 'Villars has withdrawn all the garrisons from Mons, Tournai and Ypres, and has sent them to join the main army. This shows an attack is feared.'[11] By drawing upon his garrison troops, the Marshal bolstered the strength of the field army – clearly the prudent thing to do – but he now made the wrong choice. Watching either for a frontal attack on his position, or an Allied advance on the secondary fortresses of Aire and St Venant on the Lys, Villars shifted towards his left, thus lengthening the distance between his army and Tournai. The French commander even drew troops out of the garrison there in order to reinforce the field army. In this way, his misjudgement over where the Allied blow would fall was compounded by a weakening of his strength at the critical point.

On the evening of 26 June, Eugene was on the march with his troops towards La Bassée, but soon after midnight he turned to the east towards Tournai, which came into view at dawn: 'We marched the whole night, and early this morning invested the town on all sides.'[12] The Allied siege train began the return journey downstream to Ghent before being hauled back up the Scheldt. By evening the following day, Tournai was invested in what had been a very skilful and subtle operation, luring the French army commander into putting his weight to the west, while simultaneously shifting the whole focus of the Allied army towards the east. Villars could not hide the fact that he had been duped by Marlborough, and he tried too late to send in reinforcements to the town. The garrison commander in Tournai

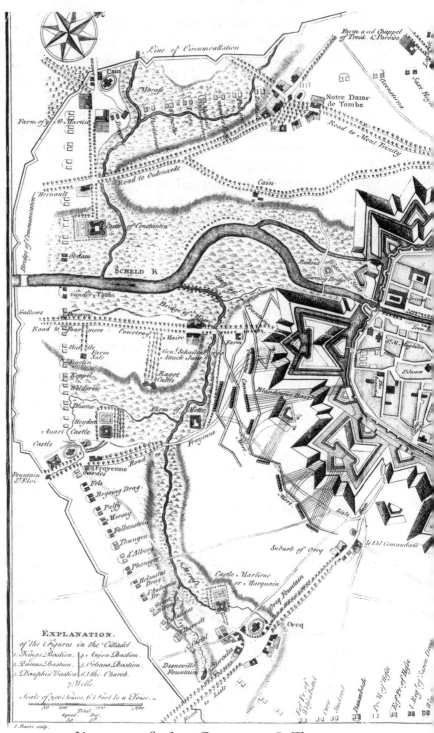

PLAN of the SIEGE of TOURNAY.

For M.r Tindal. Continuation of M.r Rapin's History of England.

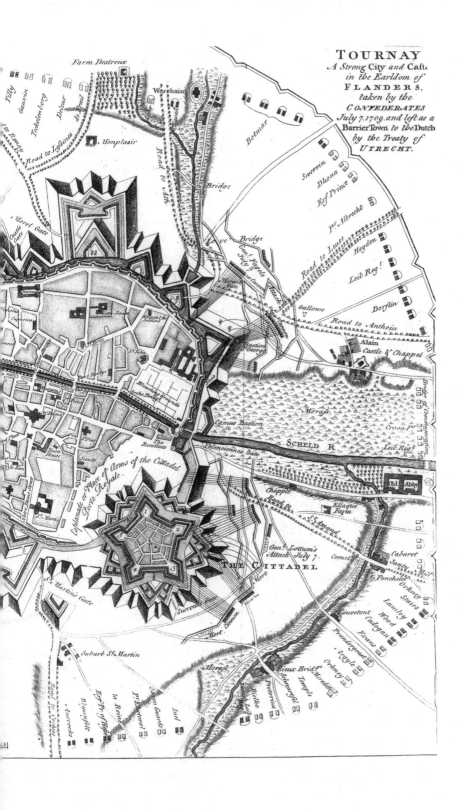

TOURNAY
*A Strong City and Castle
in the Earldom of*
FLANDERS,
taken by the
CONFEDERATES
July 7. 1709. and left as a
BarrierTown *to the* Dutch
by the Treaty of
UTRECHT.

Farm Destreux

Tilly
Gauvin
Teckelenbvrg
Detour
Road to Renly
Road to Iessins de Frail

Monplasir
Road to Ath

Warehain

Botniar

Bridge

Swerrin
Dhona
ErfPrince
Pr. Albrecht
Road to Leuse
Heyden
Leib Regt.
Dorflin

Morel Gate
Castle Gate

Louve Bridge
Geni. Vogels
July 7.

Gallows

Road to Anthoin

Alain
Castle & Chappel

St. Nicholas
Capucins
Ste. Iesuse
Little Iesuse
Holoin Che.
Soldiers
St. John

Bastion Poterne

Bridge of Tournymyton

Camus Bastion

Moraß
Croon Pr.
Leib Regt.

SCHELD R.

The Recollets
Valenciennes Gate

Old Abby

Chappel
Road &c.

St. Martin Street
Ferry Black Street
St. Marie

Esplanade or Place of Arms of the Cittadel
Porte Royale.

St. Martins Gate

THE CITTADEL
1
2
5
4
3

Geni. Lottum's
Attack July 7.

St. Amand
Elliaque
Farm

Cornet
Cabaret
Santz

le Poncheler
Orkney
Stairs

Succours Gate

Mort Esmon

Lumley
Wood
Cadogan
Evans

Suburb St. Martin

Moraß

Rieux Bridge
Pretorius
Schomygk
Temple
Orkney
Orkney
Argyle
Meredith
Prandergrast

Road to Orchies
in Reine
Wemynghe
Ancverkes
Egr. Pr. of Hesse
Dutch Guards
Iull

Bridge
King's Leiff

was the Marquis de Surville (Hautfois): 'Wounded at the siege of Lille, and has the reputation of a good officer.'[13] He had only about 7,000 troops left under his command, the rest having been drawn off by Villars in the preceding week. The surprise had been so great that de Surville had no time to clear the country around the town of cattle and forage, and some of his soldiers engaged in rounding up the herds were taken prisoner by the Allied advanced guard. Others who managed to evade capture made their escape to Condé. Even at this late stage, three infantry battalions and several squadrons of dragoons were drawn up in the town square, ready to march off to further reinforce the French field army; instead, they now hurried to help man the defences.

The Duke wrote optimistically to his wife of the whole operation: 'They expected our going to another place, so that they have not half the troops in the town they should have to defend themselves well, which makes us hope it will not cost us dear.'[14] At the same time as Marlborough and Eugene were investing Tournai, the Prince of Orange had been sent with a detachment of thirty squadrons of cavalry and ten infantry battalions to screen the minor fortresses of Mortagne and St Amand to the south. They managed to intimidate the small garrison in St Amand into abandoning the place without much resistance, and a small but inexpensive success was thus gained.

Villars and the Chevalier de Luxembourg tried to push reinforcements into Tournai from Mons and Condé to the east but were generally unsuccessful. One of these attempts was evidently a quite desperate endeavour, and Marlborough wrote to Henry Boyle on 4 July: 'M. de Villemore, a French brigadier [general], with a captain of his regiment, were taken in our camp on Tuesday morning disguised in peasants' habits, endeavouring to throw themselves into the town.'[15] The risk that the two officers ran in being taken for spies or saboteurs in this way, with all the terrible attendant punishments, was shocking. Marlborough's hope that Tournai was to be had cheaply proved to be in vain. De Surville was a tough commander; his garrison, although rather fewer than were ideal, were veteran troops; and the fortress was simply a defensive masterpiece. Richard Kane remembered: 'It was one of the best fortified places by art that is in the world, there being more works a great deal under ground than above, which made our approach very difficult.'[16]

The siege of this formidable modern fortress was to prove to be a nightmare for the Allied soldiers. Marlborough's close friend Sidney Godolphin expressed his own doubts at the prospects for early success when he wrote from London on 4 July: 'I am glad to find you continue to have so hopeful an opinion of the siege of Tournai; the people are a good deal prejudiced against it here.'[17] Villars in the meantime could be assured that with so tough an assignment before them, the Allied armies would be held in place for precious weeks in the year's short campaign season. Given the circumstances things might have been much worse for the French, whose quartermasters were still struggling to feed their troops: 'One can accustom oneself to anything, but I believe the habit of not eating is not very easy to acquire' wrote Villars, a noted epicure, at this time.[18]

When all is considered, Villars had made a perfectly good appreciation of his opponents' intentions, but been proved wrong over the choice of Tournai for a target. As it was, an Allied success against the town, if and when it came, would probably be less advantageous than one against the fortresses on the Dyle to the French left, by which route it would have been open to Marlborough to threaten the Channel ports of Gravelines, Nieuport, Dunkirk and Calais. Louis XIV recognised this, perhaps making the best of a bad job, when he wrote encouragingly to the Marshal:

By your wise dispositions and the precautions which you have taken all the vast projects [of the Allies] are reduced to the single enterprise [against Tournai] and you could not at the beginning of this campaign render me more important service.[19]

In the meantime, the digging of the approach trenches at Tournai began on the evening of 7 July. The work progressed well with the cover of darkness while the Allied siege train was being brought up the Scheldt. Although the French tried to block the route with large stones, these were soon cleared away, and by 10 July, despite heavy rain, the big guns with their ammunition and powder had arrived in the Allied camp. Prince Eugene manoeuvred with the Imperial troops to prevent Villars interrupting the operations, while Marlborough commanded at the siege itself. The weather continued to be bad, which impeded the entrenching works, and the soldiers were often knee deep in mud. Matters were made worse when the French governors of Condé and Valenciennes opened the sluice gates on the Scheldt, causing the flooding of the Allied trenches. The garrison was also able to vary the level of water in the ditches by manipulating the sluices in the town so that the conditions were absolutely miserable. In the meantime, Villars attempted a diversion by seizing Warneton and attacking Fort Rouge on the Lys, but he did not put enough weight into the effort, and he drew off when Eugene sent a relieving force to the area. Instead, the Marshal began breaking the banks of the Scheldt and Haine rivers to impede any subsequent Allied advance.

Three main attacks were mounted against Tournai under Count Lottum, Baron Fagel and Count Schulemburg; no fewer than sixty Allied battalions (perhaps 35,000 men) were engaged in the siege. Lottum's Prussian troops were directed against the citadel, while Schulemburg's Saxons went in against the St Fountaine gate. Fagel's effort with the Dutch against the Marville gate was made particularly difficult by a deep water obstacle. The French resistance was stiff, aggressive mining and counter-mining operations were soon under-way, and casualties mounted rapidly amongst the besiegers. 'By the enemies daily springing of new mines our engineers advance so very slowly' Marlborough wrote in one of his letters at this time.[20] It was soon found that the French were more adept at this kind of subterra-nean warfare than their opponents, and Marlborough's commanders struggled both to curtail the mining efforts of de Surville's engineers and to maintain the morale of their men in such awful and treacher-ous conditions. Schulemburg wrote:

> This is a siege quite different from any hitherto made; the most embarrassing thing is that few officers even among the engi-neers have any exact knowledge of this kind of underground work, and even less of the way of attacking them.[21]

Despite these difficulties, progress was gradually made, although hand-to-hand fighting took place in the dark whenever the working parties stumbled on each other in the mining and counter-mining galleries. Christian Davies, whose husband was engaged in the siege with Orkney's Regiment, commented on the brutal effectiveness of a sharpened spade for such close-quarter work in the darkness, rather than the more clumsy sword or bayonet.[22] Fagel's attack on the Marville gate failed to make progress at all, so Marlborough concen-trated his efforts on those commanded by Lottum and Schulemburg. On 26 July, a ravelin near the gate on the Valenciennes road was stormed, and the covered way from there to the Scheldt was occu-pied. For all the efforts of the garrison troops, De Surville's defences were slowly starting to fail, but the cost was high. Donald McBane remembered: 'We stormed their outerworks in the night-time, when they saw what we had done, they planted a gun directly on our flank through the wall, with one shot they killed forty-eight men.'[23]

A practicable breach in the main defences was made by the batter-ing artillery, and a major defensive position, a hornwork known as the Seven Fountains, was captured on 27 July. Almost the whole of the counterscarp on that side of Tournai was now in Allied hands. The next day, de Surville averted a general storm, with all the mayhem and destruction that would be entailed, and withdrew the survivors of his garrison (about 4,000 men) into the citadel. The governor of the town submitted on 29 July, with the Lille gate being given up straight away. De Surville was entertained to dinner by Marlborough and Eugene that evening, before taking his leave amidst mutual salutations and expressions of esteem and going into the citadel to rejoin his surviving soldiers.

Eight hundred French wounded and sick were permitted by the Allies to go to Douai, and a number of their unwounded troops hid themselves in the town and surrendered rather than fight on in the citadel. The cost so far to the besieging army was about 3,000 troops killed and wounded. The citadel of Tournai was a massively strong defensive work with five stout bastions – a regular pentagon in shape, sitting on rising ground with a gentle ascent from the town. Battery and counter-battery firing began again almost as soon as de Surville had entered the citadel but, as before with the attack on the town, mining operations soon became the most ferocious part of the siege. Robert Parker remembered: 'Our approach against the citadel was carried on mostly under ground, by sinking pits several fathoms deep, and working from these, until we came to their casemates and mines.'[24] The captain went on to describe the grim conditions in which the soldiers grappled with their opponents: 'In them our men and the enemy frequently met and fought it out.'

Schulemburg commanded the operations, which were concentrated against the St Martin's gate of the citadel, and Matthew Bishop wrote:

Of a sudden the enemy sprung a mine, which made the earth tremble under us; but it ceased in a moment ... We were prodigious hard at work in sapping the enemy, who sapped under us, and sprung several mines, which stifled great numbers of our men. Then those above would work with all their might, in order to give them below air. By that means we did save some alive.[25]

Efforts to cut off the water supply to the citadel proved ineffective, and the casualties in the muddy trenches and in the gloom of the underground workings continued to be heavy. Worst of all was the uncertainty of the sudden explosive eruption of the ground beneath the soldiers' feet as the mines, laid both by defender and, to a lesser degree, by the attackers, were blown. Both sides suffered in this way, for the Allied pioneers had begun to dig more counter-mines to foil the defenders, and Marlborough wrote that he was having bombs rolled down into the French galleries to dislodge their miners. On 5 August, a party of 150 Allied soldiers were blown up all together by the French, a day when Marlborough wrote to the Duchess:

> We should have marched this day, but for a proposition M. de Surville has made to Prince Eugene and myself of sending an officer [the Marquis de Ravignan] to Paris, for the obtaining of the King's leave for the surrendering of the citadel of the 5th of next month, in case they should not be relieved before that time … I should be glad the King would approve of this proposition, since it will save the lives of a great many men, and we cannot hope to take it much sooner.[26]

In another letter sent the same day, the Duke wrote: 'We are carrying on our attack, and this afternoon the enemy made a sortie, but were immediately repulsed.'[27] De Ravignan's mission proved fruitless, as Louis XIV would only agree to a suspension of fighting at Tournai – not a capitulation at all – as a part of a general cessation of hostilities and as a preliminary to a peace settlement. This was unacceptable to the Allies and the fighting went on.

A few days later forty men were buried when the defenders blew down a wall on them. 'We continue to push on the siege with all the caution that may be', Marlborough wrote to Henry Boyle on 22 August. 'Yesterday a new battery of fifteen mortars began to fire at [from] M. Schulemburg's attack.' The Duke went on to refer to the ever-present threat of counter-mining by the garrison: 'Our miners had the good fortune the day before to discover a mine under this battery, out of which they took eighteen barrels of powder, the enemy deferring to spring it till we should begin to fire.'[28] The very next day another massive French mine was discovered; but while it was being examined a second mine, buried beneath the first, was blown, killing and injuring many in a Hanoverian battalion gathered nearby.

At the same time that these grim subterranean operations were being pressed forward in the trenches, the Allied commanders fought their equally demanding and constant battle to supply their army. Foraging parties ranged far and wide to fill the wagons of the army, and they often encountered savage resistance from the local population, exasperated as they were at the never-ending depredations committed on their storehouse and barns; their herds and flocks; and their supply of horses. John Deane of the 1st English Foot Guards remembered that on 16 August a foraging party of Hanoverian and Hessian troops ran into an armed party of 'Boors' (peasants). After some fighting, the soldiers drew off and were forced to abandon several prisoners to the locals. These soldiers were promptly treated with great savagery. 'One man', Deane wrote, 'they cut off both his hands and put them into his haversack and bid him go home and show his comrades.'[29]

The French described the trenches and mining galleries at Tournai as an infernal labyrinth, and this was not far from the truth. The staunch resistance of the garrison and the undeniable skill of their engineers slowed the Allied operations to an agonised crawl, while the daily cost in powder, shot and soldiers' lives was daunting. A report published on 20 August 1709 went:

> Our miners and the enemy very often meet each other, when they have sharp contests till one side gives way. We have got into three or four of the enemies great galleries, which are thirty or forty feet underground and lead to several of their chambers and there we fight in armour by lanthorn [lantern] and candle, they disputing every inch of the gallery with us to hinder our finding their great mines. Yesterday we found one which was placed just under our bomb [mortar] batteries in which were 18cwt of powder besides many bombs, and if we had not been so lucky as to find it, in a very few hours our batteries and some hundreds of men had taken flight in the air.[30]

The next day a major new battery comprising fifteen large mortars was established on the covered way, at Schulemburg's attack. Adam Cardonnel, Marlborough's secretary, remembered that the troops were still up to their knees in water, but the Allied siege operations against Tournai ground steadily forward all the same. On 25 August, the Duke felt able to predict: 'Either by our advances or the enemy's want of provisions, we shall soon be masters of the place.'[31] The garrison was more than sufficient in numbers to hold the citadel but began to run short of provisions. Marlborough wrote to the Secretary of State on 31 August: 'We were agreeably surprised at six o'clock this morning by the enemy's beating the chamade and desiring to capitulate.' Aware of the poor condition of the garrison, the Duke was reluctant to grant terms: 'Their provisions are almost spent; we conclude they will be obliged to surrender in a few days on any terms.'[32] Sure enough, de Surville agreed to yield the citadel on 3 September, although he failed to gain Villars's prior approval for the decision. The French army commander would quite understandably rather have kept the Allies tied up in the expensive siege as long as possible. On 5 September, the citadel was occupied by Marlborough's weary troops. De Surville's devoted garrison had lost 3,191 men in defending the fortress and citadel, and the survivors were permitted to march away to Condé, not to serve again until formally exchanged. The officers took their swords and personal baggage, but the regimental colours, artillery and all the remaining stores had to be left in the fortress. Marlborough's casualties were 5,340 killed and wounded.

The defence of Tournai had been very well handled, even though the garrison had been unable to resist quite as long as might have been expected. De Surville's grim battle to hold out in the citadel, even though he yielded without the express permission of Marshal Villars, had held up the Allied campaign through much of the short, valuable, months of summer. This was without doubt a tactical achievement of some importance, as the options left to Marlborough and Eugene in what remained of the campaign season were now few in number.

As soon as Marlborough knew that the citadel of Tournai would yield, he sent a strong advanced guard under command of the Prince of Hesse-Cassell and Lieutenant-General Dedem to invest Mons. The capture of this fortress would almost complete the expulsion of the French from the Spanish Netherlands, restore to the Dutch the last of their cherished Barrier towns and lay the way open for the next year's campaign, perhaps with the Allies thrusting deep inside northern France. Such an eventuality must surely make the French generals stand and fight. Louis XIV was alert to the danger and sent instructions to Marshal Villars that the fortress was to be saved: 'Should Mons follow on the fate of Tournai, our case is undone ... The cost is not to be considered, the salvation of France is at stake.'[33] As Marlborough's troops prepared to take formal possession of the citadel of Tournai, Earl Orkney was sent with twenty cavalry squadrons to mask the smaller fortress of St Ghislain on the Haine river to the west of Mons. In the early morning of 6 September Hesse-Cassell's cavalry forded the Haine river at Obourg. The weather was foul and the troopers in hourly expectation of being attacked by the French army, which was reported to be on the move to the south and west. In the event, the Allied advance was not challenged, and by that evening the investment of Mons was almost complete.

Marshal Villars had quite reasonably not marched until Marlborough's intentions were clear; but spurred on by the King's instructions, he was moving forward from his lines of defence with the main army to challenge the Allied advance against Mons. The Marquis de Cheldon, taken prisoner by Allied cavalry, had no hesitation in confirming to his captors that this was so. In the afternoon of 8 September, the French commander closed up to the straggling woodland belt that lay to the south and west of Mons, initially feinting towards the north where the Allied lines of supply were most vulnerable. The following day he began to entrench a strong position in the Gap of Aulnois, between the Bois de Sars and the Bois de Lanières, near to the village of Malplaquet. Prince Eugene brought his Wing of the Allied army to combine with that of Marlborough, opposite the French position in the Gap that evening, thus interposing their full strength between Villars and the preparations for the siege of Mons. It was open to Marlborough to simply hold his ground, fending off the Marshal and his troops with one hand, while besieging the fortress with the other. However, the chance to strike at the French field army, so long sought and so long denied him, was too tempting. Villars and his army were in position nearby and disposed to fight a battle, and Marlborough would engage him where he stood.

Preparations for the emplacement of the Allied artillery were made difficult by the boggy ground, which was unfamiliar to many of Marlborough's officers. The attack was also delayed while a powerful detachment of troops under Henry Withers closed up along the road from the mopping-up operations at Tournai. During the evening of 10 September the minor fortress of St Ghislain, where the garrison was commanded by the Marquis de Legal, was stormed by a German brigade under Colonel Haxhusien. It was only on 11 September 1709 that the Allied army was ready to assault the French position in the Gap between the woods, in what became notorious as the battle of Malplaquet.

The French defences in the woods on either side of the Gap were well sited and exceptionally strong. When the fighting began, Marshal Villars's troops put up an extremely stout resistance. The initial Allied attacks were beaten off with heavy losses, but they were renewed with great bravery, and as the day wore on the French infantry were forced out of the woods on their left. That flank was then turned by the independent column, under Henry Withers, that marched onto the battlefield direct from the line of march from Tournai. Withers's attack was first blunted and then thrown back with great effort by Villars, who stripped infantry away from his centre to shore up his left flank. The Marshal was amongst those who were gravely wounded. The French centre was then pierced by British and German infantry, and an enormous cavalry battle erupted

MONS

For Mr. Tindal's Continuation of Mr. Rapin's History of England.

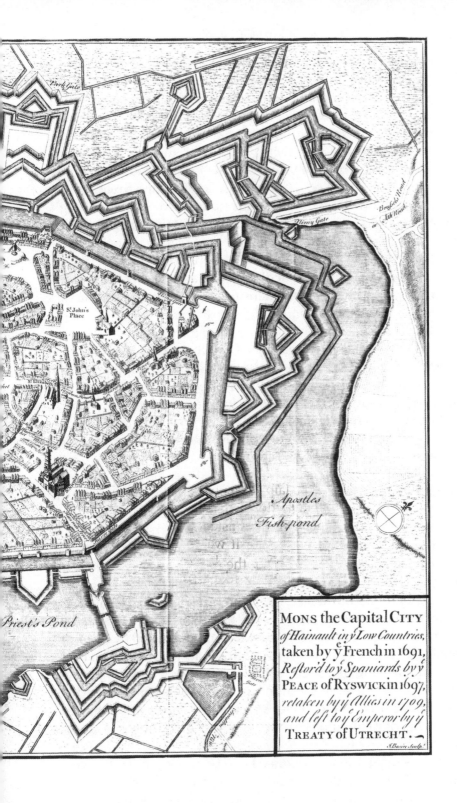

Park Gate

Brysock's Pond
or Ash Road

Pleny Gate

St John's
Place

Apostles

Fish-pond

Priest's Pond

Gate

MONS the Capital CITY
of Hainault in ȳ Low Countries,
taken by ȳ French in 1691,
Restor'd to ȳ Spaniards by ȳ
PEACE of RYSWICK in 1697,
retaken by ȳ Allies in 1709,
and left to ȳ Emperor by ȳ
TREATY of UTRECHT.

I.Basire Sculp.

in the afternoon across the plain of Malplaquet. After eight hours of the most ferocious fighting, the French had to withdraw to their lines of defence. Marlborough held the field, but his losses at some 20,000 killed and wounded were nearly twice those suffered by the French (Eugene was also injured by a musket ball, but he soon recovered). The Duke attracted heavy criticism in London (but not in Holland whose infantry bore the brunt of the losses) for his handling of the battle. The slander of a 'bloodbath' at Malplaquet found a ready audience and the notion that he had squandered his soldiers lives through complacency and incompetence – ill conceived and ill considered as it was – took hold.[34]

Field deputy Sicco van Goslinga – although so often a critic of Marlborough – wrote quite heatedly to the Hague in answer to comments reported to be made by Hiensius concerning the conduct of the battle:

> We shall be very well pleased if we finish by taking Mons. Is it, in fact, such a small thing to take two of the strongest places in Europe [Tournai and Mons], and win one of the most obstinate and bloody battles ever fought? You appear, however, to suppose that we can march straight to Paris. In truth, let me tell you; an army does not march like a traveller, finding bed and board at every stage.[35]

Villars had sought a battle at Malplaquet in order to prevent the siege of Mons, and this he failed to do. Marshal Boufflers commanded while he recovered from his wounds sustained in the battle, but the garrison was in effect left to its fate. It was of obvious importance to Marlborough and Eugene, after the heavy losses sustained at Malplaquet, that Mons should fall without much delay. The French field army, battered but intact, fell back to shelter itself behind the Rhonelle stream between Quievrain and Bavai, and the Marshal despatched troops to the lines of defence being constructed to cover the town of Mauberge to the south-east. He attempted little more other than reinforcing the garrisons at Douai, Charleroi and Landrecies. Boufflers also managed to slip three battalions of infantry into Mons on 19 September before the investment by the Allies was complete; the following day it would not have been possible, as the grip around the fortress tightened.

The garrison of Mons comprised 4,280 troops under the command of the Marquis de Grimaldi, a tough veteran of many such operations. The weather had turned foul again. Sorties mounted by

Grimaldi hindered the digging of the parallel trenches and the laborious preparations for the siege artillery to get into place. Boufflers' concern was now almost entirely on the security of Mauberge and Le Quesnoy. He realised that he had insufficient strength to impede the immediate Allied operations; the French troops, although they had fought stoutly in the woods at Malplaquet, were weary and not in good condition. Ammunition was short, the condition of the horses was poor due to lack of forage, and the soldiers still had insufficient to eat. Boufflers had little option but to bide his time, allow his men the chance to recover their strength, and wait for Villars to be well enough to resume the command. Despite these deficiencies, the Chevalier de Luxembourg was sent to Charleroi with a strong cavalry force to try and threaten Marlborough's lines of communication and supply to Brussels.

One Scottish dragoon wrote that Mons was 'much stronger than was thought at first, if we have it in three weeks, we shall be very well pleased.[36] The Allies deployed a total of fifty-eight infantry battalions and thirty-six squadrons of cavalry, under the overall command of Prince Eugene, although the Prince of Orange oversaw the day-to-day operations. Marlborough relieved eighteen of the hardest-hit battalions, and sent them off on garrison duty to rebuild and reconstitute themselves from their Malplaquet losses. In exchange, twenty-four fresh battalions were drawn out from various garrisons to augment the strength of the field army and its operations. The Allied siege train (sixty 24-pounders and ten large mortars) had been sent from Tournai by water to Brussels, and then dragged by teams of oxen along the sodden roads to Mons. Luxembourg's cavalry found themselves unable to interrupt the cumbersome operation.

The trenches were first opened in front of the hornwork protecting the Havre and Bartamount gates, while Marlborough commanded the covering army, in position to the south and west of the town. He wrote from Jemappes on the Trouille stream to the Secretary of State on 26 September:

Yesterday our great convoy of artillery and ammunition arrived safe at the camp, having by the precautions that were taken, met with no disturbance on the road, and the horses and wagons were immediately sent back to Brussels for another convoy, after which we shall be obliged to have a third before all can be brought up. In the evening we opened the trenches at two several attacks, one at the port of Be[a]rtamount and the other at the port of Havré, with very good success, only Mr Cadogan had the misfortune, at the breaking ground at the latter, to receive a shot in the neck.[37]

This injury was a particular concern for the Duke, who greatly valued the Quartermaster-General's tactical abilities and sound advice. Marlborough went on:

> We hope he is not in any danger, but the surgeons will give no judgement till the third or fourth dressing; they cannot find where the ball is lodged. Today at Noon, the French made a sortie at the port of Havré, and put our workmen in some disorder, but were soon repulsed.

One of the newly arrived units, Hill's Regiment, played a key role in repulsing the fierce sortie by the French garrison, at a loss of sixty men killed and wounded. The Allied soldiers were at first forced back some way by the briskness of the attack, but then rallied when the Hessian Regiment of Prince Albert came forward to restore the situation. Two days later the French tried again, but the besiegers were on the alert this time and promptly drove the sortie back into the fortress. The Prince of Orange had pioneers drain the inundations between Mons and St Ghislain, with the result that very soon the water level had fallen by over six feet. At the same time a fortified water-mill on the Trouille stream to the north-west of Mons, which had been used by the garrison as an outpost, was seized. The twenty-five French soldiers posted there promptly surrendered, evidently not feeling that their duty required them to sacrifice themselves for such a meagre place. On 27 September, a redoubt adjacent to the Nimy gate on the eastern side of the fortress was also stormed.

Marshal Berwick, who had come from Briançon to assist Boufflers while Villars was still recovering, probed Marlborough's covering force and found it to be too strongly posted to make an attack worthwhile. The Duke had his troops firmly in place between the Trouille and Haine rivers, with St Ghislain strongly held on his right flank; Eugene meanwhile was quite confident that the French were in no condition to make a really determined attempt to relieve Mons, and did not even trouble to erect protective lines of circumvallation for the besieging army. Accordingly, the soldiers were spared the effort and labour.

The French army was slowly gathering its strength again, Louis XIV having ordered that each garrison town in France should provide a draft of fifty soldiers to fill out the ranks of the depleted regiments. However, the Duc de St Simon wrote of the state of the troops army at this time:

> Men were without bread and without pay; the subaltern officers were compelled to eat the regulation bread, the general officers were reduced to the most miserable shift and were, like the private soldiers, without pay ... Under the circumstances it was impossible to persevere in trying to save Mons.[38]

A preliminary bombardment by two small batteries of Eugene's artillery had succeeded in dismounting several of the defenders' guns, and on 1 October the major battery, comprising thirty 24-pounder guns, was ready and the bombardment proper could begin. The covered way protecting the Havré gate on the south side of the fortress was stormed almost immediately, and the hornwork protecting the Park gate on the north side was attacked at the same time. The Allied soldiers advanced waist-deep through the water obstacle with such determination that the 450 French troops stationed at the gate promptly threw down their weapons and gave themselves up. Their officers protested that this was contrary to the commands they had given, but had which been disregarded; three of them, but not their soldiers, were permitted to withdraw into the fortress to continue the struggle.

The next day, the outer defences of the Bartamount gate on the west side up against the citadel, were captured and another great battery of thirty-two guns was then established to begin the serious breaching work. The Espinlien redoubt, beside the Park gate where the Trouille stream ran into the outer defences, was captured and seventy prisoners taken with slight loss to the Allies. The bombardment grew in intensity as the days passed, and the three salient angles of the hornwork protecting the Bartamount gate were reached by the besiegers by 8 October:

> About nine in the morning, in a heavy soaking rain, a great body of the besiegers vigorously attacked the high counterscarp and after two hours short and sharp dispute of assaults and repulses, they took it and also the most of the outer-works in the front of their approaches.[39]

Five days later, in driving rain that made the approaches slippery and treacherous, the Allied soldiers stormed part of the counterscarp at the Havré gate on the southern side in two hours of fierce hand-to-hand fighting. Marshal Boufflers in the meantime was torn between the natural desire to relieve Mons, which would almost certainly bring on a general action that he could hardly hope to win, and the sure knowledge that once Mons fell, the attentions of Marlborough and Eugene would very soon turn elsewhere, probably to Mauberge or Le Quesnoy. If Grimaldi could hold out long enough, however, the campaign season would have passed before this could happen.

Late in the evening of 17 October, a strong party of grenadiers seized a small ravelin on the edge of the main defences of the Bartamount gate with very little loss. Two batteries of heavy guns could as a result be manhandled forward to widen, at almost point-blank range, a major breach that they had already begun to make in the defences near to the citadel. The battery commander, Captain Pettit, showed great initiative in getting his guns forward across the rough ground, swept as it was with scorching defensive fire. He was struck several times by musket balls but was saved by his breastplate each time. Work began at this time to drain the extensive flooding on the south side of the fortress. The defences at the Bartamount and Havré gates were all coming to pieces, and rather than face a storm, which could not be long delayed, the Marquis de Grimaldi beat the chamade and asked for terms at noon on 19 October. Hostages were exchanged while the negotiations progressed, and the Nimy gate was surrendered on 21 October. John Millner recorded in his journal:

> At break of day, all the batteries accordingly began to play, and played a great deal of vigour and fury ... which so scared and terrified the besieged, that Monsieur Grimaldi, the same day about noon, beat a parley, and capitulated on honourable terms, whereupon, the next morning, [he] delivered to the besiegers one of the gates of the city; and on the 12th [Old Style dating – see Appendix 1] they marched out thereof, with the usual marks of honour, to the nearest garrison viz: eight battalions and one squadron to Charleroi, and six battalions and one squadron to Namur.[40]

The Marquis also had to leave all his artillery, munitions and stores in the town. James Cathcart, who took part in the operations with Stair's Dragoons, left an account of the poor condition to which the garrison was reduced as they marched out 'The miserablest wretches that ever carried arms.'[41] They might have appeared so, but Grimaldi's garrison had lost 980 killed and wounded in the defence of Mons, while the Allied casualties were 2,201, of whom 555 were killed.

Marlborough now considered the chances of advancing to engage the French forces in the lines of defence covering Mauberge but thought better of it – the weary state of his troops, the general lack of forage for the horses, and the deteriorating weather were not at all encouraging. Boufflers (Villars was still convalescent) feared just such an attempt, if not against Mauberge then perhaps Valenciennes or Le Quesnoy, and manoeuvred his threadbare army to meet any renewed Allied advance. The Duke felt that his army had done enough that year, and so the siege train was sent away to Brussels on 26 October; two days later the field army began to disperse to winter quarters. The strains of this grim campaign were beginning to show, and cases of indiscipline in the ranks of both armies had risen noticeably. A French observer wrote of the events of the summer and autumn:

> Thus ended a campaign which had begun under the most terrifying circumstances for France and the most difficult for the general charged with the defence of the frontiers ... Marshal Villars, through his genius and activity, found the means to form an army out of nothing and resources in the middle of a general famine ... Although forced to give way before the superiority of his foes, he was able to stop the exploitation of their victory and the execution of their vast projects, by denying them entry into the kingdom, and reducing them to the capture of two towns [Tournai and Mons] which did not belong to France.[42]

Perhaps understandably, this overstates Villars's achievement to a certain degree. After the fall of Tournai, Louis XIV had directed the Marshal to save Mons without regard to the cost, and yet Villars had failed. Some Allied soldiers recalled that the French, after Malplaquet, had lain very quiet, not trying at all to relieve Mons, appearing to have lost more in the battle than they admitted. Perhaps so – not in numbers of the fallen, but in the manner in which they allowed Marlborough and Eugene to continue to dictate the pace of operations after the battle. The capture of Mons did offer some genuine compensation for the great Allied effort in the campaign, as it gave a measure of protection to Marlborough's left flank and rear, shielding the otherwise exposed territories in Brabant and Limburg if the Duke chose next to move closer to the Channel coast. However, the desperate condition in which the French had started the year had not been turned into disaster. The Allied campaign had proved overall to be an expensive disappointment, made more bitter by the appalling casualties suffered at Tournai and Malplaquet.

The French Minister for Foreign Affairs, Torcy, had written on 27 September: 'The last battle has rather raised the courage of the nation than weakened it.'[43] The critics of the Duke of Marlborough, bold now that his friendship with Queen Anne was faltering and no longer gave him protection, were given strong ammunition with which to trammel his reputation and service and to lay fresh slanders about his motives and conduct, in wait for the increasingly difficult campaigns to come.

NOTES

1. G. Murray, *Letters and Dispatches of the Duke of Marlborough*, Vol IV, 1845, pp. 481–482.

2. *Ibid.*, p. 476.

3. A. Alison, *Military Life of Marlborough*, 1848, p. 244.

4. Murray, *Letters and Dispatches*, p. 499.

5. *Ibid.*, p. 504.

6. C. Petrie, *The Marshal Duke of Berwick*, 1953, p. 236.

7. Murray, *Letters and Dispatches*, p. 507.

8. Vendôme had been dismissed from his command in Flanders when the extent of his indolence and the deceitful way he had reported the disaster at Oudenarde had become known at Versailles. That he was also on the worst possible terms with the Duke of Burgundy, heir to the throne, also counted against him. However, Louis XIV could not afford to lose the services of such a gifted, if flawed, man for long, and he was soon sent to command the French armies in Spain. There he did rather well, battering the Allied armies at Brihuega and Villaviciosa in December 1710, before dying of food poisoning in the following year.

9. G.M. Trevelyan, *Peace and the Protestant Succession*, 1932, p. 6.

10. W.S. Churchill, *Marlborough, His Life and Times*, Vol II, 1947, p. 571.

11. *Ibid.*, p. 570.

12. Murray, *Letters and Dispatches*, p. 520.

13. *Ibid.*, p. 520.

14. Churchill, *Marlborough*, p. 575.

15. Murray, *Letters and Dispatches*, p. 529.

16. R. Kane, *Campaigns of King William and Queen Anne*, 1736, p. 83.

17. Churchill, *Marlborough*, p. 577.

18. C.T. Atkinson, *Marlborough and the Rise of the British Army*, 1921, p. 386.

19. Churchill, *Marlborough*, p. 576.

20. *Ibid.*, p. 581.

21. *Ibid.*, p. 577.

22. J. Fortescue, (ed.) *Adventures of Mother Ross*, 1929, p. 128.

23. D. McBane, *The Expert Swordsman's Companion*, 1728, p. 139.

24. D.G. Chandler, (ed.), *Captain Robert Parker and Comte de Merode-Westerloo*, 1968, p. 84.

25. Churchill, *Marlborough*, pp. 579–580.

26. W. Coxe, *Memoirs of John, Duke of Marlborough*, Vol III, 1848, p. 425.

27. Murray, *Letters and Dispatches*, p. 569.

28. *Ibid.*, p. 577.

29. D.G. Chandler, (ed.), *Journal of John Deane*, 1984, p. 86.

30. F. Myatt, *The British Infantry*, 1983, p. 40.

31. Murray, *Letters and Dispatches*, p. 580.

32. *Ibid.*, p. 585.

33. D.G. Chandler, *Marlborough as Military Commander*, 1973, p. 251.

34. The opposing armies got into position during 9 September 1709 in woods on either side of the Gap of Aulnois near to the village of Malplaquet. Marlborough gave serious consideration to mounting an attack on the French the following day, but the artillery train of the Allied army would not be in position properly by then, and the Duke and Prince Eugene wanted to make a careful reconnaissance of the ground, which was unfamiliar to them both. The ground at Malplaquet posed several significant problems for the Allied commanders. The Gap between the Bois de Lanières and the Bois de Sars lay along a slight ridge that is a watershed, and forms the border between Belgium and France. The many creeks and boggy streams running away to the north (the Allied side) in particular, made the ground unsuitable for the siting of heavy guns without a great deal of preparation. The delay this work entailed could not easily be avoided. In addition, Henry Withers, in command of a powerful corps of cavalry and infantry, was conducting 'mopping-up' operations at Tournai and covering the huge supply trains for the Allied army. He would not arrive until 11 September, and Marlborough had an ambitious plan to throw this unmarked force onto the left flank of the French army while the battle was already in progress. Eugene referred to this in a letter sent to the Emperor in Vienna as a 'special project'. See Chandler, *Marlborough as Military Commander*, p. 257. So for good reasons, the Allied attack was delayed by two days, and the French had time to massively strengthen an already good defensive position. Had the Duke attacked on either the 9 or 10 September, when his own preparations were far from complete and his guns were not in place, he would have been rightly criticised; by waiting until all was ready, and attacking on 11 September he was still criticised, but he had been right to do so.

35. Churchill, *Marlborough*, p. 632.

36. W. Burn, *A Scots Fusilier and Dragoon under Marlborough*, 1936, pp. 92–93.

37. Murray, *Letters and Dispatches*, pp. 606–607.

38. B. St John, *Memoirs of the Duc de St Simon*, Vol II, 1879, p. 111.

39. J.A. Millner, *A Compendious Journal 1701–1712*, 1736, p. 284.

40. *Ibid*.

41. C.T. Atkinson, *Gleanings from the Cathcart Mss*, 1951, p. 100.

42. Chandler, p. 268.

43. Churchill, *Marlborough*, p. 637.

IX

This Defence was the Best:
Douai, Béthune, St Venant and Aire, 1710

The new campaign in 1710 opened with all attention on the vital theatre of war along the northern border of France. Negotiations to find a peace settlement acceptable to all parties continued and Marlborough was often, quite apart from his military duties, called on to participate in these discussions, but there was no real progress. Clause 37 remained incapable of resolution: the Allies insisted and Louis XIV could not accept it. The tone of the discussions had also noticeably changed. Marshal d'Harcourt had done well in holding Imperial forces in check on the Rhine while the Allied campaign in Spain languished, even though large numbers of French troops had been drawn away to help hold the line in the north. The French, aware that Allied power and Marlborough's influence in particular had passed its zenith, were noticed to be more confident and forthright in the discussions than in the previous year.

France still staggered under the enduring effects of the Great Frost and famine, and the memory of the rough handling that Marlborough and Eugene had repeatedly dealt out to the French armies over the previous two years was fresh and painful. Louis XIV's treasury was empty and the French people war-weary. Despite this, their success in the woods at Malplaquet, highly qualified though it undoubtedly was, had put heart back into the French generals, although they understandably remained cautious if not actually nervous. Their soldiers had stood and fought, had endured and marched off in good order, and without doubt would do so again.

The armies of the Grand Alliance stood deep in the French fortress belt. Marlborough and Eugene had achieved a great deal – at a cost – but the region was barren of forage. The Allied quartermasters had to reach back well into Brabant and Limburg for the supplies required for their army, which now comprised 155 infantry battalions and 262 squadrons of cavalry. With close on 40,000 cavalrymen and dragoons to provide for, the vast Allied array had almost reached the limit of what could be sustained in the war-ravaged and congested region. For all the illusion of their successes in the preceding two years (Oudenarde, Lille, Tournai, Malplaquet, Mons), the Allies were increasingly enmeshed in the coils so carefully laid thirty years before by Marshal Vauban. Three years after that great military engineer died, discarded by the King he had served so well, Vauban's plans for the protection of northern France were taking slow effect, as the nimble feet of the Allied commanders were made leaden. Louis XIV needed time in which to succeed in Spain itself, and Vauban gave it to him.

Marlborough's mood was made sombre by troubles in London, where his political opponents grew in strength and influence, and his wife's friendship with Queen Anne, so valuable in the past, gradually fell to pieces. 'I am so discouraged by what I see that I have never during the war, gone into the field with so heavy a heart', he wrote on 14 April.[1] Such low spirits were often felt by the Duke before the actual hard business of campaigning got underway. Once with his army though, his customary close attention to details took hold; as in the previous year, Marlborough had the option to swing right or left at the French. If he went to the right against Ypres and St Venant and Aire on the Lys river, then Brabant and Brussels would be exposed to a French raid. This was a chance that the Dutch would not readily accept, a consideration that had persuaded Marlborough to turn towards Tournai and to Malplaquet the previous year. The Duke had to cover Brussels or conduct a campaign at such a pace that his opponent had no chance to go raiding. Alternatively, an advance against Douai on the Scarpe or Béthune on the Deule would avoid such risk and lead the Allied commanders to more open terrain, better suited to the employment of their powerful cavalry – a region incidentally that was relatively untouched by war and where supplies and forage should be plentiful. At first glance it appeared that with one final heave, the Duke could achieve the long-awaited overthrow of his opponent and then be able to move out onto the wide plains of Artois and Picardy.

Villars was still recovering from the gunshot wound to his knee received at Malplaquet, and Charles de Baatz, Marshal d'Montesquiou (formerly Comte d'Artagnan) commanded in his absence. He had inspected the frontier fortresses and found that many of them were under manned and poorly stocked with ammunition and provisions. Montesquiou recommended to Versailles that a major withdrawal be undertaken to the general line of the Deule and Lys, but Louis XIV instead ordered that the fortresses were to be strengthened and held at whatever cost. Marshal Berwick had been offered the command, but he would only accept this if permitted in the right circumstances to attack Marlborough and Eugene if the chance arose. Louis XIV would not agree, and so Berwick went to command the scratch French forces in the Dauphiné instead. Uncertain just where the Allied blow would fall, Montesquiou had to reinforce both Ypres on his left and La Bassée in the centre, where, chronically short of both food and fodder, he could only initially deploy a slim force of forty infantry battalions and forty squadrons of cavalry. By the time the new campaign really got underway, this had only increased to fifty-eight battalions and seventy squadrons and many of the units were under strength. Both commanders had difficulty concentrating their armies that spring, but the Allies had made better time than their opponents.

Marlborough arrived at Tournai to take command of operations on 12 April. He had already sent an instruction to his close friend Earl Albemarle to seize Mortagne on the Scheldt, which had been by-passed by the Allies in their hectic march from Tournai to Mons the previous September. The place was seized two days later on 14 April, but lost to the Chevalier de Luxembourg the next day. Albemarle captured Mortagne for a final time on 18 April, but a simultaneous attempt against St Amand failed on account of extensive flooding of the fields nearby. Two days later, Marlborough wrote:

> We learned at the same time our having taken Mortagne, and the enemy's retaking it. On Friday [18 April] we repossessed ourselves of it, but I am every hour apprehensive of their attack-ing it again, having a great advantage of us by the help of their galleys from Condé, while the waters are exceptional; however we shall do our best to preserve it. We should have been glad to have made ourselves masters likewise of St Amand.[2]

The Duke completed the initial concentration of his army at Tournai. His full strength was not yet available, but he was also aware that d'Montesquiou was very short of provisions and, as a result, would also not fully concentrate his army for some weeks. Marlborough did not want to wait for all his own troops to arrive. He had decided to move against Douai despite its strong location; sheltered by the

Scarpe river to the north and the inundations of the Senseé to the south and east. Possession of this town should open up the roads leading towards Arras, Valenciennes and Cambrai.

On 19 April, Marlborough began his advance in four columns, each comprising about 20,000 troops, heading south over the forty miles or so to the river crossings over the Deule and Scarpe and the canal that linked the two rivers between Pont à Vendin, north of Lens, and Douai. The Duke wrote the next day:

> The troops are advancing with all diligence. We have now a good part of the army in the plain of Lille, and having made the necessary disposition of bread and forage, we propose to march this evening towards the [French] lines, in hopes to find the enemy the less prepared to defend them than if we delayed it till the whole army can join.[3]

Crossing points were successfully established at Pont à Vendin, Courrieres and Sart, but an attempt to cross at Pont Auby, closest to Douai, failed. Montesquiou had not expected such a rapid advance by Marlborough, and he promptly fell back over the Scarpe at Vitry – off-balance and outnumbered, he had little option other than to do so, and Douai was exposed in the process. On 22 April, Marlborough wrote:

> We passed the Scarpe this afternoon, in the same manner we passed the Deule yesterday. M. d'Artagnan was with his troops on the other side, but marched away in so much confusion that the soldiers found a good deal of baggage in his camp.[4]

So sudden was Marlborough's approach to the river crossings that much of the French cavalry, who should have been placed to give warnings, were dispersed and engaged in the humble, but necessary task of gathering forage. In the scramble to pull back, the French officers lost their baggage as their own servants were also out gathering forage and could not get back to camp in time.

The Chevalier de Luxembourg brought his cavalry detachment from Arras and Béthune to combine with Montesquiou, but the Marshal thought it necessary to fall back on Cambrai. Having lost the line of the Scarpe, his troops needed a fresh place to form and this was plainly the best course. Marlborough sent the Prince of Hesse-Cassell on ahead with a strong detachment to harry the French withdrawal, but apart from some skirmishing with their rear-guard there was little contact. Some hard words were exchanged between the French commanders at this point; Luxembourg protesting that Montesquiou should not have abandoned the river crossings quite so readily, while Luxembourg was in turn accused of being slow in marching up in support, despite urgent requests to do so.

That same day, 22 April, Prince Eugene invested Douai on three sides. The covering army commanded by Marlborough, comprising the British, Hanoverian and Dutch troops, encamped that evening to the south of the Scarpe near to Vitry, able to move rapidly to foil any late French attempt to reinforce the garrison from the vicinity of Arras. John Millner remembered that two days later:

> The better to prevent the enemy's surprisals after the siege was formed, and to maintain the same when formed, and to make it the easier for the besiegers, who set apart thereto, the Duke immediately caused a line of circumvallation, to be begun and carried on round the city, where most need required, and was soon after accomplished.[5]

Douai was a powerful fortress; well supplied and held by about 7,700 French troops commanded by the veteran campaigner, the Marquis d'Albergotti, who was well known to both Marlborough and Eugene. He was supported by the expert engineer officer Major-General de Valori and the Chevalier de Jaucourt who commanded the artillery.

'This town was an important one to us', Colonel De La Colonie remembered, 'as it covered all Artois, had magnificent arsenals, and was the headquarters of the Artillery school.'[6] The formidable fortifications of the place included a double water-filled ditch and a strong outwork known as Fort Scarpe, which was manned by three infantry battalions with thirty-eight guns and twelve large mortars, and also protected by extensive flooding. This out-work covered the north-eastern side of the town on the road leading to Lille, and was quite an obstacle in its own right. It also guarded the northern end of a canal, cut by the French between the Scarpe and Deule rivers in the late seventeenth century, soon after they took possession of Douai, to facilitate the easy movement of guns and stores towards the border with the Southern Netherlands. This strong place would have to be taken before the most promising angle of approach to Douai could be attempted; and to make matters worse, the artillery in Douai swept the approaches to Fort Scarpe. However, the breaching of the banks of local waterways to create the defensive inundations, had the unintended benefit for the Allies that the routine crossing of local rivers and streams was made easier by the lowering in the water levels.

Forty infantry battalions under command of the Prince of Orange were employed in the siege operations. The Allied pioneers and labourers were soon hard at work, and it was possible to drain the town's double ditch, formed by the Scarpe river, into the Sensée. This, coincidentally, flooded a wide area to the south of the town, which effectively prevented any relieving French force from approaching from that direction. The construction of the lines of circumvallation was begun on 25 April and for additional security a fortified post was also set up at Arleux on the Sensée. By 28 April, the Allied army was able to occupy the siege lines, and John Millner wrote the next day:

> All the horse and dragoons of our army, and a competent number of the besiegers, were busily employed in the making and bring-ing of fascines etc., for the expeditious carrying on of the said siege against Douai and Fort La Scarpe.[7]

As usual, operations could not really begin until the Allied siege train had come up, and Marlborough wrote the same day: 'It will be at least ten days before we can expect it; in the meantime we shall have little to do here.'[8] The Duke's forward supply base was at Tournai, and the French made fresh attempts to disrupt the daily convoys coming up the Scarpe by using armed galleys. So the Duke ran his wagons along the rutted roads while this problem was dealt with and also established another water route up the Deule and then along the canal to Pont Auby.

Early on 1 May 1710, Eugene's infantry stormed a French outpost at Pignonville, near to Fort Scarpe, taking 100 prisoners in a sharp little action. Four days later the trenches were opened opposite the defences on the north and west sides of the town. This was contrary to normal practice as the guns of the siege train were not yet up, but Marlborough was striving to push things forward, writing on 5 May with some impatience: '[A] good part of our artillery is arrived at Tournai, and may be here in four or five days.'[9] The two attacks directed against the town, commanded respectively by the Prince of Orange and the Prince of Anhalt-Dessau, were pushed to within 250 yards of the defences two days later.

At about 9.00 pm on 7 May, d'Albergotti sent the Duc de Montemar with 1,200 grenadiers and dismounted dragoons through heavy driz-zle on a grand raid on the Allied works. The operation was a complete surprise and appeared to catch the Allied soldiers fast asleep; Sutton's

Regiment broke and was scattered and Smith's Regiment was badly mauled. John Deane remembered: 'They came out of the town very strong upon us, sending out two regiments of dragoons all afoot and all the Grenadiers in the garrison, who threw in abundance of hand grenades & bombs amongst us.'[10] The French troops were eventually driven out by reinforcements sent in by Eugene, under the command of Brigadier-General Macartney, but the bitter fighting took all night long, and it had still been a humiliating rebuff for the besiegers.[11] 'There was on our side 500 men killed upon the spot and 200 and odd wounded. Most of Colonel Sutton's men being killed or wounded. The Colonel himself being taken prisoner.[12] A few days later d'Albergotti tried to repeat the success, but this time the Allies were alert and drove off the attempt with heavy losses. However, a party of fifty Allied soldiers, engaged in extending a trench, were ambushed by the French, and all were killed or captured. Accidents, inevitable and terrible in the confines of the siege works, caused havoc on several occasions: 'The commanders of both [parties] with several of their men, were accidentally blowed up by some loose powder, which lay carelessly on the ground', wrote John Millner.[13]

Montesquiou was instructed by Louis XIV in one of his many, not always appreciated, instructions to his field commanders to take up a position between Arras and Péronne, and to hinder the siege of Douai from there. To insist on such specific tactical details cannot have been helpful to the Marshal, who should have been left with enough discretion to choose his own dispositions within the overall context of his instructions. He was also strictly ordered to await the return of Marshal Villars to the army before getting involved in any general engagement. On 9 May, the big guns of the Allied train arrived in the camp; these included eighty of the powerful 24-pounders, and the real work of reducing the fortifications of Douai could begin. Two days later Eugene's troops had pushed their saps to the outer ditch, and a forward grand battery of twenty-four guns was erected there, together with four big siege mortars at each attack. They opened fire in earnest on 14 May, and the days of the garrison were now numbered, unless the French field army could achieve something quickly. Within five days of the commencement of firing the Allied bombardment had done much of its preparatory work, and the batteries in the garrison were mostly disabled, with fires raging through parts of the town. On 17 May, the French attempted another sortie, this time directed against the Allied left attack. Nine companies of grenadiers led the assault and they came on with great energy, but were met by Preston's

Regiment who were drawn up in good order and drove the French soldiers back out of the trenches with heavy loss, including nearly 100 unwounded prisoners. The sortie, gallant as it was, had achieved nothing other than to weaken the garrison. An attempt by the French at this time to flood the Allied trenches was foiled by Marlborough's engineers who diverted the Scarpe river again, further enlarging the water obstacle on the exposed flank of the besieging army.

Marshal Berwick had rejoined the French army at this time to give support to Villars, whose energy was sapped by the leg wound which proved frustratingly slow to heal, so that he was obliged to use crutches and found it almost impossible to mount a horse. He had resumed the command on the day the Allied bombardment began, but his mangled leg was held fast in an iron brace. Having made no serious attempt yet to interfere with Marlborough's preparations, Villars had now got permission from Versailles to fight a battle to save Douai. The French commander gathered his army, which reportedly comprised 155 infantry battalions and 272 squadrons of cavalry, and edged towards Arras, looking to manoeuvre the Allies away from the fortress. With a distinct numerical inferiority, the French commander had to be alert that Marlborough did not suddenly turn aside from the siege and fall on his army while it was on the move. He plainly had to take care just how he confronted the Allies, for Bouchain, Arras and Cambrai also had to be covered against any Allied raid.

Villars had three possible courses open to him, all potentially promising, but each having a real element of risk in the face of such formidable opponents. If he adopted the most obvious course and moved directly across the Sensée to confront the Allies, Marlborough could at little risk draw additional troops out of the siege works by the shortest route and meet him. Given the Allied superiority in numbers, a pitched battle there to the south of Douai held out little prospect of easy success. If Villars swung around Arras instead to approach Douai from the west, then Eugene was in place and the Duke could either threaten the right flank of the French army as it came forward, or march against Bouchain, which would have been left exposed by the French turning movement. Any such move by Marlborough, with little risk to his own army as he would be moving on interior lines to his opponent, would bring Villars back in haste, having to march around the outside of a curve to get into place again. Alternatively, if the Marshal went to the east, moving past Bouchain to try and turn the left flank of the Allied army, then Arras was exposed to a raid, in just the same way as Bouchain would be if Villars went to the west. In both cases, the Marshal would be operating on exterior lines, with all the additional exertion and delay involved. Marlborough and Eugene, by comparison, could swing in whichever direction was necessary to meet him, with relatively little effort. If, in order to counter the threat to Arras and Bouchain while he manoeuvred, Villars left strong garrisons in those two places, his army's strength in the field would be seriously reduced. He would be unable either to dictate matters to the Allies and lift the siege of Douai, or be able to stand a battle in the open. None of the options was very enticing, but, having considered everything, the Marshal concluded that the approach across the Scarpe to the west offered the best chance, albeit rather slim, of success in lifting the siege.

The operations against Douai progressed steadily. On 26 May, Marlborough wrote:

> We are advanced at the siege within a few paces of the pali-
> sades, but being obliged to go on by the sap, it is more tedious
> than were to be wished ... The enemy made a sortie, and being
> perceived by our men, we let them come very near before we
> gave them our fire at which they immediately retired into the
> town, leaving about twenty men dead upon the spot.[14]

By the end of the month, the Allied troops had reached the covered way and laid bridges over the avant-fosse. Preparations were made to bring the siege guns forward onto the glacis, and d'Albergotti began indicating his increasingly precarious plight to French observ-ers on high ground to the south, by having signal flags raised over the fortress. There was little Villars could do immediately to help him; although he did move to threaten the Allied detachment at Arleux, nothing much came of the attempt.

The garrison blew several large defensive mines to impede the siege operations, and mounted regular sorties to disrupt their dig-ging; on one occasion they even managed to round up a herd of cattle that had been allowed to graze too near to the fortress, and drove them back into Douai to supplement the rations. John Deane of the 1st English Foot Guards wrote of the continuing operations in the trenches, while the opposing field armies marched to and fro:

> On the 20 of May [1 June New Style dating] our [be]siegers threw in
> their bombs and grenades, cannon balls and small shot at a furious
> rate, and they at us. But it happened that some of our bombs fell
> into a great magazine of theirs of loaded bombs and grenades, and

did the enemy a world of damage, killing abundance of men and made such a hurricane, yet the very earth shook in our camp.[15]

The French army crossed the Scarpe, near to Arras, on 28 May and began the approach over the plain of Lens. Villars's soldiers carried four days' bread in their knapsacks, and the guns were well to the fore as if to challenge the Allies to give battle. Marlborough and Eugene had been aware of the French approach, and the Duke had moved his covering army towards Mont St Eloy two days earlier. Now Eugene joined him, leaving only thirty battalions of infantry at the siege works. The construction had begun between Vitry and Montigny of a stout line of entrenchments covered with advanced redoubts. It was a time of high tension as the two active field armies manoeuvred in close proximity to each other. A slip by either commander could bring catastrophe. Villars came to a rest less than two miles from where Marlborough had occupied his defensive position, and Robert Parker commented 'He seemed determined to give the Duke battle, and began to cannonade us with great fury, and this brought Prince Eugene from the siege with as many men as could be spared.'[16] The French commander was of course looking for an opening, while Marlborough's tactical dispositions were hampered to a certain degree by having to shield the operations around Douai, while simultaneously countering the movements of the French. The Duke also felt it necessary to detach Tilly with twelve squadrons of cavalry towards the south, to guard against any attempt by Villars to get a detachment between his army and the troops in the trenches at Douai.

Although it was a hard decision, Villars soon thought better of attacking the Allies when in such a good position, which could not easily be assaulted or turned. The Douai garrison made several sorties hoping to divert Marlborough's attention, and twenty battalions of infantry had to be sent back into the trenches to counter these attempts. Despite this, on 5 June, the Marshal began to pull back, sending troops to reinforce Ypres, Béthune, St Venant and Aire instead. By reducing his field army in this way, he tacitly accepted that the siege could not be lifted. Louis XIV approved this caution, even though Douai would be lost; little though he relished seeing his fortresses fall, he could not risk the army. D'Albergotti, dug in behind the battered defences of Douai, was giving the King what he needed most: time, while the growing staleness in the Grand Alliance took effect.

By 15 June, both the covered way and counterscarp on both attacks had been reached by the Allied infantry despite vigorous attempts by the defenders to drive them back. Marlborough wrote to the Secretary for State, Henry Boyle: 'We have been battering the ravelins at both attacks for three days past ... tonight we intend to attack.'[17] The forward breaching batteries were now able to engage the four demi-lunes that protected the main walls of Douai, adjacent to the Eereclein gate. On 22 June, Eugene opened trenches before Fort Scarpe; saps were quickly pushed forward right up to the defences, and a small detached redoubt between Douai and Fort Scarpe was carried by assault. D'Albergotti took careful stock of the situation and consulted his senior officers; he asked for terms on 25 June rather than face a storm, which was clearly in preparation. He tried, without success, to retain possession of Fort Scarpe while offering to yield the town itself, but the Allies took possession of both Douai and the fort at noon two days later. The garrison had been reduced to 4,527 men by this time, scarcely enough to properly man the defences in the face of a real assault, and they were granted honourable terms, being permitted to march away to Cambrai to await formal exchange. Marlborough entertained d'Albergotti and his senior officers to dinner the following day and then wrote to his wife: 'Douai and the fort of Scarpe's being surrendered; the giving up of the latter will save us a good deal of time, and a great many men's lives.'[18] This had been an expensive operation for the Allies all the same, as no fewer than 8,009 of their men were killed or wounded; while French casualties were only 2,860, and Marlborough had to employ sixty-three days in the siege, rather than the thirty days he had rather optimistically predicted. Such was the effect of Vauban's engineering genius when allied to the formidable professional competence of a robust commander like d'Albergotti.

As soon as Douai capitulated, Marlborough had intended to move against Arras, the capture of which would see the Allied army moving towards more open country once more. Regiments that had suffered heavily in the Douai trenches were replaced with fresh units brought out from garrison duty. Villars had, however, deployed his army into a good position to shield the fortress, and lines of defence had been constructed between the Somme and Scarpe rivers. Rather to Marlborough's frustration, his opponent had proved able to anticipate his next move. It seemed unlikely that the Allies could force these lines without heavy casualties – the memory of Malplaquet cast a long shadow, and no one wanted to make the attempt. The French commander had also swept the area clean of forage. Instead, Marlborough's army, after spending several days resting and levelling the siege works before Douai, advanced through heavy rain and clinging mud towards Vimy. The Duke halted on 11 July just to the east of the Scarpe, both to allow the bread wagons to catch up and in the vain hope of provoking Villars to stand and fight. The Marshal, however, was not to be tempted, although he had been reinforced by a strong detachment that had been covering Bouchain under command of the Chevalier de Luxembourg. The French stayed back behind the Crinchon stream and took up a position between Arras and the Somme. As Villars was now placed he could not really be forced from the spot. A number of important towns had been left exposed, but the Marshal was conducting his campaign with skill, saving the strength of the field army while allowing his fortresses to take the brunt of Marlborough's campaign.

The Duke turned aside to Béthune, described as being a small but well-fortified town, with six strong bastions and walls entirely protected by a water obstacle. The citadel was also strengthened with a secondary water defence. The garrison of 3,220 troops was commanded by an Irishman in the French service, Major-General Michael Roth. The Marquis de Puy-Vauban, nephew of the late Marshal, was governor of the town.[19] After some delay to allow the trains of the army to close up, the Allied investment of the place by Baron Fagel with thirty infantry battalions and twenty squadrons of cavalry was completed on 15 July. This was achieved just before the French had an opportunity to properly resupply the garrison. Vauban wrote in his journal of the siege:

> At 4.00 pm [we] saw a lot of infantry and standards, so we assumed the siege was about to begin. We therefore began to fill the covered ways and the Place d'Armes with troops and set fire to the faubourgs [suburbs] and houses outside the town. We also began to flood areas.[20]

A week later, the lines of circumvallation were reported to be finished, and the Allied soldiers had begun to dig the approach trenches. As usual, two attacks were pushed forward: one with Dutch troops under Fagel against the Arras gate, and the other with Saxons and Prussians commanded by Count Schulemburg at the Aire gate. The digging work at first made very good progress, getting to within 200 paces at the Arras gate with hardly any loss. The Allied covering army meanwhile took up position near Villars-Brulin. It was soon evident that the investment of Béthune was actually far from complete, and Vauban continued for some time to be kept informed of the Allied movements by local peasants who made their way into the town to sell provisions.

The guns of the Allied siege train arrived on 25 July, and operations could begin in earnest. As if in reply the garrison sprang into life, and on 26 July Vauban wrote:

> Brigadier Miromesnil made a sortie at the head of five companies of grenadiers … the enemy guards stood firm with their bayonets fixed waiting for us to fire, our troops had orders not to fire until the enemy [fired] … a terrible carnage followed. All this was done with audacity and in splendid style, which gave a good example to the rest [of the garrison].[21]

This sudden French attack had fallen squarely on two Prussian battalions, who were caught by surprise, scattered and ran for safety. Orrery's Regiment was nearby and made a stand – hence Vauban's reference to a 'carnage', for the British unit alone lost 202 men killed and wounded in the brief affair before the French soldiers withdrew. Vauban wrote that the next day 'A drummer was sent to return two wounded officers taken prisoner in the trenches.'[22]

On 1 August, Marlborough led his cavalry forward in a reconnaissance force and found that Villars was busy at work on constructing a new line of defences, apparently resigned to leaving Béthune to its fate. This line would in time stretch from the Meuse to the Channel coast and become famous in tales of military success. At the siege, Schluemburg's attack was delayed by the need to drain off the flooded ground. Roth's soldiers still put up a strong resistance, and mining operations of course were undertaken on both sides. Vauban commented on a particularly successful attempt at counter-mining by the defenders: 'Our miners heard the enemy sappers very close and gave them a *camouflet* of 300 pounds of powder which blew off better than we hoped, and flames came right out in their parallel.'[23]

In some exasperation, Marlborough wrote to James Stanhope on 18 August: 'I am almost ashamed to tell you that we are still before Béthune, but we lie under a great misfortune of being obliged to carry on the war here by siege almost without engineers.'[24] Villars, on the other hand could, be quite content with this pace of operations, for the real peril for France lay in the potential loss of Arras, while Béthune, valuable prize though it might be, represented a secondary target. The French commander, aside from some manoeuvring to try and catch Marlborough off-guard, confined his activities to strengthening his lines of defence. On 24 August, Villars pushed a strong force of cavalry and dragoons forward to harry

PLAN OF BETHUNE.

For M.ᵈ Tindal's Continuation of M.ᵈ Rapin's History of England.

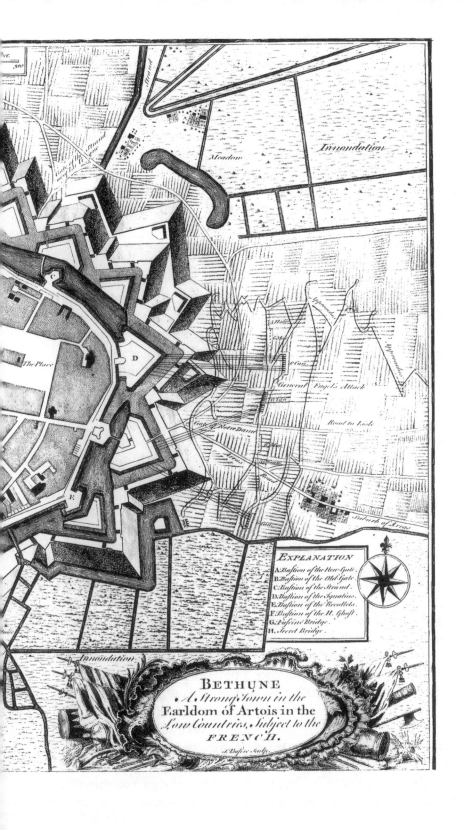

Meadow

Innondation

Strand

The Place

D

D

E

General Engel's Attack

Gate of Notre Dame

Road to Lisle

Suburb of Arras

Innondation

EXPLANATION

A. Bastion of the New Gate.
B. Bastion of the Old Gate.
C. Bastion of the Strand.
D. Bastion of the Ignatius.
E. Bastion of the Recollets.
F. Bastion of the H. Ghost.
G. Fascine Bridge.
H. Secret Bridge.

BETHUNE

A Strong Town in the
Earldom of Artois in the
Low Countries, Subject to the
FRENCH.

A. Basire Sculp.

Marlborough's foraging parties, and a day of brisk skirmishing followed. The Allied soldiers, outnumbered in the opening clashes, fell back towards their camp and quite a number were taken prisoner. When the French tried to follow this success in the afternoon, they were met by fresh Hessian and Danish infantry that came forward to support the foragers, and were soon driven off. John Deane wrote: 'The enemy having lately attempted to disturb our besieging army, with about 30 squadrons of their cavalry, designing to have secured a pass; but now our folks have spoiled their designs and hindered them.'[25]

Apart from this rather half-hearted French attempt to disrupt the siege operations, Béthune was left to its fate. A week or so after Schulemburg's troops bridged the *avant-fossé* in a dawn attack and got a foothold on the counterscarp, Roth had to capitulate on 28 August. The garrison was running short of ammunition anyway, and John Millner remembered: 'Two great breaches in the main walls of the town, in order for a general grand storm, [and] the fear and dread thereof so terrified the governor.'[26] In fact, neither Vauban or Roth had to be 'terrified', as Millner put it, to wish to spare their faithful soldiers the horrors of a storm and sack when the place could no longer be held. A rather unusual argument broke out over the capitulation, however, as Roth beat the chamade and hung out signal flags at the breach opposite the attack commanded by Schulemburg. The other Allied attack was not so far advanced towards the covered way, partly, Marlborough remembered, because Baron Fagel was so apprehensive of French mines. Roth's decision was accordingly quite logical, but Fagel took this as an insult to both himself and his Dutch soldiers. He refused to stop firing at the breach even though Roth, Vauban and Schulemburg were standing near the counterscarp with their officers, out in the open, discussing the terms of the capitulation. This of course was both counter to the 'rules' of siege warfare and ill-mannered at the very least. Schulemburg hurriedly asked Vauban to have the chamade beaten and signal flags hung out at Fagel's attack also, so that the Dutch general could have his share in the success and report the same to the States-General. This was duly done. The Allied army took possession of Béthune the following day, having lost 3,365 killed and wounded in the whole operation. Vauban, Roth and their 1,700 surviving troops were granted good terms and permitted to march away to St Omer with two pieces of artillery but without giving their parole. The simple fact that the garrison had lost nearly half its strength in the defence of the place speaks volumes for their bravery and the valiant and aggressive defence put up by Roth and Vauban.

At once Marlborough moved against the fortresses of Aire and St Venant on the Lys river. Once these were taken, not only would the line of the river be open for a renewed advance into France ,but the Duke would have greater access to the Channel coast and could put both Dunkirk and Calais under threat. Such a move, however, would put his own left flank at some risk, with the renewed possibility that Villars's cavalry would go raiding into Brabant. For the moment the Duke put these concerns to one side. With Aire and St Venant in his hands, the prospects for a successful campaign, supported by the Royal Navy, along the coast the next year, as he had planned in the high summer of 1708, would be so much the greater. The approach march began on 2 September, after close reconnaissance showed that two simultaneous operations were possible. William Cadogan and Daniel Dopff commanded one of the advanced parties and they surprised two French outposts near to the village of Lambre, taking three officers and over 100 men prisoner. Aire was held by 5,700 troops commanded by the Marquis de Goesbriand, but St Venant, at first sight, was not so formidable an obstacle, with a garrison only about 3,000 strong under command of Brigadier-General de Seloe. The error at Béthune was not repeated, and the two French garrisons were well supplied, in good time.

Prince Eugene's army took up a covering position near to the Lys, while Marlborough made his headquarters close by at Willers. Leopold, Prince of Anhalt-Dessau, was appointed to command the siege of Aire, the Prince of Orange commanded the operations against St Venant. The towns were both invested by 7 September, while the ponderous siege train came up by water from Menin. The weather had turned wet and cold as the season advanced, and the Allied trenches and encampments were often running with water. Marlborough wrote on 11 September: 'At St Venant the Prince of Orange has turned the course of two rivulets which supplied the inundations before that place, and he is now busy in turning likewise the course of the Lys above the town.'[27] Sickness took hold amongst the troops, and morale fell noticeably. Despite this, the siege operations were pressed onwards by the weary soldiers – the Duke remembered that there was little alternative, as the big guns of the siege train could not be moved once in place, being soon sunk up to their axle trees in the clinging mud, despite standing on massive baulks of timber.

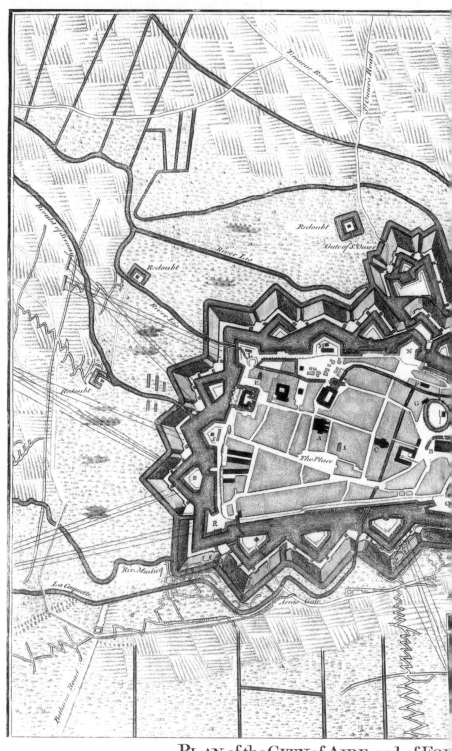

PLAN of the CITY of AIRE and of FO[...]

For. For Mr Tindal's Continuation[...]

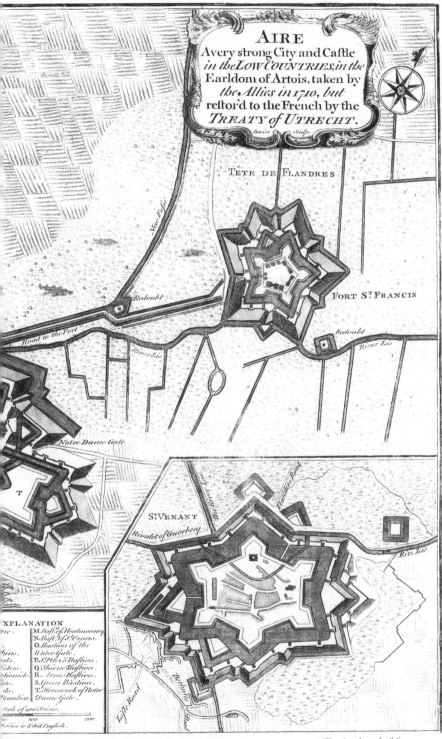

AIRE
A very strong City and Castle
in the LOW COUNTRIES, in the
Earldom of Artois, taken by
the Allies in 1710, but
restor'd to the French by the
TREATY of UTRECHT.

Basire. Sculp.

TÉTE DE FLANDRES

River Felsbe

Redoubt

Road to the Fort

River Lis

FORT St FRANCIS

Redoubt

River Lis

Notre Dame Gate

T

St VENANT

Rivulet of Guerbecq

Flanders Road

Riv. Lis.

Lisse Road

Bethune Road

Bethune Road

FRANCIS with a VIEW of St VENANT

1. The Attack on the Left.
2. The Attack on the Right.

Rapin's History of England.

Gloom was cast into the Allied camp when one of the river convoys on the way to supply the siege operations was destroyed by a French raid in the third week of September, despite having an escort of over 1,200 troops under the command of Brigadier-General Ginkel. The Marquis de Ravignan advanced from Ypres on the evening of 18 September with a strong force of grenadiers and dragoons. Avoiding the attention of the Allied garrisons in Menin and Courtrai, he intercepted the convoy near to St Eloy the following afternoon. Driving off the escort, who were apparently taken completely by surprise (Ginkel and no fewer than 600 of his men were taken prisoner), the French then set fire to the barges, three of which were loaded with ammunition. These began to explode in a series of devastating detonations, the force of which broke the banks, diverted the course of the Lys for a while, and broke windows as far away as St Quentin. De Ravignan then withdrew and, neatly evading Allied pursuit, successfully made his way through Rousselaer back to Ypres by the evening of 20 September.

The Duke wrote to London a few days later: 'Having defeated our escort they blew up the powder in the boats. Most of those with corn and meal for the army have escaped.'[28] He was particularly annoyed by the failure to protect the convoy, for the French raid had been well handled and the Allied response was feeble. Although the loss could quickly be made good, this was the first and only outright defeat on any real scale suffered by troops under his command during almost nine years of constant campaigning. He went on in his letter: 'I have sent to our neighbouring garrisons to know what supply of powder and ball they can afford us, and I hope this misfortune, which is the first that has happened to us during the whole course of the war, will not disappoint our sieges.' Despite this setback for the operations, Marlborough had been able to assure the Secretary of State that at Aire, 'several of our batteries, cannon and mortars, began to fire on Friday morning early, and had such good success that the enemy have done us very little damage since, most of their artillery being dismounted [disabled].' The Duke went on: 'Our batteries began to fire yesterday morning at St Venant, where they are advanced in their approaches to the avant-fossé and are preparing to fill it up.' Despite all this, the important daily use of the river was undoubtedly hampered by the destruction of the convoy and the debris that was left littering the waterways. The Duke wrote to local authorities two days later: 'The misfortune that happened this past week to our boats on the Lys having blocked the passage of that river, I want you to send straight away those numbers of workmen necessary to lift those boats which are sunk, and to clear the river.'[29]

The Allied army was becoming worn down with the repeated siege operations, tactically successful though each one proved to be. The failure to anticipate or prevent de Ravignan's raid might be seen as a result of this fatigue. Some feared that a fine fighting instrument was in the process of being ruined, and one of Marlborough's field officers had written to London late in August: 'If we pretend to take any more towns, our infantry will be quite destroyed and our horse so much out of order that we shall be obliged to stay as long in garrison next spring as the enemy.'[30] The Allied soldiers were undoubtedly weary, and had become resigned to continuing the arduous campaign – how different it all was to the post-Ramillies glory of the summer of 1706. Still, the soldiers' loyalty to the Duke and their faith in him did not noticeably diminish, and they responded to the demands made of them. The effects were more pronounced in London, where exasperation was growing at the seemingly interminable war, together with the suspicion, that could not quite be laid to rest, that Marlborough was engaging in pointless siege operations to prolong the campaign and maintain his own lucrative position at the head of the Allied armies.

St Venant was not a fortress of the first rank by any means; its defensive works comprising as they did a simple levelled earthen parapet in the shape of a hexagon. It was well protected by flooded meadows and marshes, but could not stand a siege for very long once these had been drained off. The weather had turned fine for a while, and the siege operations were pressed forward so well that the garrison capitulated to the Prince of Orange on 2 October after three days of negotiations. Although the French troops were not thought to have performed particularly well, it was recognised that they had faced an impossible task, and they were granted good terms and marched away to Arras to await formal exchange. The besiegers suffered 177 killed and 762 wounded in the operation. Meanwhile, Marshal d'Harcourt had come from the Rhine to take over the command of the French field army, to permit Villars to rest. There might be a chance to fall on and overwhelm at least one Allied detachment while the two sieges were carried on, but d'Harcourt was warned to be cautious by Louis XIV. The King had come to rely on time and the deadening effect of the prolonged siege operations, and did not want to put the field army at risk.

The simultaneous operations against Aire (the more formidable of the two fortresses on the Lys and, according to Richard Kane, a place 'very strong by art and nature'[31]) went on in appalling conditions. The capture of St Venant had taken three weeks, but that of Aire would entail two months of murderous fighting. The governor, de Goesbriand, was a staunch opponent with fifteen infantry battalions and seven squadrons of dismounted dragoons under command. The defences of the town were extensive and intricate, comprising regular stone-faced bastions and demi-lunes, with a particularly strong hornwork at the gate of Our Lady. There was also an outwork called Fort St Francis, protected by the Lys river on one side and extensive inundations on the other. This fort also had a large detached redoubt, sited to protect the entrenched path from Aire itself.

The Allied soldiers were immediately set to digging trenches and draining away the water. John Deane of the 1st English Foot Guards wrote that the troops were employed to 'march with a design to cut all the marsh ditches and waters that run in and about Aire [and] turn several of the waters another way and drained off what waters they possibly could.'[32] On 12 September, the cavalry and dragoons of the army were sent out cutting fascines in the surrounding hedgerows, and the ground around Aire was broken and the digging of approach and parallel trenches began at 11.00 p.m. that night. Deane remembered: 'The enemy … did fire very thick both cannon and small shot – but it was then too late for our men was under cover.'[33] Two weeks later, the Comte d'Estrade, who had a reputation as a bruising infantry commander, led a powerful sortie against the besiegers. Shortly after dark, the French troops suddenly came pouring out of the fortress into the Allied trenches, making deadly use of sharpened spades, bayonets and the long-handled hatchets of the grenadiers, in a brutal and very well-handled attack. Although taken by surprise, the Allied soldiers quickly rallied and stood their ground; after a bloody affray, d'Estrade pulled his men back, and John Deane wrote:

> A great part of the garrison sallied out and did beat our men from the trenches for a while at a sad rate, and was very near taking a battery of our guns which they designed to have nailed up … A great many men were killed on both sides at this attack.[34]

The sortie failed to delay the siege operations very much, but d'Estrade tried once more a few days later. He attempted now to regain the redoubt beside the path from Fort St Francis to the town, which had just been stormed by the Allies, and tried to seize one of the forward breaching batteries. The attack was only repulsed after bitter and costly close quarter fighting. In the meantime, on 22 September, d'Harcourt had sent a strong detachment of cavalry to raid the Allied communications. The squadrons were promptly intercepted and forced in a scrambling battle to draw off, leaving 220 prisoners behind. The Chevalier de Luxembourg also attempted, without success, to surprise and capture Fort Scarpe near to Douai.

The troops on both sides lived and fought calf deep in mud; all their clothing and equipment was soaked through, while stores of gunpowder became damp, making sustained battery and counter-battery firing difficult. Marlborough again wrily commented towards the end of the month that as the siege guns could not be dragged out of the mud into which they had sunk, they might as well go on firing:

Take it [Aire] we must, for we cannot draw the guns from the batteries. But God knows when we shall have it; night and day our poor men are up to their knees in mud and water, which is a most grevious [sic] sight.[35]

The technical complexities of siege warfare were apparent when Marlborough wrote at this time:

At the attack on the side of Lambre we have joined the lodgement on the avant-fossé, and made several saps in order to a descent; but one of these, being pierced too low, let the water into our trenches, which will put us a little backward, but it is repaired.[36]

By 5 October, part of the covered way at the angle between the hornwork and the glacis was in Allied hands, and a small redoubt covering the Béthune road was captured in a surprise attack. It took a further ten days of continuous hand-to-hand fighting to get posses-sion of the hornwork itself. A week later, in pouring rain, the Allied soldiers got across the water-filled ditch to gain a foothold beside the Arras gate, from where they drove off, with heavy casualties, a determined counter-attack by the garrison.

The wet weather made the roads hard to use, and bread rations were sometimes short. The siege batteries had closed up to the Arras gate by 29 October, and began to widen a breach that had been made in the main defences. The Allied commanders were concerned at the slow rate of progress, and the troops were looking forward to their winter quarters. By 5 November, the saps had been pushed far enough forward for the besiegers to begin to prepare for a storm of the breach; at last, to general relief in both armies, de Goesbriand asked Anhalt-Dessau for terms three days later. The garrisons in Aire, and Fort St Francis (which still held out) capitulated on 9 November, and the Arras gate was handed over as a token of submission. The gruelling siege had taken sixty-four days, and Marlborough wrote to Queen Anne with news of the hard-won success:

> I have the honour to acquaint Your Majesty with the surrender of Aire. Our bridges being made and everything in readiness to storm the place, the governor thought fit to beat the chamade yesterday in the evening, and to send out hostages with the capitulation, which being agreed to, and signed this afternoon, one of the gates is delivered to us, and the garrison is to march out on Tuesday to be conducted to St Omer.[37]

The 3,628 survivors of the garrison marched out on 12 November, leaving about 1,600 sick and wounded in the town. The cost to the Allies of this limited success, against what was at best a fortress of secondary importance, was disproportionately heavy: some 6,400 men killed and wounded, with another 14,000 now sick in hospital. The foul weather had taken its toll.

By any measure, this had been a grim campaign, with at least a quarter of the Allied troops engaged in the four sieges of Douai, Béthune, St Venant and Aire becoming casualties. At 19,119 killed and wounded, to say nothing of the sick who were absent from the ranks, the price paid for limited tactical gains was quite startling, while the French, by comparison, had suffered far fewer casualties (just 5,860), although it could be claimed they were steadily losing ground. Well, ground was what the French had. They could give way at this coldly measured pace, intending to baffle the intentions of the Allied commanders long enough for the protracted peace negotiations, both overt and covert, to take effect. The Duke, with good reason, wrote of the operation against Aire in particular: 'This defence was the best we have seen.'[38] The powerful dynamics of the advantages of scientific defence in depth over even the most accomplished attacker was evident, and those who questioned whether this was a war that was capable of being won, at least in this particular fashion, were growing in number. Their voices were made stronger as the Allied campaign in Spain faltered and failed, particularly when

Archduke Charles (Carlos III) took the Imperial throne in Vienna on the unexpected death of his older brother.

At the end of the year's campaign, Marlborough returned to London, on 6 January 1711; the man who, obedient to his instructions, was pushing on with a war that no-one now wanted, although few had the courage to say so openly. He found a poor welcome from the Queen and those who at one time had been his confidantes, admirers and supporters. Advised, contrary to custom, not to seek the thanks of Parliament for his efforts in the recent campaign, the Duke cut a lonely figure.

NOTES

1. W. Coxe, *Memoirs of John, Duke of Marlborough*, Vol III, 1847, p. 39.

2. G. Murray, *Letters and Dispatches of the Duke of Marlborough*, Vol IV, 1845, p. 722.

3. *Ibid.*, p. 724.

4. *Ibid.*

5. John Millner, *A Compendious Journal 1702–1711*, 1736, p. 290.

6. W. Horsley, (ed.), *Chronicles of an Old Campaigner*, 1904, pp. 348–349.

7. Millner, *A Compendious Journal*, p. 291.

8. Murray, *Letters and Dispatches*, Vol V, p. 11.

9. *Ibid.*, p. 18.

10. D.G. Chandler, (ed.), *Journal of John Deane*, 1984, p. 103.

11. Brigadier-General George Macartney had been deprived of his regiment earlier in the war for misconduct. He served on with the army as a volunteer, and his almost suicidal bravery at Malplaquet restored him to his command.

12.Chandler, *Journal of John Deane*, p. 104.

13.Millner, *A Compendious Journal*, p. 291.

14.Murray, *Letters and Dispatches*, p. 34.

15.Chandler, *Journal of John Deane*, p. 107.

16.D. Chandler, *Marlborough as Military Commander*, 1973, p. 279.

18.Murray, *Letters and Dispatches*, p. 53.

19.Michael Roth was an émigré Roman Catholic officer, who had served under the Earl of Tyrconnel in 1686 before going to France after the Treaty of Limerick. He was made Comte de Roth by Louis XIV and became a Lieutenant-General in the French Army in 1720.

20.J. Reeve, *The Siege of Béthune, 1710*, 1985, p. 203.

21.*Ibid.*, p. 207.

22.*Ibid.*

23.Reeve, *Siege*, p. 204.

24.Murray, *Letters and Dispatches*, p. 105.

25.Chandler, *Journal of John Deane*, p. 113.

26.Millner, *A Compendious Journal*, p. 303.

27.Murray, *Letters and Dispatches*, p. 135.

28.*Ibid.*, p. 147. See also Coxe, *Memoirs*, p. 148.

29.*Ibid.*, pp. 159–160.

30.W.S. Churchill, *Marlborough, His Life and Times*, Vol II, 1947, p. 700.

31.R. Kane, *Campaigns of King William III and Queen Anne*, 1745, p. 87.

32. Chandler, *Journal of John Deane*, p. 115.

33. *Ibid.*, p. 116.

34. *Ibid.*, p. 117.

35. A. Alison, *Military Life of John, Duke of Marlborough*, 1848, p. 313.

36. Murray, *Letters and Dispatches*, p. 183. This is an example of sappers digging down through earth fortifications, to get to a defensive ditch with some element of cover from fire. In this case they went too far down, and flooded their own works.

37. *Ibid.*, p. 212.

38. Coxe, *Memoirs*, p. 149.

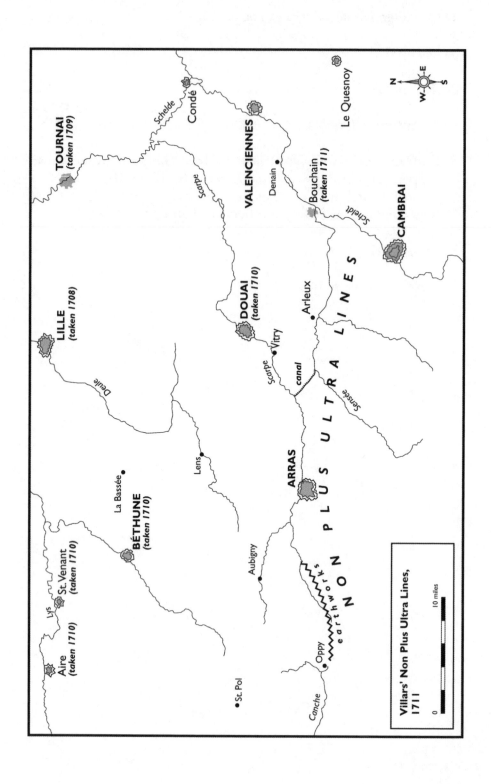

TOURNAI
(taken 1709)

Schelde

Condé

Scarpe

VALENCIENNES

Denain

Bouchain
(taken 1711)

Le Quesnoy

Scheldt

CAMBRAI

LILLE
(taken 1708)

Deule

DOUAI
(taken 1710)

Arleux

L I N E S

Vitry

Scarpe

canal

U L T R A

Sensée

Lens

ARRAS

P L U S

La Bassée

BÉTHUNE
(taken 1710)

Aubigny

N O N

earthworks

Lys

St. Venant
(taken 1710)

Lys

Aire
(taken 1710)

St. Pol

Oppy

Conche

Villars' Non Plus Ultra Lines,
1711

0   10 miles

N
W · E
S

X

Make War Like a Fox: Marlborough's Final Triumph at Bouchain, 1711

Despite political troubles in London, the Duke of Marlborough was confirmed in command of the Anglo-Dutch armies for the new campaign in 1711, and fresh funds were voted by Parliament, which was apparently keen to press the war onwards to a victorious conclusion. The Duke was anxious to get the spring campaign in the Low Countries underway with as little delay as possible, and he wrote on 19 February: 'General Lumley will have acquainted you that the general officers and all others belonging to the forces in Flanders are to hasten over and embark by the first week of March at the furthest.'[1] In March, he could report that that the troops were assembling under the control of William Cadogan on the plain of Lille and were ready to move forward once their supplies had come up by river and canal. In mid-April, the Duke was sending all his excess baggage away and preparing to join the troops, but the unexpected death of Emperor Joseph in Vienna on 17 April inevitably upset the Allied preparations for the new campaign.

The Emperor's death also neatly answered the thorny question of just who should be King in Spain. Archduke Charles, perhaps understandably, preferred the Imperial throne, now suddenly vacated by his older brother, to the more uncertain prospect in Madrid. Prince Eugene was called to Vienna, and by early summer he had drawn most of the Imperial troops in the Spanish Netherlands away to the middle and upper Rhine, where their presence was required to reassure the German princes of the Empire at this uncertain time of transition. Louis XIV had been swift to make the most of the news, sending fresh troops to Alsace, and the Grand Alliance was temporarily in some difficulty. Peace negotiations edged forward, as they had done for some years, but playing his hand with some care, the French King might, despite the many mistakes that had been made, win the war for Spain after all. However, his strong frontier fortress defences had been seriously eroded by Marlborough over the preceding three years. The security of northern France increasingly rested on the long-improvised lines of field defence constructed by his commanders. If these should be lost, it was not certain that Allied armies might not still erupt out onto the plains of Artois and Picardy and carry fire and sword to Versailles and Paris.

Marlborough's army, soon to be reduced in numbers, took the field early in May; despite the inevitable disruption caused by the Emperor's death, he was concerned to avoid possible criticism if he delayed opening the campaign. The French were active too and in mid-May a party of their dragoons intercepted and wrecked a convoy of thirty supply barges near Marchiennes on the Scarpe. The approach of the French soldiers was shielded from observation by a dense morning mist, and the Allied escort was easily driven off. Fifteen barges were set alight and destroyed before the raiders hurried back to their lines to avoid capture. They need have been in no such haste, as their exploit went almost completely unnoticed by the Allied army, and the French dragoons got clean away, meeting no trouble.

The control of the waterways in the region, as so often before the key to ease of movement, caught the attention of the opposing commanders, and Marlborough wrote on 14 May:

> The enemy have made two dams in the Sensée, near Arleux, to overflow the borders of the river and stop the waters coming to Douai … Twenty squadrons of horse and six battalions of foot are ordered to encamp between St Amand and Mortagne to cover the men employed in clearing the Scarpe of the boats that were burnt and sunk the other day.[2]

These steadily escalating but comparatively minor operations, necessary to both maintain the waterways as avenues for Allied transports, and the continued flow of water to the mills in Douai, would have far-reaching consequences. On 18 May, Marlborough wrote to the Secretary of State: 'We have cleared the Scarpe of the late accident, and the boats now come up as formerly. We had a great convoy of boats with artillery and ammunition move up the Lys last week from Ghent.'[3] His concern at his lack of numbers once Eugene took his troops away is shown letter sent to Lord Raby, Queen Anne's ambassador in Berlin, on 1 June: 'What we are obliged to leave in garrison at Douai, Aire, Béthune and St Venant, we are thirty battalions weaker in the field than we were last year, while the enemy are a good deal stronger.'[4] Eugene parted from Marlborough on 13 June 1711; they would not meet again while the Duke remained in command of the Anglo-Dutch armies, and their great partnership in war was over. With his friend and colleague, and his valuable veteran Imperial soldiers, gone, the Duke of Marlborough was now clearly outnumbered by Marshal Villars.

The Duke moved to confront Villars in the area between Arras on the Scarpe and Bouchain on the Scheldt. The conditions for the marching troops were particularly arduous as the weather was very hot, and several men collapsed and died of heat-stroke on the way. The French defensive lines were part of the extensive system known as the Lines of Non Plus Ultra (sometimes given as Ne Plus Ultra – Nothing Further is Possible)[5] stretching from the Channel coast past Arras and Valenciennes to Namur on the Meuse, making use of the extensive waterways of the region; only in the vicinity of Arras were the water obstacles not really complete. Reconnaissance had also shown that a convenient crossing place over the Sensée was offered by a causeway crossing marshy ground near to the small village of Arleux, where the road from Douai led south towards Paris. Here the French had a small fortified post to the north of the river and slightly in advance of the lines of defence. It was also clear that Villars would reinforce the garrison in the post at Arleux if he believed it to be seriously threatened, or the causeways about to be used by the Allies. The place was bound to attract attention anyway, for the French had built a number of dams in the area to try and interrupt the flow of water to the mills in Douai, where Marlborough's bakers laboured to supply his army with bread. It was only a matter of time before the Allies moved against Arleux and its neighbouring hamlet, Aubenchuel-au-Bac.

On 6 July, the Duke sent a detachment of troops to seize the post at Arleux, a task which was soon accomplished:

The enemy having, since our coming to this ground, repaired the dike and sluices we had demolished near Arleux, by which they have again diverted the current of the water from running out of the Sensée into the canal of Douai ... I ordered 700 men of the garrison of Douai to march out in the night. They were supported by the pickets of the army, and attacked the post at break of day that morning and having made themselves masters of the castle and of a redoubt at the mill of Arleux, wherein were 115 men that were all made prisoners; we are now opening the sluices and breaking the dams which the enemy had made.[6]

Work also began under Colonel des Rogues to strengthen the rather sketchy defences at Arleux while Hompesch, one of the ablest of the Dutch commanders, covered the works from a position near to Douai with a detachment of ten infantry battalions and twelve squadrons of cavalry. To no great surprise, however, Villars soon struck back at this impudent incursion into his defensive lines. Early on 12 July, he surprised and mauled Hompesch's troops, who were caught in their camp entirely unawares with their senior officers apparently asleep in a nearby town. Heavy casualties were suffered, although the fort at Arleux itself was not taken by the French. Robert Parker remembered:

> They fell upon the right flank of our horse trampling and cutting down all before them, and had they not fallen to plunder too soon they might have driven through our entire detachment … They suffered little or nothing, but killed and wounded many of our troopers, and carried off a considerable number of our horses.[7]

In fact, ninety-seven horses were captured by the French dragoons – a considerable haul, given the increasing difficulties that the remount officers in both armies had in meeting their quotas. Marlborough, in response, then strengthened his forces in the area; the garrison at Arleux, in particular, was increased to 600 men under Colonel Savary. The Duke's army then resumed its foraging operations. On 22 July, the French advanced through a misty night and recaptured the crossing and fortified post at Arleux on the fourth attempt, wading waist-deep through the marshy waters to make their attacks. William Cadogan and Baron Fagel, detached by Marlborough to support Hompesch, came up too late to interrupt the French attack. According to Richard Kane, 'He had an account that Arleux was taken, and that the enemy were hard at work demolishing it'.[8] This fairly minor success was hailed in Versailles and Paris as a great tactical achievement with Villars apparently getting the better of Marlborough, whose tactical deftness seemed to have suddenly failed him. The French report of the affair ran: 'The besieged defended themselves very bravely, and yet the mill and the fort were taken by storm, at one in the afternoon, and the garrison made prisoners of war … The officers and soldiers showed an extraordinary valour, wading through ditches up to their middle.'[9] In fact, the Duke was about to be handed a gift by his opponent.

While all this fierce but relatively small-scale fighting was going on around Arleux, the main armies had gathered some 20 miles to the westwards. Marlborough deployed his troops to the south of Lillers, as if a major assault on the Lines of Non Plus Ultra might be attempted from there. Not wanting a repetition of the seemingly pointless skirmishing around the supposedly unimportant post at Arleux to be a distraction, Villars had the fort demolished and drew the small French garrison back to the south of the Sensée river to carry out some foraging in that area. He also laid plans to send Montesquiou, with a strong force of cavalry, raiding deep into Brabant, tearing up the Allied lines of supply and communication if Marlborough attempted a major attack in the area of Arras. This would certainly alarm the Dutch and drag the Duke's campaign to a halt soon enough, even if he did succeed in the hazardous business of fighting his way through the Lines of Non Plus Ultra. To counter such an incursion into Brabant, Marlborough reinforced Hompesch's cavalry detachment around Douai still further. With Villars actively contemplating making that raid around the left flank of the Allied army, the cavalry that the Duke kept at Douai aroused no suspicion in the Marshal's mind. His opponent was simply guarding against such a French attempt against his communications and supply lines. The concern for the security of Brabant was by no means trivial or feigned, and Marlborough wrote on 30 July: 'We have been alarmed by the march of a detachment of the enemy consisting of seventeen battalions and twenty squadrons ... and by further intelligence of their having some design in Brabant.'[10] The Duke also received messages full of alarm from the civic dignitaries in Brussels, as rumours of an impending French raid grew. Whatever else might be intended, it plainly did no harm to hold Hompesch and his cavalry off from the main army near to Douai, where it could cover the approaches to Brabant, or be available for other tasks as they arose.

Everyone was expecting a battle to the west of Arras, one that would be just as bloody as Malplaquet, and quite understandably there was a certain gloom in the Allied army. Villars drew in the troops who had been foraging to the south of Arleux to augment his main strength at the point of most threat. On 4 August, Marlborough carried out a very conspicuous reconnaissance of the French lines in the area opposite Avesnies-le-Comte, as if an attack there was imminent. Richard Kane rode with the Duke's party that day, and wrote:

He often stopped and showed the General officers how he would have the army drawn up before day [break] next morning, and pointing with his cane to the several places the attacks should be made ... He returned to camp, and gave orders for the army to prepare for battle.[11]

Villars warned his commanders to be on the alert that night, expecting to be attacked with the dawn. At the same time, Marlborough sent a force of cavalry under Earl Albemarle farther to the west, to threaten the left flank of the French position. This was done in broad daylight and was too obvious to be a serious threat to turn Villars's position, but the Marshal could not ignore it altogether and he accordingly marched some cavalry squadrons to the west to match the movement. At the same time and more discreetly, Allied pioneers under Brigadier-General Sutton were laying pontoon bridges over the Scarpe at Vitry, and this particular activity went quite unnoticed by the French. Marlborough had seen that in demolishing the fort at Arleux, the causeway crossings in that area had been left by Villars and could now be used to get across the Sensée river and marshes by whichever commander could get his army there first.

On the same evening that Marlborough carried out his final and very overt reconnaissance of the formidable French defences (4 August), William Cadogan was riding fast with a small escort to meet Hompesch at Douai, where a strong force of horse and foot, mostly drawn out from the local Allied garrisons, had now quietly been gathered together. They moved forward quickly, so that before dawn on 5 August Cadogan and Hompesch were back at the undefended causeway near Arleux with their advanced guard. Unobserved or impeded by any French scouts they 'passed the causeway of Arleux without opposition, and were in possession of the enemies lines.'[12] At the Allied camp near Villers Brulin, the soldiers were roused from their bivouacs just before midnight and set to marching eastwards along the line of the Sensée, curving south of Vimy ridge, then swinging to the north to cross over the pontoon bridges at Vitry and on at a good pace towards Arleux. Before long, French troops could be seen marching on the other side of the river, parallel with, but always a little behind, the Allied solders. They had started out later, when Marshal Villars realised that, far from attacking him in position, his opponent was now moving to turn his right flank and breach the defensive lines. As the sun came up Marlborough received a message from Cadogan that the crossing places around Arleux were safely in the hands of his dragoons, and the Duke sent word to his generals that he would be obliged if the infantry would step out. They did so, but the effort was extreme, with hundreds of men falling out with exhaustion at the roadside. Albemarle's cavalry and dragoons, forming the Allied rearguard, were detailed to take the exhausted men up and bring them along, draped over their horses. No matter how hard the French commander drove his men on – and he did – Villars still could not make up the lost ground.

Robert Parker remembered: 'It was a perfect race between the two armies, but we, having the start of them by some hours, constantly kept ahead … Had not the Sensée and the morass been between us, we could not have avoided coming to blows.'[13] Villars got to within sight of Arleux shortly after noon on 5 August, to find the Allied army already flooding across the causeways; the Marshal's escort got into a scrambling skirmish with some of Marlborough's cavalry, and he had to hurry away to avoid capture, although a number of his dragoons were cut off and taken prisoner. By mid-afternoon, when French troops in substantial numbers were at last arriving, Villars found that the entire right Wing of the Allied army had crossed the causeway and were drawn up in a good position stretching between Oisy and the Scheldt. The left Wing of the army and the stragglers who had been unable to keep up during the thirty-six-mile forced march, were closing up to the crossing place. 'Almost as soon as I got hither', Marlborough reported, 'he [Villars] appeared with the head of his army, and immediately put 100 dragoons into the castle of Oisy, a musket-shot from this place, who were all made prisoners.'[14]

In this daring and dramatic way, Marlborough took advantage of the series of apparently rather pointless operations around the river crossings at Arleux, to decoy his opponent away and then break clean through the vaunted Lines of Non Plus Ultra, with the cost of hardly the life of a single soldier. It was a very skilled display of tactical ability, wrong-footing Villars and very publicly throwing the Marshal's misplaced self-confidence and lack of judgement into sharp relief. The French commander blustered, as well he might, and complained of heavy rains that he said had both shielded Marlborough's movements and slowed his own march to Arleux. Most of the Allied soldiers just across the river had maintained their pace well enough, however, and everyone knew it. The simple truth was that Marlborough got his troops marching to the crossing places a good two hours before his opponent did, and the Marshal, who was caught out while waiting in place for an attack that was never to come, could not recover that lost time.[15]

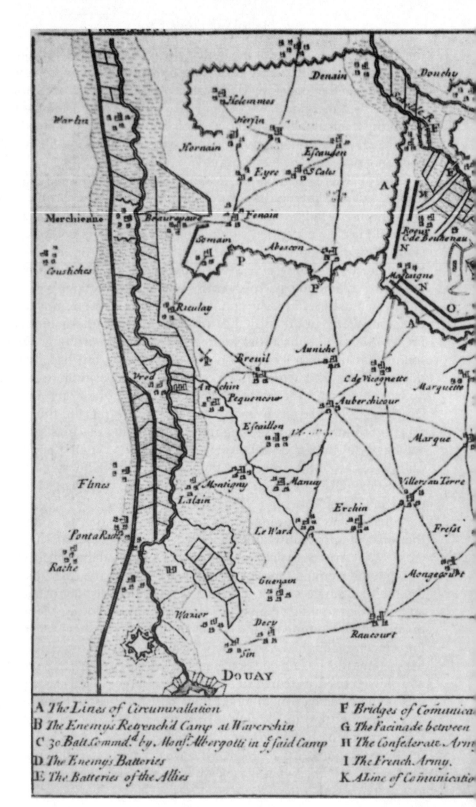

Warbu

Merchienne

Coustiches

Vred

Flines

Pont a Rache

Rache

Helemmes

Sienfin

Hornain

Somain

Rieulay

Breuil

Autchin

Peguencour

Escaillon

Montigny

Lalain

Le Ward

Wazier

Denain

Escauden

Eyre

65 Cates

Fenain

Abscon

Auniche

Auberchicour

Mannu

Erchin

Guenain

Dery

Sin

DOUAY

Donchu

Roguc
C de Bouhenau

Montaigne

C de Vicognette

Marquette

Marque

Villers au Terre

Fresst

Mongeroult

Rancourt

Note: the North compass point appears to show East.

AN
EXACT PLAN
of the Seige of
BOUCHAIN
is humbly Dedicated
to the Rt Honble
WILLIAM VISCOUNT
BATEMAN
by his most humble Servt
Thomas Lediard.

Haspre

Noyelle

H

Lieu S.Amand

Avene le Secq

D. of Marlborough
Quarters

H

Kerdaing

Estrun

Pallion
cour

M. Villars
Quarter

I

Thun l'Evecq

Thun S. Martin

Schelde R.

Ewars

Escaudevre

CAMBRAY

Entanglet

Bantigny

Cuviller

Flivg

Neuvilla

Abancourt

Fresi

Blecour

Saucour

Bachan Bencheul

Sailly

Raillecour

ubigny

Espiazy

Maincourt

One League

1/4   1/2   3/4   1

n the Schelde.
le and Senfette.

nd by ÿ Enemy.

1. The Enemys Comunication in the Morasse, Cut off
M 40 Squadrons Comanded by Genl Dopsst.
N The Beseiging Army 30 Batt & 12 Squadrons.
O 20 Batt to guard ÿ line from Marquett to ÿ Senfette
P Lines of Comunication with Marchiennes.

The formidable French fortress of Bouchain lay a few miles to the east of Arleux at the confluence of the Scheldt and the Sensée and was now exposed to Marlborough's attack. In response to the Duke's moves, Villars quickly brought his army into a good position at Bourlon Wood, covered by the marshy ground between the village of Inchy and Cambrai. From here, with vigilance, he should be able to prevent any move to besiege either Bouchain or Cambrai. On 6 August, Marlborough advanced from Aubencheul-en-Bac as if to confront Villars, but then turned smartly away to the left. He moved his army across the Scheldt on eight pontoon bridges laid below Etrun into a position near to Avesnes le Sec to begin an investment of Bouchain. In this way, he kept between Villars and the fortress, neatly placing the French on the outside of any marching curve necessary to get themselves properly into position and making difficult any late reinforcement or supplies being sent into the garrison. Once across the Scheldt, he was also reasonably secure if Villars should suddenly throw caution to the winds and attack. The lines of communication and supply for the Allied army from Douai now lay around the north and western sides of Bouchain. They were screened from direct French interference unless Villars moved to his left and cut them.

Marlborough received some critical comments for making this fresh move and not closing to attack Villars in position there and then. He wrote to Vienna a couple of weeks later with his reasons:

The same day in which we passed the lines, Marshal Villars appeared at the head of his army, behind the marshes of Marquion. He encamped there that night, and the next day continued his march, in four columns, towards Cambrai, covered by the marsh which extends to the village of Inchy, a league and a half from Cambrai; so that his troops, passing the village, formed on the right towards that town, behind the villages of Sailly and Rolencourt, and the hollow roads, and his left by the march of Inchy … In this situation it was impracticable for us to attack him, and we had no other measures to take than first to pass the Scheldt, lest he should anticipate us, by crossing and taking post on the other side, in our front [between Marlborough and Bouchain], by which movement we should have been deprived of all the advantages of our passage of the lines, and should have been obliged to retrograde by the way we came.[16]

Villars was temporarily baffled, unaware of Marlborough's full intentions for several days, and by 7 August, the Duke had begun the investment of Bouchain, moving around the eastern side of the fortress. Richard Kane wrote that it was: 'strongly situated in the great morass that was the barrier of the kingdom [France], at which place the Scheldt and Sensée joins.'[17] The very capable Marquis de Ravignan commanded the garrison, and the place consisted of an upper and a lower town, defended by a particularly large extended hornwork, which lay across the Scheldt from the main fortress. Due to the close proximity of the two rivers, the Marquis also had the advantage of extensive water obstacles, marshes and flooded meadows, both natural and man-made.

The French commander was in something of a dilemma, although he did manage to slip some reinforcements into the garrison: 800 grenadiers under command of the Comte d'Offrey with four battalions of infantry and dismounted dragoons and a resupply of several hundred sacks of flour. If Villars moved from Bourlon Wood to the eastern bank of the Scheldt, as he must if the Allied operations against Bouchain were to be seriously challenged, then Marlborough might counter-march to the west, in a kind of Arleux operation in reverse, to threaten Arras once again. This important town was almost undefended now, and the Marshal's recent humiliating experience at Arleux left him with little optimism that he would spot his opponent's next move in time to intercept him on the road. Nor could Villars detach a sizeable portion of his army to return and cover Arras, just in case Marlborough suddenly switched his effort back there, for all the French strength was now required to save Bouchain, in itself an important place. For all the Duke's worries and the practical disadvantages he suffered at this time, not least of which was the relative lack of numbers in his army, he was the more alert commander and dictating the pace of the campaign. Marlborough held the initiative, and Villars was reduced to watching for, and reacting to, his opponent's moves.

While the Marshal studied his maps, he established his headquarters at Paithencourt (Palliencour), near to Etrun, just to the southwest of Bouchain, not far from the recently vacated Allied encampment. On the evening of 7 August, Marlborough had more pontoon bridges laid across the Scheldt at Neuville, to the north of Bouchain, and pushed a strong detachment of sixty squadrons of cavalry under command of Daniel Dopff forward across the river to screen the place from that side. The main camp for the Allied army was established at Avesnes-le-Sec between the Scheldt and Sensée rivers to the east of Bouchain. Here the Duke received a large convoy of supplies from Douai, escorted by cavalry under command of General

Cornelius Wood. The next day, Villars, satisfied that no immediate Allied march towards Arras was in prospect for the time being, began his response and moved to challenge Marlborough's investment. He sent the Marquis d'Albergotti forward across the Sensée, moving around the southern side of Bouchain with a powerful force of 12,000 infantry, to Wavrechain to forestall Dopff's encroaching deployment. The Marquis lost no time in entrenching his troops, with a ditch and palisade on the hill between Wavrechain and a hamlet known as Wasne-aubac. His back was to the Sensée, but the position was strong and he was in no great danger while Villars and the main French army was so close. Artillery was brought up and a deep ditch and palisade were constructed. D'Albergotti was separated from the garrison in Bouchain only by the wide wet meadows of the Sensée, but these were quite an obstacle, only crossed by a two-mile-long farm track which became known as the 'Cow-path' (*le Sentier aux Vaches*). French pioneers gradually began to improve this track with fascine bundles and wicker hurdles, and in this precarious and fragile way d'Albergotti's detachment and de Ravignan's garrison could communicate with each other. This path would become the scene of many sharp battles in the weeks to come.

Marlborough faced several simultaneous challenges as the siege got under way, quite apart from the simple fact that most of his commanders thought the operation obviously doomed to failure. 'Everybody except my Lord Duke and Cadogan are against the siege' an artillery officer wrote home.[18] The heavy guns of the siege train had to be brought forward from Tournai, and as Valenciennes remained in French hands, closing the upper reaches of the Scheldt to Allied boats, these had to be ferried up the Scarpe to Douai, then laboriously dragged along the fifteen miles or more to Bouchain. The munitions, food and materiel which the 90,000-strong Allied army depended on for existence had to come by the same difficult route. D'Albergotti, situated at Wavrechain to the south-west of Bouchain, was well placed to strike at this vital supply line, upon which all Marlborough's plans now rested. It was also still possible that Villars might suddenly abandon any attempt to disrupt the siege operations at close quarters and try to seize the initiative by moving with his whole army across the Sensée, using the convenient crossing places at Arleux once again to straddle Marlborough's lines of supply and communication with Douai and Tournai. He could select and occupy a good defensive position with his larger army and invite Marlborough to attack him there; otherwise the Duke must draw off from the attempt on Bouchain and abandon his campaign for the season all together.

However, Villars decided against a campaign of manoeuvre to dislodge Marlborough's growing grip on Bouchain. The French main army was well closed up to the inundations astride the southern approaches to the fortress, which was itself only about two miles' distance from their camp. D'Albergotti, soon to be reinforced with Montesquiou's corps, had established a strong entrenched camp on Wavrechain hill, in close proximity to, and in contact with, the garrison. This was entirely in accord with the maxims laid down by Vauban for setting out the requirements for an active, rather than entirely passive, defence of a fortress; with forces operating together in concert, both inside and outside the formal defensive works. These arrangements seemed to be good; Villars even managed to slip some more reinforcements into the garrison, and Marlborough still had the smaller army with the far greater task to perform. It was difficult to see how, with Villars and his army quite so close and active, the Allied siege could ever succeed. The doubts expressed by many of Marlborough's officers seemed to be well founded. However, the choice made by Villars was the least enterprising of those open to him. Had he been more active (and his debilitating leg-wound must have played a part in this), he might have done well to maneouvre against Marlborough's communications instead of staying close to the fortress. The Marshal's recent and very public failure at the Arleux crossings may also have played its part, inclining him to make the more cautious choice: hampering the Allied siege while running no great risks. This may be seen as significant, for Marlborough expressed doubts at this time as to whether, with his army's lack of numbers, he could really stand a battle in the open against Villars. The Duke was playing a dangerous game, simultaneously operating against a powerful fortress in close proximity to a larger French army under a skilled commander he could not expect to overcome in battle, if that should be offered. Marlborough read his opponent and the course chosen by France at this stage in the war (he did not expect Villars to stand and fight from choice), and laid his plans accordingly. The Marshal had become a spectator.

Marlborough's obvious first step was to try to dislodge d'Albergotti from Wavrechain hill, for now the Marquis had established batteries there he would be able to rake the Allied parallel trenches on the western side of Bouchain, once these were opened. On 9 August, the Duke sent Baron Fagel across the Scheldt with sixteen infantry battalions to reinforce the troops that Dopff already had in place facing the hill. An attack on the French position was generally expected, and the next day Robert Parker remembered: 'We were posted in a large, high-grown field of wheat, about seventy or eighty paces from their works ... I must confess I did not like the aspect of the thing. We plainly saw that their entrenchments was a perfect bulwark, strong and lofty, and crowded with men and cannon pointed directly at us.'[19] The Allied infantry detailed for the task were formed up and ready to step off, under command of Lord North and Grey (who lost his right hand at Blenheim), but Marlborough's own observations, from close quarters and at some risk from French sharpshooters, convinced him of the futility of an assault. D'Albergotti was a wily commander, and had carefully kept a strong reserve of infantry near Wasne-aubac to threaten any such attempt by the Allies. The operation was called off at the last moment, to Parker's evident relief; he saw the Duke scouting the French position and was afraid for his safety:

> The Duke of Marlborough rode up quite unattended, and alone, and posted himself a little on the right of my company of grenadiers, from which he had a fair view ... We were in pain for him while he stayed, lest the enemy might have discovered him, and fired at him ... The corn we stood in was high, we slipped off undiscovered and were a good way down the hill before they perceived that we were retiring, and then they let fly.[20]

It was clear to Villars that Marlborough's army now lay astride the Scheldt to the north and west of Bouchain; with the main encampment at Avesnes le Sec, but with Dopff and Fagel confronting d'Albergotti at Wavrechain hill. The Duke's army was split into several parts, each separated by water obstacles, and was accordingly vulnerable to a forthright movement by the French. Even if this was not going to be attempted, at the very least he could be made to call off any attempt to overwhelm d'Albergotti's position. Villars moved forward with his army towards where the Scheldt and Sensée began to converge, and Marlborough, in response, withdrew his troops from in front of Wavrechain hill for the time being. As the Allied infantry pulled back, their opponents were encouraged to push cavalry forward and attempt to turn the movement into a rout. The French horsemen came on rather too far, however, and got badly cut up for their trouble; Villars rode forward to carry out his own reconnaissance with a dragoon escort, and became involved in the action, as Richard Kane recalled:

> As soon as Villars appeared on top of the hill, they charged him with such resolution that they broke through those that first

appeared, and had certainly killed or taken Villars had not a brigadier, who seeing the general in this danger, come up with some fresh squadrons to his relief, which saved the Marshal, but the brigadier and his squadrons paid dear for it; for he was desperately wounded and taken prisoner.[21]

As chance would have it, the French officer Kane referred to had taken William Cadogan prisoner during the Allied operations against Menin in August 1706, and had treated him with great civility. Now Cadogan could repay the compliment, sending his own coach to take the wounded man to his quarters, and making sure that every possible care was taken of him. The officer recovered very well, and he was soon returned to the French army without being asked to give his parole.

Wavrechain hill was plainly not to be easily taken by storm, so Marlborough set about neutralising the position. On 12 August, Colonel John Armstrong, his chief engineer, oversaw a vast project to construct an entrenched position facing d'Albergotti's troops and to install twenty-four heavy guns to challenge the French batteries. This backbreaking and hazardous work was accomplished in a single night by 5,000 workmen and pioneers under the colonel's direction – a considerable feat of engineering, and one which met with no interference from the French nearby. This was timely, for doubts were growing about the wisdom of the whole operation. The States-General in particular were concerned, and Marlborough wrote on 13 August: 'The greatest number of them thought the difficulties we should meet with could hardly be overcome.'[22]

Work had also begun to construct the lines of circumvallation around parts of Bouchain, and over the next ten days some thirty miles of fortification would be completed, extending to secure the Allied flank on the Selle stream. The massive gun emplacement confronting Wavrechain hill was enlarged and the lines extended to the Scheldt near to Neuville to cover the approaches to the Lower Town. Two lines of communication were constructed which stretched north-westwards between the Scarpe at Marchiennes and the Scheldt to provide an enclosed, easily defended area in which the Allied army could gather forage without French interference. Because of the closeness of Villars's army sitting in the angle between the Scheldt and the Sensée, d'Albergotti's entrenched position at Wavrechain, and the adjacent marshes; the Allied lines of circumvallation were not as perfectly complete as would usually be the case, but they were certainly extensive.

While this work by the Allied troops and labourers progressed, Villars was also busy. The Cow-path across the Sensée marshes from Wavrechain hill was enlarged and improved by d'Albergotti's soldiers, and other secondary parallel paths were cut. The footpaths were several feet deep in water in places, and hundreds of fascines were laid to make them passable. If these tracks could be opened out and sufficiently strengthened to be used regularly as temporary roads, then the siege of Bouchain would become a broken-backed affair, with the garrison reinforced and resupplied by Villars as he pleased. Marlborough could not allow this, and so Dopff's infantry was sent in to disrupt the work, advancing through the brackish water to come to grips with the French troops guarding the paths.

With the cover of darkness, an attack was made on 17 August under a cross-fire from the French soldiers on Wavrechain hill, the garrison in Bouchain, and those soldiers guarding and working on the Cow-path itself. Despite this, the Allied casualties were surprisingly light – probably no more than six or seven killed and wounded, indicating that surprise was entirely achieved. After a brief struggle at bayonet point, the grenadiers drove the French off, and the path, so vital to the French defence of the fortress, was securely in Allied hands. John Millner wrote: 'At night, a small party of 400 grenadiers of the besiegers waded through a little part of the bog, and boldly attacked [and] after a small dispute beat them out.'[23] With this means of communication cut the garrison was isolated, even though the outposts of the French army were within hailing distance. On 20 August, the investment of Bouchain was in place as far as it could be, and two days later, once darkness fell, the digging of the Allied trenches could begin. Fifty 24-pounder guns and thirty mortars of the siege train had now arrived despite a French attempt to cut the road, and work on setting up the batteries began immediately.

This was a significant tactical success for Marlborough, and a great demonstration of his skill, energy and enterprise – Villars really should have been able to prevent this from happening at all. The Duke, in the face of a numerically stronger enemy who was standing behind formidable defensive lines, should not have been able to get that close and to invest the town. He had shouldered his opponent aside, then marched around the front of a hostile fortress to occupy a good position, with flanks secure and his lines of supply open, from which to begin his formal siege. He had then brought up his guns and emplaced his batteries, while cutting through the means of communication between the garrison and the relieving army. Villars could not prevent the bombardment now. It simply should not have happened, and the Marshal had never failed more obviously. At this time, Prince Eugene wrote to Marlborough from Muhlberg: 'Marshal Villars will have the mortification to witness the capture of this important fortress, which will increase the glory of the enterprise.'[24]

The Allied commanders opened the trenches properly on 23 August, with three lines of attack against Bouchain: one against the lower town under command of Lieutenant-General Schwartz, and two against the upper town under Fagel. Henry Withers commanded a reserve force of twenty infantry battalions and twelve squadrons of cavalry to support Fagel's efforts. By 30 August, the batteries were ready and the breaching work began. The French gunners, both in the garrison and in the field army, tried to suppress the Allied batteries but with little success: 'The French, from their camp cannonaded us but to no purpose, for we secured ourselves with good trenches', McBane wrote.[25] On 1 September, Villars made an attempt to shake Marlborough's grip on Bouchain, sending General de Chateaumourant with a strong force of cavalry and dragoons to raid the Allied camp and retake the Cow-path. The bridge at Etrun was briefly lost to the French, and four Allied infantry battalions were taken by surprise and routed near to the hamlet of Houdaing. The effort then rather ran out of steam. The French cavalry drew off over the captured bridges, and the Allied siege operations and their grip on the Cow-path went on as before. The besieging batteries were hard at work, and the French gunners did their best to hamper them. Marlborough wrote: 'Our army which attacks the town is bombarded by the enemy [army] and we have several posts so near that the sentinels have converations.'[26] Having captured a part of the covered way of the lower town, the besiegers took the right counter-scarp of the lower town during the evening of 6 September. The left counter-scarp fell two days later.

The Comte de Villars (the Marshal's son) was detached by d'Albergotti from the operations on Wavrechain hill, and led 5,000 troops on a fresh raid towards Douai on 7 September, once again hoping to draw the Allies off from Bouchain. William Cadogan was sent with a detachment to intercept the movement and this robust response was enough to have the Comte hurriedly drawing back on Wavrechain hill, avoiding being cut off from the main French army. By 10 September, the right-hand detached bastion covering the lower town was taken by the Allies, and the garrison soon abandoned the bastion on the left as a result. Major breaches were now being broken in the walls of the fortress by the artillery, and the garrison could not hold on for much longer. The breaches were reckoned to be almost practicable, and the Marquis de Ravignan felt forced to parley with the besiegers on 12 September. Although he asked that hostages be exchanged while negotiations for a submission proceeded, Marlborough refused the request and the bombardment resumed: 'All our batteries began again afresh and played three rounds very furiously into the town.'[27] The Marquis quickly gave way and agreed to capitulate, apparently without insisting on conditions. He wrote with some understandable bitterness that Villars 'stood looking on with an army much superior to that of the Allies, and yet could suffer him to be drove to these dishonourable terms.'[28]

The Allied occupation of the fortress on 14 September, was soon followed by a rather undignified squabble between Marlborough and the French, over the precise terms of the surrender and whether or not the garrison were to be regarded as prisoners of war. This was no mere matter of semantics as the outcome would have a significant impact on the professional reputation of de Ravignan and his officers. He claimed that Bouchain had only yielded on the garrison being offered honourable terms by the besiegers, but as far as the Duke was concerned, the French had yielded with no such understanding and were, as a result, his prisoners, only to be offered for exchange when he saw fit. Marshal Villars now attempted to argue the point, partly to cover his own chagrin at having failed to save the fortress, and the matter was even referred to Versailles, from where Louis XIV found time to write to Marlborough and raise the question as a matter of honour. The Duke was unmoved; he had discussed the terms of the surrender in careful detail with his generals, and was in no doubt that nothing was offered in advance to the garrison that was not performed in practice. He would not be brow-beaten by his opponent, but the story was eagerly seized upon by the Duke's critics, who claimed it was more evidence of his duplicity and lack of good faith and fine feelings.

The fall of Bouchain was quite naturally hailed as a major Allied victory: at the cost of just over 4,000 casualties the fortress had been taken, while the garrison and Villars' main army lost 2,550 killed and wounded, with some 3,100 of the garrison being marched away as prisoners of war. The success had been achieved with force ratios in the opposing armies that simply defied contemporary military logic and which in other circumstances would have been seen as most unsatisfactory. Villars had been able to deploy about 96,000 troops in addition to the garrison in Bouchain. For Marlborough to proceed with a successful siege he should, according to conventional wisdom, have had at least 130,000 men under command, whereas in fact, with

Eugene absent, he had only 90,000 troops. This numerical imbalance should have rendered his success impossible. This was a significant achievement, made more so as the besiegers' entrenchments had often been under fire – not from just one direction (that of the fortress) but from the French field army to the south and the batteries on Wavrechain hill as well. Marlborough could justly claim a significant success, while Villars' failure to prevent the fall of Bouchain was starkly evident. A Dutch officer wrote of the siege: 'The garrison was numerous and wanted nothing, it was supported by the French Army; and yet in the sight of a hundred thousand fighting men, they were made prisoners of war.'[29] Marlborough has been described as the giant of his times, and it is plain why this was so.

Marlborough wrote to London with the news: 'I am sure you will be very pleased with the good news I send you of our being masters of Bouchain, and that Marshal de Villars has done us the honour of being witness of the garrison being made prisoners of war.'[30] Tactically, the capture of a first-rate fortress such as Bouchain was undoubtedly a victory for Marlborough, but in a rather narrow sense. The French, pursuing their strategy of fighting only defensive warfare for the time being, had once more gained time – a commodity that the Duke did not have in abundance, as enthusiasm for the war and his own reputation trickled steadily away. Villars, for all his tactical maladroitness on occasions, knew how to play this game – a game that his opponent could neither afford to play nor, when he did play, could win. The Duke, while he was aware of this, had little choice but to press doggedly on, looking as ever for the chance to confront the French in the open but knowing that they were not to be caught in that way. He also knew that he was no longer included in the most confidential discussions over the terms for a peace agreement, and wrote with some bitterness on 21 October 1711:

> You cannot but imagine it would be a terrible mortification to me to pass by the Hague when our plenipotentiaries are there, and myself a stranger to their transactions; and what hopes can I have of any countenance at home if I am not thought fit to be trusted abroad.[31]

Marlborough's influence in London had by this time become very fragile; his fiery wife, the Duchess Sarah, was now completely estranged from Queen Anne, who had tired of the seemingly endless war and was apparently more exasperated than exhilarated by the Duke's efforts on campaign. In her correspondence she increasingly referred to those of her advisers who preferred peace to war – a plainly disparaging reference to her old friend, the Duke. The tactical successes at Arleux and Bouchain did cheer Marlborough's dwindling band of supporters but, unsurprisingly, did not impress his enemies that much. These opponents were in the ascendant now as, critically, the Duke no longer enjoyed the favour of the Court. The war for Spain had gone on too long; the costs, and the taxes that paid those costs, were generally regarded as a scandal, particularly as it was now plain who would sit on the throne in Madrid, with Archduke Charles (who might have been Carlos III) happily settled in Vienna as Emperor. Better, it seemed to all concerned, to have a less than perfect peace (especially if that peace should guarantee favourable concessions to British traders), than the prolongation of a pointless and broken-backed war. Yet Marlborough's only hope to save himself from professional ruin was victory: an outright victory over the French – and that was not to be had, at any price, in the time left to him in command.

As the operations around Bouchain wound down, Marlborough had intended to move forward and threaten Le Quesnoy. With the onset of increasingly wintry weather, the Dutch and many of his own commanders were reluctant to prolong the campaign. With his own diminished prestige, the Duke could not insist, and so on 27 October he left Earl Albemarle and William Cadogan with the army and returned to London to face his critics and enemies. On the way he was magnificently entertained in Antwerp by the civic worthies, led by the governor, the Marquis de Tarazena, who had proved so troublesome in the operations against Dendermonde in 1706. Although Villars attempted a number of sharp cavalry raids to disrupt the Allied dispositions near Bouchain, particularly breaking down the sluice gates on the Sensée and Scheldt rivers to flood the area, Albemarle proved quite capable of handling these, and one of Marlborough's last letters in command congratulated the Earl of the success of his recent operations against the French raiders: 'We had an account of the precipitate retreat of the enemy, which everybody allows is chiefly owing to your Lordship's great care and diligence.'[32]

The Duke, in the meantime, had received a frigid reception when he went back to London in the middle of December. No one wanted to be associated with his impending, widely-expected downfall, and he cut a lonely, shunned figure amongst people who so recently had clamoured for his attention and favour. On the last day of the year the blow fell, and Queen Anne wrote to Marlborough in her own hand – in itself an unusual honour – dismissing him from all his posts and appointments. Marlborough threw the letter in the fire. At Versailles of course, everyone rejoiced at the glad news, and Louis XIV wrily commented that this would do everything for him that he desired. The Duke stayed in England only until his ailing friend Sidney Godolphin died late in 1712, and then went to live abroad with the Duchess. Queen Anne, who had been served so long and so well by her Captain-General, thought that he was very prudent to go. Marlborough had been increasingly subjected to politically motivated charges of corruption and peculation. Questions had been raised, with the startling clarity given by hindsight, over the wisdom or otherwise with which he had handled public funds while conducting vast and complex military campaigns. He was subjected to a sustained, government-inspired public campaign of criticism and villification. The Queen's advice was a good indication of the peril in which he stood and of the limited degree to which she could protect him – if indeed she would have even stirred herself to do so. Marlborough may well have remembered Strafford's caution to Crown servants not to put not their trust in princes.

NOTES

1. Murray, *Letters and Dispatches of the Duke of Marlborough*, Vol V, 1845, p. 259.

2. *Ibid.*, pp. 342–343.

3. *Ibid.*, p. 348.

4. *Ibid.*, p. 363.

5. The curious expression 'Non (or Ne) Plus Ultra' (nothing further is possible) is said to have been used by Villars's tailor when asked to let out the marshal's breeches to accommodate his increasing waistline. Other accounts ascribe the comment to the Duke of Marlborough's tailor when asked to perform the same service!

6. Murray, *Letters and Dispatches*, p. 413.

7. D.G. Chandler, (ed.), *Captain Robert Parker and the Comte de Merode-Westerloo*, 1968, p. 98. See also J. Brereton, *History of the 4/7ᵗʰ Dragoon Guards*, 1982, p. 79.

8. R. Kane, *Campaigns of King William and Queen Anne*, 1745, p. 91.

9. T. Lediard, *Life of John, Duke of Marlborough*, 1736, p. 147.

10. Murray, *Letters and Dispatches*, p. 425.

11. Kane, *Campaigns*, p. 93.

12. *Ibid.*, p. 94.

13. Chandler, *Captain Robert Parker*, p. 103. See also W.S. Churchill, *Marlborough, His life and Times*, Vol II, 1947, p. 849.

14. Murray, *Letters and Dispatches*, p. 429.

15. Both Hilaire Belloc and John Hussey have written with conviction that this operation was not a deliberate plan by Marlborough as many of his biographers assert, but that the French in fact initially caught Marlborough out at Arleux, inflicting a number of minor tactical defeats on their less alert opponents – van Hompesch in particular seemed not to be on good form at this time. They acknowledge that Marlborough then made a virtue of necessity with his brilliant night march on 5 August 1711 to break the Lines, but argue that this was in response to French attacks, not part of a pre-thought-out and cunning plan to have Colonel Savary fortify the place and in that way goad Villars into coming back and demolishing it. See H. Belloc, *The Tactics and Strategy of the Great Duke of Marlborough*, 1932, pp. 213–230, and also J. Hussey, *Marlborough and the Loss of Arleux*, 1986.

16. W. Coxe, *Memoirs of John, Duke of Marlborough*, Vol III, 1848, p. 231.

17. Kane, *Campaigns*, p. 97.

18. Churchill, *Marlborough*, p. 857.

19. D.G. Chandler, *Marlborough as Military Commander*, 1973, p. 294.

20. Chandler, *Captain Robert Parker*, p. 108.

21. Kane, *Campaigns*, p. 99.

22.Churchill, *Marlborough*, p. 863.

23.J.A. Millner, *A Compendious Journal, 1702–1711*, 1733, pp. 329–330.

24.Coxe, *Memoirs*, p. 239.

25.D. McBane, *The Expert Swordsman's Companion*, 1728, p. 148.

26.Churchill, *Marlborough*, p. 865.

27.Millner, *A Compendious Journal*, p. 326.

28.Chandler, *Captain Robert Parker*, p. 299.

29.T. Lediard, *Life of John, Duke of Marlborough*, London, 1736, pp. 202–203.

30.Coxe, *Memoirs*, p. 241.

31.A. Alison, *Military Life of John, Duke of Marlborough*, 1848, p. 343.

32.Murray, *Letters and Dispatches*, pp. 572–573.

Epilogue

Better an Imperfect Peace, 1712–1713

The Allied campaign in the Spanish Netherlands and along France's northern border never regained its sparkle once Marlborough left the scene. His successor as commander of Queen Anne's army was James Butler, 2nd Duke of Ormonde, a man who was brave enough but did not possess the same high abilities. He was described by Richard Kane as 'Good natured, but a weak and ambitious man, fit to be made a fool of by a set of crafty knaves.'[1] Confidential discussions were going on between Britain and France to draw this seemingly interminable war to an end. Ormonde was quietly encouraged by ministers in London not to engage the French too closely, or even at all if he could manage it. He perfectly competently, although without exerting himself too much, covered Prince Eugene's siege of Le Quesnoy during June 1712, and Marshal Villars protested that this operation by Ormonde was against an understanding reached in the discussions which were still in progress between Britain and France.

Before long this encouragement to Ormonde not to engage the French became an instruction: 'It is the Queen's positive command to Your Grace, that you avoid engaging in any siege, or hazarding a battle.'[2] Of course in private, the Dutch and Austrians knew all about this, while pretending not to know, and naturally resented that the British should apparently try to negotiate a separate peace for themselves. This avoided the awkward question which many were curiously reluctant to face: whether or not the war was any longer worth the enormous effort, or whether it was now being pursued for its own sake, with the parties on both sides lacking the wit or the will to bring things properly to a negotiated close.

The counterscarp at Le Quesnoy was stormed by Eugene on 1 July and the 3,000-strong garrison made prisoners of war soon afterwards. The Prince then moved forward to lay siege to Landrecies, but in doing so he was stretching his communications too far and was obliged to reduce the garrisons covering his rear areas to perilously low levels. In mid-July, the British troops were withdrawn from operations on insructions from London, and the pace of French activity quickened accordingly. At least an element of collusion seems likely. Villars struck suddenly and hard at the now over-extended Allies, and a serious defeat was suffered by Earl Albemarle and his Dutch corps at Denain on 24 July. The Marshal was able to go on and in a remarkably adept campaign recover a lot of what had been lost by the French over the preceding three years. The enormous effort and expense devoted by Marlborough and Eugene and their soldiers to drive through Vauban's fortress belt was swept aside without much trouble.

The war had become rather pointless now anyway, as Archduke Charles was installed as Emperor in Vienna. The Allied campaign in Spain, so expensive in men, treasure and materiel – and so ill-managed – had foundered. The Spanish people on the whole were very content with their young French King; with his grandson secure in Madrid, Louis XIV was prepared to be accommodating in other respects. Peace came to a weary Europe with the Treaties of Utrecht, Rastadt and Baden agreed between 1713 and 1715.[3] Philip V, the French claimant, remained on the throne in Madrid, but the enormous empire had been divided – not least in that the Spanish Netherlands (Belgium) now became an Austrian Province (at least until the Revolutionary and Napoleonic wars swept it away). The Habsburg encirclement, which might have been a mirage but had so concerned Louis XIV, was avoided, although valuable French-held fortresses on the eastern bank of the Rhine had to be given up – in some respects the most lasting of the effects of the war. France's borders, in the process, were confirmed more or less where they stand today.

Significant trade concessions in Spain's empire were granted to Britain (as well as confirming possession of such territories as Gibraltar, Minorca and Newfoundland). Austria increased her holdings in northern Italy as a kind of compensation for not getting Spain, while the Elector of Liège and Cologne and his brother, the Elector of of Bavaria, were reinstated in their domains. Holland, after lengthy negotiations with Vienna, eventually agreed a reduced Barrier in the Southern Netherlands, but the trade concessions to Dutch merchants operating in the Spanish empire were less advantageous than those granted to Britain. These were meagre gains, and Holland, valiant, obstinate and loyal, had been ruined as a major power by its immense efforts in the war. For all its faults, this was a pragmatic settlement – to prolong the conflict would plainly have been futile. Although no-one was entirely satisfied with the result of eleven years of conflict, in the widest sense a curb was seen to have been put on what, rightly or wrongly, had been regarded in much of Europe as the over-mighty and growing power of Louis XIV on the one hand, and a dangerous encirclement of France on the other.

Marlborough returned to England two years later, on the death of Queen Anne. King George I immediately reappointed him to be Captain-General. William Cadogan, who had gone into exile with the Duke, was also reinstated in his offices and appointments. The Duke was never very close to the German King, who never forgot or forgave the snub he was carelessly given when left out of the plans that led to the victory at Oudenarde in 1708. Marlborough never went on campaign again, staying in London during the 1715 Jacobite Rising, while Argyll, Cadogan and Joesph Sabine handled things. The King nonetheless accorded the Duke the honour that was his due, and Marlborough was able to manage the reduction of the British Army to peacetime establishments, without too much harm being done in the process.[4] As Master-General of the Ordnance, Marlborough instigated the formation of the Royal Regiment of Artillery – the arm that had served him so well during almost ten years of siege operations. The Duke suffered a stroke in 1716, the first of several. He retired from public life, and lived in increasing ill-health until June 1722, when he died at Windsor Lodge.

NOTES

1. R. Kane, *Campaigns of King William and Queen Anne*, 1745, p. 102.

2. W. Coxe, *Life of John, Duke of Marlborough*, 1848, Vol III, p. 302.

3. The main provisions of the Treaties of Utrecht, Rastadt and Baden (1713–1715):

   (a) Philip V to be recognised as King of Spain and the Indies. The crowns of France and Spain to be kept separate.
   (b) Naples, the Milanese, Sardinia and the Southern Netherlands to come under Austrian rule. The Dutch Barrier to be restored, in revised form.
   (c) France to surrender Kehl, Freiburg and Briesach on the right bank of the Rhine, but retain Strasbourg and Alsace. The fortifications of Dunkirk to be demolished.

(d) The Elector of Bavaria, and the Elector-Bishop of Liège and Cologne to be restored to their domains. (Marlborough lost the principality of Mindleheim, granted to him by the grateful Emperor in the aftermath of Blenheim, in the process, but he kept the title.)

(e) The Protestant succession in Great Britain, on the death of Queen Anne, to be assured. The Pretender, James III, to be expelled from France.

(f) Britain to retain Minorca, Gibraltar, Newfoundland, Hudson's Bay, Arcadia and St Kitts.

(g) Holland and Britain to be permitted exclusive access to trade with certain Spanish ports.

(h) Kingdom of Prussia to be recognised, and to receive Upper Guelderland. The Duke of Savoy to receive part of the Milanese and Sicily.

4. Amongst the innovations that resulted was the numbering of the infantry regiments (not the Foot Guards who were always numbered), rather than having the units known by the names of their colonels. Robert Parker's regiment, the Royal Irish (Ingoldsby's and Sterne's) became the 18th Regiment of Foot, although the captain thought that because of their length of service, they should have been accorded a lower (and therefore more senior) number. Orkney's Regiment (The Royal Militia, or the Royal Scots), became the 1st Regiment of Foot.

Chronological List of Marlborough's Siege Operations

Dates given for the commencement of sieges, and therefore the duration of the operations, have to be treated with care. Some commentators use the day on which a fortress was invested or cut off, and others the day that the besieging army arrived on the ground, or even when the trench-digging and bombardment began. In the same way, a fortress might capitulate on a certain date but the garrison not actually give up possession until several days later, so there are varying interpretations when a siege can be said to have ended. Not surprisingly, different accounts often give conflicting dates for the same operation. I have tried to be consistent in using the date of investment as the start of a siege and the date of formal agreement for a capitulation as being the end. Care should also be taken whether the New Style or the Old Style (eleven days earlier) of dating is being used in an account, most particularly by British commentators of the time (John Deane, for example, consistently used the Old Style). Also, the new year did not start until March 25 (Lady Day), and so January 1709 (as we know it) might well be stated to still be 1708 in contemporary accounts, although later editors will have often amended this for convenience and clarity.

1702

29 August–25 September	Venlo
25 September–2 October	Stevensweert
29 September–7 October	Ruremonde
13–29 October	Liège

1703

25 April–15 May	Bonn
15–26 August	Huy
9–27 September	Limburg

1704
8–16 July   Rain
19 September–26 November   Landau
4 November–20 December   Trarbach

1705
6–11 July   Huy (recapture from French)
29 August–6 September   Leau (St Loewe)

1706
19 June–9 July   Ostend
22 July–22 August   Menin
29 May (blockade)–9 September   Dendermonde
16 September–1 October   Ath

1708
12 August–9 December   Lille
18 December–1 January 1709   Ghent

1709
27 June–3 September   Tournai
6–10 September   St Ghislain
6 September (blockade)–20 October   Mons

1710
23 April–25 June   Douai
15 July–8 August   Béthune
5 September–2 October   St Venant
12 September–8 November   Aire

1711
7 August–12 September   Bouchain

APPENDIX II

Glossary of Siege Terms

Abattis	Embedded obstacles made from sharpened branches and sticks.
Approaches	Trenches dug towards a fortress to give cover to besieging forces.
Attack	Trench approaches directed against a specific part of a fortress.
Avant-fosse	An entrenchment in advance of the main defences.
Bagnette (Banquette)	An infantry fire-step.
Bastion	A pentagonal work that projects outwards from the main defensive curtain, with guns sited to sweep along the face of the walls.
Bonnet	A small quadrangular outwork designed to protect the flanks of a demi-lune.
Breach	An opening in defences made by artillery bombardment or mining. A 'practicable' breach was capable of being mounted by a fully equipped foot-soldier, with both hands on his musket, without too much difficulty. A breach that was reasonably capable of being defended was therefore not thought to be 'practicable'.
Caltrops	Iron spikes scattered on the ground as anti-personnel, and anti-horse, obstacles.
Camouflet	An explosive charge intended to be used as a counter-mine to demolish enemy mining galleries.

Capitulate	To agree to give up a fortress on negotiated (usually good) terms.
Casemate	A fortified point used to shelter artillery from enemy fire.
Chamade	A request, usually by beat of drum, to negotiate terms of submission.
Cavalier	Raised breastwork, constructed at intervals along a sap or trench.
Chamber	Space hollowed out in mine-working to take an explosive charge.
Circumvallation	Besieging lines, constructed to face outwards to open country, around a besieged town or fortress, to deter any attempt at a relief.
Citadel	A strong self-contained defensive work, usually the key part of a major fortress. Often based on the original medieval castle on the site. Frequently referred to as 'the castle' in contemporary accounts.
Contravallation	Besieging lines, facing inwards to town or fortress to deter any sortie by the garrison.
Counter-Approach	A trench dug by a garrison out towards siege works.
Counter-Guard	A triangular outwork, similar to a demi-lune, protecting a bastion.
Counter-Scarp	A tunnel loop-holed for musketry fire, running along the inside of the outer face of a ditch, allowing defenders to fire back into that ditch if it is captured by attackers.
Covered Way	The first line of defence on the counter-scarp, usually held only by infantry, intended to absorb the first shock of an attack.
Crownwork	A major outwork with two flanks, and a front with bastion and two demi-bastions, forming a semi-pointed 'crown'. This was a refinement of a Hornwork defence.
Curtain	The stretch of rampart wall running between two bastions.

Cuvette	Man-trap ditch, within the main defensive ditch.
Demi-bastion	A half-bastion with one flank and one face.
Demi-Lune	A 'half-moon' outwork protecting a stretch of wall between two bastions. Often protecting a main entrance with a 'chicane' approach to give protection against direct fire.
Discretion	To surrender without negotiated terms, at the mercy of the victor.
Embrasure	A flared opening in a wall designed for artillery use.
Enceinte (pregnant)	Continuous curtain wall, bowed outwards like a belly.
Enfilade	To fire at an angle against the side or flank of attacking troops. Soldiers suffering this are caught in a 'defile', a narrowed and therefore concentrated arc of fire.
Fascine	A bundle of sticks used as temporary bridging or flooring material.
Fausse-Braye	A low earthern rampart, rather obsolete by 1700.
Fougasse	A dug-in anti-personnel mine, sometimes only packed with gunpowder but often also with stones and grapeshot, pointing towards attacking troops. Usually fired by means of a set fuse.
Gabion	A wicker basket which, when filled with earth or stones, which could be piled with others to make a wall or barricade.
Gallery	Main type of underground mine tunnel.
Glacis	The slope running from the covered way of a fortress towards open country.
Grenade	A cast-iron, glass or clay-cased bomb, lit by fuse and thrown into enemy troops and buildings. Usually only used by 'Grenadiers'.
Hornwork	An outwork with two flanks and a front with two demi-bastions. Usually protecting a bastion or demi-lune.
Loophole	A slit cut in a wall, through which sol-

	diers can fire their muskets from shelter.
Lune(tte)	A triangular work placed in advance of main fortifications, sometimes protecting a demi-lune.
Mantlet	A wheeled timber screen to protect the leading men working in a trench.
Mine	An explosive charge placed in the ground underneath defences, usually (according to Vauban's teachings) to a depth of at least ten feet. Counter-mines could be used by defenders against attacking troops, with the charge placed under their trenches. Mining could also involve cutting away the earth around foundations of buildings or siege works to cause a collapse. Counter-mining was undertaken to intercept and disrupt the mining efforts of an opponent.
Mortar	A high-angle artillery piece, used to lob bombs into fortifications and towns.
Palisades	A line of sharpened stakes on top of a covered way.
Parallel	One of series of trenches 1st, 2nd etc, dug by besiegers at roughly equi-distant intervals from the covered way of a fortress.
Parapet Firing	A highly regulated technique of keeping up a continuous musketry fire against an attacking enemy. Ranks advanced to a parapet to fire, then having done so, turned away and returned to the rear to reload and prepared to advance again when the turn came. An alternative method was for those in the rear ranks to pass their loaded muskets forward to the best shots who would be grouped in the front rank.
Rameau	A secondary mine tunnel.
Ravelin	A triangular detached defensive work, in front of a curtain wall.
Redan	A v-shaped defensive work, open at the rear.

Redoubt	An enclosed defensive work.
Sally-port	A gate or opening, capable of being swung aside quickly, through which a counter-attaack could be launched.
Sap	A narrow siege trench, pushed forward under cover of gabions, usually at zig-zag angles.
Scarp	The outer slope of a rampart.
Tenaille (allion)	A low defensive work in the ditch, in front of the curtain wall.
Traverse	Blocking positions and obstacles, placed at intervals to prevent enemy fire sweeping down trenches, parapets or covered ways.

Bibliography

(JSAHR - Journal of the Society of Army Historical Research)

Alison, A.	*The Military Life of John, Duke of Marlborough*, London, 1848.
Anon.,	*Relation de Siege de Douay en 1710*, Paris, 1827, (RE Library, Rochester).
Atkinson, C.T.	*Marlborough and the Rise of the British Army*, London, 1921.
	Marlborough's Sieges. JSAHR, London, 1933.
	Marlborough and the Dutch Deputies, JSAHR, London, 1935.
	(ed.) *Gleanings from the Cathcart Mss*, JSAHR, London, 1951.
	Wynendael, JSAHR, London, 1956.
Barnett, C.	*Marlborough*, London, 1974.
Belloc, H.	*Tactics and Strategy of the Great Duke of Marlborough*, London, 1933.
Bidermann, G.	*In Mortal Combat*, Kansas, 2000.
Blomfield, R.	*Sebastien le Prestre de Vauban*, London, 1938.
Brereton, J.	*History of 4/7ᵗʰ Dragoon Guards*, Catterick, 1982.
Burn, W.	*A Scots Fusilier and Dragoon Under Marlborough*, JSAHR, London, 1936.
Burton, I.	*The Captain-General*, London, 1968.
Burrell, S.	(ed.), *Amiable Renegade, Memoirs of Captain Peter Drake*, London, 1960.
Carman, W.	*The Siege of Lille*. JSAHR, London, 1940.

Chandler, D.   (ed.), *The Marlborough Wars, Captain Robert Parker and Comte de Merode-Westerloo*, London, 1968 and 1998.
Marlborough as Military Commander, London, 1973.
The Art of Warfare in the Age of Marlborough, London, 1976.
(ed.), *Journal of John Deane*, JSAHR, London, 1984.
Blenheim Preparation, Tunbridge Wells, 2004.

Childs, J.   *Warfare in the Seventeenth Century*, London, 2000.

Churchill, W. S.   *Life and Times of the Duke of Marlborough*, (two book reprint edition) London, 1947.

Clarke, G.   *Fortification*, London, 1907.

Courvisier, A.   *La Bataille de Malplaquet 1709*, Paris, 1997.

Coxe, W.   *Memoirs of John, Duke of Marlborough*, London, 1847.

Cronin, V.   *Louis XIV*, London, 1964.

De La Colonie, J-M.   (ed. W Horsley), *Chronicles of an Old Campaigner*, London, 1904.

Drake, P.   *Memoirs*, Dublin, 1745.

Duffy, C.   *Stone and Fire, Science of Fortress Warfare, 1660-1860*, London 1975 .
Siege Warfare, the Fortress in the Early Modern World, London, 1979.

Dickinson, H.   (ed.), *Correspondence of Henry St John and Thomas Erle*, JSAHR, London, 1970.

Edwards, H.   *A Life of Marlborough*, London, 1926.

Falkner, J.   *Great and Glorious Days*, Tunbridge Wells, 2002.
Blenheim 1704, Marlborough's Greatest Victory, Barnsley, 2004.
Marlborough's Wars, Eye-Witness Accounts, Barnsley, 2005.
Ramillies, 1706, Year of Miracles, Barnsley, 2006.

Fortescue, J.   *History of the British Army*, Vol I, London, 1899.
(ed.), *Life and Adventures of Mrs Christian Davies*, London, 1929.

Hamilton, G.	*Letters of 1ˢᵗ Earl Orkney*, English Historical Review, London, 1904.
Hatton, R.	*Louis XIV and His World*, London, 1972.
	George I, Elector and King, London, 1979.
Henderson, N.	*Prince Eugen of Savoy*, London, 1964.
Hogg, I.	*A History of Artillery*, London, 1974.
	Fortress, London, 1981.
Hughes, Q.	*Military Architecture*, London, 1974.
Hussey, J.	*Marlborough and the Loss of Arleux, 1711*, JSAHR, London, 1986.
Johnston, S.	(ed.), *Letters of Samuel Noyes, 1703-1704*, JSAHR, London, 1959.
Kane, R.	*Campaigns of King William and Queen Anne*, London, 1745.
Langallerie, M.	*Memoires*, London, 1710.
Lazard, P.	*Vauban 1633-1707*, Paris, 1934.
Lediard, T.	*Life of John, Duke of Marlborough*, London, 1736.
Louda, J. and MacLagan, M.	*Lines of Succession*, London, 1981.
McBane, D.	*The Expert Swordsman's Companion*, Edinburgh, 1728.
MacMunn, G.	*Prince Eugene, Twin Marshal with Marlborough*, London, 1934.
MacFarlane, C.	*Life of Marlborough*, London, 1854.
McKay, D.	*Prince Eugene of Savoy*, London, 1977.
Maycock, F.	*An Outline of Marlborough's Campaigns*, London, 1913.
Merode-Westerloo, J.	*Memoires*, Brussels, 1840.
Millner, J.	*A Compendious Journal, 1701-1712*, London, 1733.
Murray, G.	(ed.), *Letters and Dispatches of the Duke of Marlborough*, London, 1845.
Myatt F.	*The British Infantry*, London, 1983.
Nosworthy, B.	*The Anatomy of Victory*, New York, 1992.
Parker, R.	*Memoirs*, Dublin, 1747.
Petrie, C.	*Louis XIV*, London, 1938.
	The Marshal, Duke of Berwick, London, 1953.
Phelan, I.	*Marlborough as Logistician*, JSAHR, 1989.
Porter, W.	*History of the Corps of Royal Engineers*, Chatham, 1885.

Reeve, J.	*The Siege of Béthune 1710*, JSAHR, London, 1985.
Sautai, M.	*La Siege de la ville et de la citadelle de Lille en 1708*, Paris, 1899.
Scouller, R.	*The Armies of Queen Anne*, Oxford, 1966.
St John, B.	(ed.) *Memoirs of Duc de St Simon*, London, 1876.
Taylor, F.	*The Wars of Marlborough 1702-1709*, Oxford, 1921.
Tindal, N.	*Continuation of Rapin's History of England*, London, 1738.
Trevelyan, G.	*Select Documents for Queen Anne's Reign*, London, 1929.
	England Under Queen Anne (3 Vols), London, 1932.
	Blenheim.
	Ramillies and the Union with Scotland.
	The Peace and the Protestant Succession.
Vauban, S.	*Traite des Sièges et sur l'Attacque des Places (1704)*, Musée de l'Armée, Paris, 1992.
	Traite sur la Defense des Places (1706), Paris, 1779.
Vial, J-L.	*Garrison de la ville de Diest prise par les Francais*, Paris, 2005.
Weygand, H.	*Histoire de l'Armée Francais*, Paris, 1938.
Whitworth, R.	*Field Marshal Lord Ligonier*, London, 1958.

Index